Understanding Action Learning

NEW FROM AMA

The Adult Learning Theory and Practice Book Series

About the Series

This new book series is intended to provide new thinking about adult learning theory and practice and will serve as a bridge across professions, disciplines, geographical, and cultural boundaries. The **Adult Learning Theory and Practice Series** will be organized into two components: a series for practitioners who facilitate adult learning, and a series for those who conduct scholarly research on adult learning. Each book in this series will address a new issue or theory in adult learning, identify relevant resources and practical tools for application, and present the results of new, original research that link theory and practice.

To learn more about the Adult Learning Theory and Practice Book Series, please contact the series editors or Jacqueline Flynn

Series Editors:

Dr. William J. Rothwell—(814) 863-2581; wjr@psu.edu
Dr. Victoria J. Marsick—(212) 678-3754;
marsick@exchange.tc.columbia.edu
Dr. Andrea D. Ellinger—(217) 333-0807; adelling@uiuc.edu
Ms. Jacqueline Flynn, Executive Editor, AMACOM Books
(212) 903-8379—jflynn@amanet.org

To find submission guidelines and learn more about the Adult Learning Theory and Practice series, please go to: www.amanet.org/go/AMAInnovationsAdultLearning

Understanding Action Learning

Judy O'Neil, Ed.D.

Victoria J. Marsick, Ph.D.

American Management Association

New York | Atlanta | Brussels | Chicago | Mexico City | San Francisco
Shanghai | Tokyo | Toronto | Washington, D. C.

Special discounts on bulk quantities of AMACOM books are available to corporations, professional associations, and other organizations. For details, contact Special Sales Department, AMACOM, a division of American Management Association, 1601 Broadway, New York, NY 10019.

Tel.: 212-903-8316. Fax: 212-903-8083.

Web site: www. amacombooks.org

Library of Congress Cataloging-in-Publication Data

O'Neil, Judy.
    Understanding action learning / Judy O'Neil and Victoria J. Marsick.
      p. cm. — (AMA innovations in adult learning)
    Includes bibliographical references and index.
    ISBN 978-0-8144-7395-5
    1. Organizational learning. 2. Leadership. 3. Action learning. 4. Employees—Training of.
I. Marsick, Victoria J. II. Title.
    HD58.82.O54 2007
    658.3'124—dc22

                                         2007011836

Printing number

10 9 8 7 6 5 4 3 2 1

Dedicated to our Action Learning colleagues, partners, and clients—who make this book—and the work we all do in Action Learning—a very satisfying and innovative continuous learning journey!

—Victoria and Judy

ADVISORY BOARD

Bill Gardner has worldwide responsibility for Executive Assessment, Executive & Leadership Development, Succession Planning, Learning & Collaborative Technologies, Performance Management, Corporate Learning & Development, and Organization Development for Advanced Micro Devices (AMD). Under Bill's leadership AMD's Learning & Development organization was named to *Training* magazine's Top 100 learning & education groups in 2001, 2002, 2003 and 2004. He holds a BS in Finance from Mississippi State and an MBA from the University of Southern Mississippi.

Dave Medrano is an Associate Dean for the corporate university of one of the world's leading multinational automotive companies where he directs training and development to support sales and marketing functions. He is also responsible for reconfiguring training programs for the company's global workforce. He speaks internationally to industry groups and holds a B.A. from the University of California at Los Angeles and an MBA from Pepperdine University.

Rich Wellins, Ph.D. is a Senior Vice President with Development Dimensions International (DDI) where his responsibilities include leading the Center for Applied Behavioral Research, developing and launching a new leadership development system, and building systems for internal knowledge management. He is a frequent speaker and has written 6 books, including the best seller *Empowered Teams*. He holds a Doctorate in social/industrial psychology from American University.

American Management Association

EDITORIAL BOARD

Andrea D. Ellinger, Ph.D., PHR, is an Associate Professor in the Department of Human Resource Education at the University of Illinois at Urbana-Champaign. Previously she was an Associate Research Educator at the Culverhouse College of Commerce and Business Administration at The University of Alabama, working on a two-year Kellogg Foundation research grant, and an Assistant Professor of Adult Education and Doctoral Program Coordinator at The Pennsylvania State University - Harrisburg, where she also taught in the Master's of Training and Development program. She holds a Ph.D. in Adult Education from The University of Georgia, an M.S. in Management from Rensselaer Polytechnic Institute, and a B.S. in Business Administration from Bryant College.

Victoria J. Marsick, Ph.D. is a Professor of Adult & Organizational Learning, Department of Organization and Leadership, Columbia University, Teachers College. She co-directs the J.M. Huber Institute for Learning in Organization at Teachers College with Martha Gephart. She directs graduate programs in adult education and organizational learning. Prior to joining Teachers College, she was a Training Director at the United Nations Children's Fund. She holds a Ph.D. in Adult Education from the University of California, Berkeley, and an M.P.A. in International Public Administration from Syracuse University.

William J. Rothwell, Ph.D., SPHR, is Professor-in-Charge of the Workforce Education and Development program in the Department of Learning and Performance Systems at The Pennsylvania State University. He is the author of over 50 books as well as the President of Rothwell and Associates, Inc. Dr. Rothwell received his undergraduate degree at Illinois State University, his M.A. and Ph.D. from the University of Illinois at Urbana-Champaign, and his M.B.A. from the University of Illinois at Springfield. Dr. Rothwell is also North American Editor for the International Journal of Training and Development and series co-editor of two book series with Pfeiffer: The Organization Change and Development Series and the Using Technology in Training and Learning Series.

vii

ABOUT THE AUTHORS

Judy O'Neil, Ed.D.

Judy O'Neil is President of the consulting firm Partners for Learning and Leadership, Inc., which specializes in action technologies including Action Learning. She holds an Ed.D. and M.A. in Adult Education from Teachers College, Columbia University, New York, and is on the adjunct faculty at Teachers College. She spent 30 years in the corporate world specializing in human resource development and organizational change. Her publications include *Action Learning: Successful Strategies for Individual, Team, and Organizational Development; ASTD: What Works Online; Action Learning; Real Work, Real Learning;* and *A Review of Action Learning Literature, 1994–2000, Parts 1 & 2.* Her clients have included the Government of Bermuda, VNU (Nielson Media Ratings), Berlex Pharmaceuticals, AstraZeneca Pharmaceuticals, Fidelity Investments, PSE&G, RR Donnelley, AT&T, Ernst & Young, Northwest, The Mount Sinai Medical Center of New York, New York Transit Authority, and The Hartford Insurance company.

Victoria J. Marsick, Ph.D.

Victoria J. Marsick, Ph.D. is a Professor of Adult & Organizational Learning, Department of Organization and Leadership, Columbia University, Teachers College. She co-directs the J.M. Huber Institute for Learning in Organization at Teachers College with Martha Gephart. She directs graduate programs in adult education and organizational learning. Prior to joining Teachers College, she was a Training Director at the United Nations Children's Fund. She holds a Ph.D. in Adult Education from the University of California, Berkeley, and an M.P.A. in International Public Administration from Syracuse University.

CONTENTS

American Management Association

FOREWORD

"No problem can be solved from the level of consciousness that created it," as Albert Einstein observed. Today, pressing challenges often demand breakthrough thinking and fresh insight of the kind called for by Einstein. It is AMA's hope that this new series - AMA Innovations in Adult Learning: Theory into Practice, published by the American Management Association's AMACOM division—will enable adults, and those who support their learning, to expand their thinking and find creative solutions to tough challenges at work. Books in this series are grounded in the lessons of theory, practice, and research. Authors hope to equip readers with a solid understanding of the know-why of issues, the know-what of options, and the know-how of experience in order to best inform effective solutions and action.

This series is inspired by the vision of Edward T. Reilly, President and Chief Executive Officer of the American Management Association (AMA). AMA, a recognized leader in management and learning solutions in the workplace, has joined forces with contributing academic editors to carry out the vision - William J. Rothwell (The Pennsylvania State University), Victoria J. Marsick (Teachers College Columbia University), and Andrea D. Ellinger (University of Illinois at Urbana-Champaign). Guiding the series is an Advisory Board of senior workplace learning professionals who help us meet the tests of relevance and applicability to real-life conditions. Our distinguished workplace Advisory Board currently includes Dave Medrano, Associate of Dean at the University of Toyota, Rich Wellins, Ph.D., Senior VP with Development Dimensions International, and Bill Gardner, Director, Global Talent and Organization Development at Advanced Micro Devices.

xi

About This New Series

In launching this series, we conceived of adult learning as being at a crossroads. Lifelong learning is an acknowledged need in a fast-paced knowledge era. Learners are increasingly self-directed, but they do not learn in isolation in the workplace. They work and learn together in groups and other kinds of communities to help organizations meet their goals. New insights into how the brain works, technology that enables learning any time and any place, and expanded awareness of social, emotional and cultural intelligence enable new learning strategies and solutions. Yet, faced by a diverse and global workplace, organizations still seek to understand differences in how adults take in and interpret information, acquire skills, build and share knowledge, and use what they know.

This new series offers insights into how adults can effectively learn in today's workplace, and how organizations can better support and use that learning to power their performance. We hope to bring people together across interdisciplinary, professional, geographic, or cultural boundaries to provide readers with solutions to learning challenges. Books will present findings from cutting-edge research, theory and practice. Authors will synthesize relevant research or present the results of new, original research that links theory and practice. They will identify and provide relevant resources and practical tools for application, In short, these books bridge the academic, professional and work worlds by focusing on theory-to-practice and practice-to-theory.

About This Book

Understanding Action Learning is the inaugural book in this series. How does this book represent what we hope to achieve in this new series? Why is this book needed now? Who are these authors and what contributions does their book make?

Learning at the individual, group, and organizational levels has been heralded as an important source of competitive advantage. Both scholars and practitioners are increasingly asked to develop interventions and infrastructures that help people and organizations learn. About 80% of such learning is estimated to take place informally. Yet much more is known about effective training and education than is known about just-in-time learning outside of the classroom. This book provides readers with state-of-the-art knowledge about a common intervention that is built around informal learning, Action Learning.

In recent years, Action Learning has gained currency as an approach to developing people by using "work on an actual project or problem as the way to learn" (Introduction, p. xvii). Action Learning helps people grow on the job by building a learning environment around meaningful challenges they or the organization need to address. Despite its growing popularity for developing leaders, Action Learning "means many things to many people" (Chapter 1, p. 1). This book was written to help readers: understand the essence of Action Learning; decide if and how to use it in their setting; and benefit from what is known about its effective implementation.

This book is timely as the first in this series because of the increasing demand for strategic leadership development. Action Learning is driven by line management to meet strategic goals and objectives. But there are many ways that it can be implemented. Action Learning must be adapted to suit the business needs, culture and context of each organization. The authors do not assume that a particular version of Action Learning is optimal or the only way to use it. Drs. Judy O'Neil and Victoria J. Marsick provide readers with a framework for understanding its essence and decision tools to consider the many ways Action Learning can be implemented. They share a wealth of resources and stories from organizations about its use. They provide planners, designers, and implementers of Action Learning with a "road map that practitioners can use to make choices about how to design and implement Action Learning in their own settings" (Chapter 1, p. 2).

An Invitation

We invite you to read about the many ways that Action Learning has worked for others and consider how Action Learning can best work for you. This book will introduce you to the theory, research, and the practice of these two authors and colleagues who have both researched and applied Action Learning in different settings. Infused with practical experiences, tools, and guidelines, this book will certainly enhance your understanding of Action Learning! We invite you to enjoy this book. But, as you do so, we also encourage you to think about other needs that professionals like you in this field may have. If you have a topic or issue that you believe deserves treatment in the series, we welcome you to contact us. We also encourage you to visit the website that accompanies this book series.

William J. Rothwell
University Park, PA

Andrea D. Ellinger
Champaign-Urbana, IL

ACKNOWLEDGMENTS

I t takes a community to write a book! So we would like to acknowledge the many people in our community who made writing this book possible.

First, there are our colleagues in Action Learning with whom we often work and with whom we have developed many of the ideas, strategies, and tools in this book. We especially acknowledge Dr. Karen E. Watkins, University of Georgia, Athens, who is the third principal in our research and consulting group, Partners for Learning and Leadership, Inc. Karen's expertise in action research and action science has influenced the theory base that underlies our research and practice.

Second, Judy and Victoria—along with Dr. Lyle Yorks, Teachers College, Columbia University—were lead researchers in ARL™ Inquiry, affiliated with Leadership in International Management (LIM). This research group undertook a number of studies on Action Reflection Learning that informed the ideas in this book. Other members of ARL™ Inquiry included, at that time, Bob Kolodny, Sharon Lamm, and Glenn Nilson. Lyle, Judy, and Victoria edited a book[1] that forms the framework for this volume based on research and insights gained during this period. Several doctoral students at Teachers College, Columbia University, who became interested in Action Learning, including Sharon Lamm and Robert L. Dilworth, also contributed to the work on this earlier volume. We (and ARL™ Inquiry) are indebted to LIM and Management Institute of Lund (MiL), LIM's parent, for opening doors to study of Action Learning programs over the years. Victoria's research on Action Learning would never have been possible without the generous support and assistance of Lennart Rohlin, President and founder of MiL where she first conducted research on Action Learning programs that MiL undertook for managers in Europe.

A third debt is owed to the Action Learning facilitators who participated in Judy O'Neil's dissertation study that laid the foundation for the Schools of Action Learning and the Action Learning Pyramid. Judy would especially like to acknowledge the help and guidance of Professor David Botham, who was head of the Revans Institute for Action Learning and Research at the University of Salford at the time.

Special thanks goes to Isabel Rimanoczy, a principal of LIM, who co-authored the Theory Appendix in this book. Many people contributed vignettes and stories of their Action Learning work to this volume. We acknowledge the wealth of examples they have generously shared (in alphabetical order): Kate Hoepfner-Karle, formerly with Invensys and currently with KHK Human Capital Consulting; Jeffrey S. Kuhn, Peer Insight; Sharon Lamm-Hartmann, Inside Out Learning, Inc; Holly O'Grady, formerly with VNU and currently with American Express; Janet Reid-Hector; Robert Ward, formerly with Berlex and currently President, Leadership Bridge, LLC; Chuck Williams, Pfizer, Inc., and Lyle Yorks, Department of Organization and Leadership, Teachers College, Columbia University. We take full responsibility for our interpretation and application of their stories.

Our appreciation also goes to the many clients with whom we have worked and the many participants we have met in Action Learning programs and through our research.

Many people have read versions of this book and helped us to improve the quality of the thinking and clarity of writing and illustrations. A thank you to Kate Hoepfner-Karle and Holly O'Grady for reading chapters with an eye toward making them understandable and valuable for practitioners who read this book. Thank you, also, to Dr. Andrea Ellinger, University of Illinois, and Yu-Lin Wang, doctoral student in the Department of Human Resource Education who reviewed the final manuscript and provided us with valuable suggestions to improve it. Finally, we thank Roni Bruscini who saved us many untold hours with her word processing help in preparing the bibliography; Peter Neaman who prepared several of the diagrams illustrating the four schools of action learning; and Jacquie Flynn, our helpful AMA editor.

For their patience, emotional intelligence and support of many kinds, Judy and Victoria thank their spouses, Paul O'Neil and Peter Neaman! As many an author has acclaimed, this book would not have been written without their patience, understanding, and intelligence.

INTRODUCTION

"Live as if you were to die tomorrow. Learn as if you were to live forever."
    —Ghandi
"Since knowledge is about yesterday, the real learning takes place
through questions about today and tomorrow."
    —IFAL-USA

What *Is* Action Learning?

This book is about Action Learning (AL), an approach to developing people that has become increasingly used by organizations. In the first chapter of this book, we show how AL grew out of a common interest in different parts of the world in an action-based approach to learning from experience that values the knowledge people develop by doing things. People have come to define AL in different ways, but at its core, it is:

> An approach to working with and developing people that uses work on an actual project or problem as the way to learn. Participants work in small groups to take action to solve their problem and learn how to learn from that action. Often a learning coach works with the group in order to help the members learn how to balance their work with the learning from that work.[1]

xvii

This view of learning stands in contrast to formal schooling, through which a bank of knowledge is passed on that has been accumulated over the years by experts and other guardians of society's culture. It is not that AL de-values the latter, but AL *does* turn around the way in which people access and use such knowledge through learning.

AL starts with what people already know and do, their accumulated personal experience of what works. Some programs, therefore, give participants a book entitled "Leadership," for example, that consists of blank journal pages on which the participant writes his/her own theory of leadership as it evolves through experience around doing real work. Through a collaborative process, participants test, refine, and experiment with new thinking about their challenges and problems. Expert knowledge may well be drawn upon, but only after participants have first probed their *own* experience and viewpoints. Peer questioning fuels probing. Questions grow out of views and assumptions about the world that people may not even be aware they hold. Through peer questioning, along with the freedom to hear and think about the viewpoints behind those questions without engaging in debate about final solutions, participants can open their thinking up to fresh insight about taken-for-granted courses of action.

Many training courses incorporate application-oriented activities in which action is taken to practice what has been taught. Sometimes, action *is* the centerpiece of what is being learned, for example, through ropes courses, mountain (wall) climbing, or white water canoeing. These are not what we describe in this book as AL. AL is built around real work, not activity of any kind. Participants "have skin in the game." They cannot simply walk away from the pressing challenges that are at the heart of AL. Decisions have real consequences. Participants cannot settle for less than a workable solution because they cannot walk away from the problem when the bell rings.

AL, as described in this book, builds learning environments around collaborative work on real problems. Readers are encouraged to think, however, about ways that the tools and strategies embodied in programs could be imported into just-in-time learning solutions that are applied outside of programs when work challenges arise; and/or into classroom-based training activities that are not full-fledged AL programs.

What Are Our Goals for This Book?

We have three key goals in writing this book:

- To help readers decide when AL is a good choice for their needs, and if so, how to decide on the best AL design(s) to address their needs—given their goals, characteristics of their organizational and industry cultures, and the needs of participants
- To share templates, tools, and examples from real world practice so that readers can better understand what AL is and how it can be implemented
- To provide insights based on theory and research to enable readers to ground decisions and choices in what is known through scholarship.

Our first goal is to help readers decide whether or not AL is the best strategy for the needs they are seeking to address. We offer insight into different kinds of designs, and to what should be considered in making choices about these designs, to get a best fit with goals and needs. We start with the assumption that AL programs must be organic, that is, they fit naturally with the unique context and people involved in them. We also assume that the design, implementation, and evaluation benefit from a co-design process that brings to the table lessons learned from experience in other organizations and from theory and research.

To reach this goal, we have developed the Action Learning Pyramid, a conceptual model of four different kinds of AL designs: tacit, scientific, experiential, and critically reflective. The model is introduced in chapter 1. Programs can sometimes look exactly like one of these four designs, but they may also combine aspects of these four designs to suit their particular circumstances. We have presented this model as a pyramid with core elements at the base, to which are added differentiating features. As one moves up the pyramid, a design carries with it many of the features of prior levels, but adds a feature that calls for other design considerations vis-à-vis the program, participant learning, and organizational considerations. The reader can also think of the model more as a core circle—embodying learning through work on a real project—with four spokes that represent pulls toward one or other key design features, as illustrated in Figure 1, AL Designs.

FIGURE 1 AL Designs

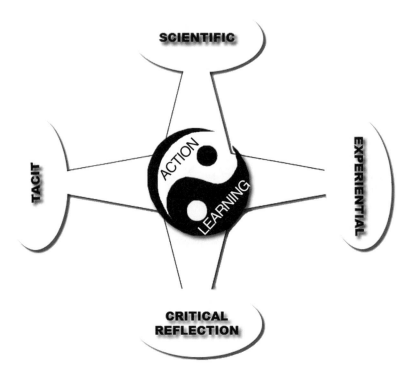

Our second goal is to share templates, tools, and examples that help AL come alive. Readers will see how different organizations have designed, implemented, and evaluated their AL initiatives. People from those initiatives share the thinking behind the choices they have made in ways that should help readers better think through the choices they wish to make about a program in their own settings. Templates and tools are shared that readers can adapt and use in developing their programs. Readers can thus take advantage of the lessons of experience from other programs.

Finally, our third goal is to ground decisions and choices, insofar as possible, in what is known from research and from theory. The Action Learning Pyramid itself is based on dissertation research by Judy O'Neil and by insights from research on AL conducted by both authors and by many of their colleagues. Research by other key scholars in the field is also drawn upon and shared to inform reader choices about their own initiatives. A Theory Appendix provides further reading for those who wish to dig more deeply into the scholarship of AL that underlies this book.[2]

What Are the Benefits of Action Learning?

AL is not a completely *new* approach to development, but an increasing number of companies have embraced it in the last twenty years or so. Key to its increased adoption is the rapidly changing global environment. Solutions that worked in the past may no longer work. Leaders in organizations are charged with finding innovative solutions to business problems, and to do so again and again and again. Things are changing so fast in the environment that it is no longer sufficient for managers to rely on their existing expert knowledge. Participants struggle with new issues in an AL program and as a result learn to look at their work and the organization differently. Having the *right* answers isn't good enough. Managers have to know how to ask the *right* questions. And AL is a question-focused approach.

Organizations adopt AL for many different reasons, but often, they use this approach because it enables them to align learning strategically with their business goals. AL is a *results-driven* learning process. Solutions to business problems provide immediate, measurable impact on organizational results, in addition to longer-term development of participant capabilities. AL provides an ongoing process that builds and supports the development of individual and team competence through the solution of actual business problems.

Leaders in today's rapidly changing environment must be resilient. In the industrial era, continuous learning was helpful, but in today's knowledge society, continuous learning is necessary for anyone in knowledge jobs. The U.S. National Center on Education and the Economy, for example, describes the knowledge world as follows:

> A world in which routine work is largely done by machines is a world in which mathematical reasoning will be no less important than math facts, in which line workers who cannot contribute to the design of products they are fabricating may be as obsolete as the last model of the product, in which auto mechanics will have to figure out what to do when the many computers in the cars they are working on do not function as they were designed to function, in which software engineers who are also musicians

and artists will have an edge over those who are not as the entertainment industry evolves, in which it will pay architects to know something about nanotechnology, and small business people who build custom yachts and fishing boats will be able to survive only if they quickly learn a lot about the scientific foundations of carbon fiber composites.[3]

But classroom education (K–12) has not adequately prepared everyone for continuous learning. In addition to the ability to continuously build one's knowledge and expertise, many leaders and employees also need help in learning how to learn from experience.

AL balances working on a problem and learning through that process. This happens through a cycle of work in the team that helps the participant look at and think about the problem in new ways, action in the workplace, reflection on that action, more work in the team, and so on. Through this process, people learn how to better learn from their experience. AL builds the ability to become self-directed in one's learning. It places participants in a situation where they must take responsibility for what and how they learn. Finally, and importantly in today's networked learning environment, participants learn through collaboration and social interaction. They learn to work and learn across silos within their teams and through conversations about their challenges with others across the organization. AL builds skills in networking and provides opportunities to extend networks with key peers and leaders elsewhere in the organization.

There is another benefit from AL that makes it attractive to organizations. A continuing challenge in organizations is transfer of learning from the classroom to the work environment. Because participants are dealing with real work in AL, the transfer of their learning to the workplace is made easier. Evaluation of AL programs, as discussed in chapter 5, indicates that this design is more likely to result in the modeling and spread of behaviors and transformation in the organization—even to people who haven't yet been a part of the program. When AL programs involve real action on the problem, inevitably teams identify and try to address organizational barriers, and look to bolster organizational supports that make it more likely a solution will be adopted. Recommendations may look good on the shelf, but real problems arise through implementation. Work on the project in the AL program means a higher likelihood that change will begin to take place before the program is over. The momentum can be capitalized upon because the way is more often paved for following through on a new way of doing things rather than the old *right* answer.

Who Should Read This Book?

We have written this book primarily for learning and organization development specialists who want to want to know more about how to design, implement, and evaluate AL programs in their settings. But this book can also be helpful to:

- executives and other organizational leaders who want to understand the implications of using AL in their organizations—especially chapters 1, 5 and 6
- managers and potential participants who want to know more about AL before they engage in it—especially the vignettes and examples showcased throughout
- coaches and consultants who want insight into how to facilitate AL, as distinct from executive coaching, that focuses on how to help people better *learn from what they do versus what people do and how to change those behaviors*—especially chapter 4
- those who teach courses in human resource development, organization development, and work-based learning and who might also engage in research and evaluation about it—especially chapters 1, 4, and 6, along with the Theory Appendix.

How Should Readers Use This Book?

This book can be read and used differently by readers, depending on one's interests and needs. We first lay out a map of the book, and then describe the rationale for several of its key recurring features. We conclude with a few words about how to use the Theory Appendix.

What Do Chapters Help Readers Learn?

Chapter 1 provides background and definitions in order to lay groundwork for readers about what AL is, and how it is differently understood.

A framework is introduced that helps the reader decide if AL is the right intervention for the organization's needs. The Action Learning Pyramid is presented and explained, and programs are described that illustrate how and why they emphasize, respectively, the Tacit, Scientific, Experiential, and Critical Reflection "schools" of AL.

In chapter 2, we identify what we think are important steps in co-designing AL programs. Co-design means that a consultant—either external or internal—the human resource or organizational development client within the organization, and the field organization are all involved in bringing specific knowledge and support to the design of the program. We identify and discuss seventeen steps in the co-design, although not all the steps are needed for each program. This chapter is intended for those who design and implement programs. It incorporates frequently asked questions about designing programs, for example, when and how to involve key leaders in the design, what makes a good project, whether a team or individual challenge model should be used, making decisions about the use of learning coaches, ensuring alignment with other HR systems, and planning for the rollout of programs.

Chapter 3 turns to implementation strategies that support success. In this chapter, we look at the elements and strategies that grow out of execution that help to make a successful program. We look at the critical roles of sponsor, participant, and learning coach. We examine strategies to prepare participants upfront for their experience and to help them better learn during the program. We describe methods for programs focused on team projects, guidelines for individual problem programs, processes for personal learning goals, and the use of learning journals to support the various types of programs. We close this chapter with a look at other execution factors that support success or contribute to failure in an AL program.

The AL coach is different from coaches who focus either on life coaching or on behavioral change. The AL coach holds the space for learning. What does that mean? And how does he/she do this successfully? In chapter 4, we look at the way that a coach's background, values, and attitudes influence his or her practice. We examine how the role of learning coach is viewed in the various schools, how the role of the learning coach might change based on the co-design that best fits an organization's needs, how the responsibilities of a learning coach help with group process and create situations for learning, how coaches might work together, and finally a discussion of how to develop an individual to work as a learning coach.

Chapter 5 answers questions around evaluation of AL programs. How can you be sure the program you've co-designed and implemented was actually successful? How can you show to the organization that their investment of time, talent, and resources is producing the intended results? We lay out theory and good practice around transfer of learning and discuss challenges that are ubiquitous in evaluating learning outcomes and linking that learning to more tangible business results. The project often provides avenues for assessing impact, but in this chapter, we also grapple with ways to understand benefits for learning and development that are key to the reason for launching the initiative.

Chapter 6 helps the reader reflect on prior chapters and reconsider AL for his/her specific organizational context. This chapter helps readers to pull together insights gained. It is both a summary as well as a guide to how to think more deeply about what was learned so that the reader can reassess and apply AL in his/her own setting. A review is included to help the reader find information in the book about key considerations in using AL. And a tool is introduced to help readers decide which of the four schools of AL might be most appropriate to their context.

What Features Can Readers Expect to Find Throughout the Book?

Several features are used throughout this book. One of these is the use of questions as headings. We use questions as headings because questions drive the power of AL. These headings, therefore, are consistent with the emphasis on questioning for fresh insight. Questions both open doors to the mind and enable their askers to live in the ambiguity caused by the fact that answers are not always readily available to tough challenges.

We use quotations and stories from various sources throughout the book to stimulate multiple ways of knowing. And finally, we include many insets with examples, vignettes, and tools throughout the book to bring voices from AL programs into the book so that readers will be exposed to a wide range of views and experience about what makes AL successful in different contexts.

How Can Readers Use the Theory Appendix?

The Theory Appendix, written jointly by Isabel Rimanoczy and Judy O'Neil, is included so that readers can delve more deeply into theory that underlies the models provided in this book. Not everyone needs to go into this depth of reading, but the appendix will be helpful to those who want to know more about the "why" and "how" of AL. The appendix first describes more fully the learning model that underlies each of the AL schools. In the second half of the appendix, readers will find more information about how adults learn from experience and how developmental considerations affect how adults take in and process what they learn through these programs.

What Is Our Wish for You?

We leave you to explore the chapters laid out above. As you take this journey, we recall advice Rainer Maria Rilke gave to a young poet:

> I would like to beg you, dear Sir, as well as I can, to have patience with everything unresolved in your heart and to try to love the questions themselves as if they were locked rooms or books written in a very foreign language. Don't search for the answers, which could not be given to you now, because you would not be able to live them. And the point is to live everything. Live the questions now. Perhaps then, someday far in the future, you will gradually, without even noticing it, live your way into the answer.[4]

Deciding if Action Learning Is Right for Your Organization

"The wisest mind has something yet to learn."
   —George Santayana
"If you don't know where you are going, any road will get you there!"
   —Lewis Carroll

Leadership development has taken front-and-center stage in organizations today, and Action Learning (AL) has become a preferred approach to developing leaders in many organizations.[1] There are a number of reasons for this preference: a rapid and ever-changing global work environment,[2] a desire on the part of organizations to see development efforts produce tangible outcomes, and a recognition that people are more motivated to learn when the experience is relevant to their lives.[3] Despite its growing popularity, AL by its very definition—learning by doing real work—means many things to many people. We are writing this book to help practitioners make sense of some of the more frequently used versions of AL so that they can choose among them when launching AL in their organizations.

We also offer lessons from experience—our own and that of others—to provide rules of thumb in working through the many challenges that arise from AL. Learning from real work is typically as messy during development initiatives as it is in the real world. It is this strength—real world work carried out within a protected environment that allows people to make and learn from mistakes—that makes AL attractive but also makes it much harder to plan for, control, and con-

1

tain. Real work appeals to managers who can get more excited about a challenge that stretches them and helps them grow while also contributing to the organization. Real work means results now and less difficulty in "transferring learning back home." Real work has real consequences that typically surface and highlight complications that extend to other people and parts of the organization. So real work also means that designers have to think differently about how to help managers learn from messy situations. We are writing this book for these planners, designers, and implementers of AL initiatives.

What Is Action Learning?

Although many organizations "do" AL, what they do looks very different. So it is hard to come to agreement about what AL really is. Its essence—learning by doing—has become a central feature of almost any good learning design that requires application and skill in addition to knowledge of facts.[4] Even universities, the guardians of facts, bring action into their classrooms, via case studies, role playing, and analyses of one's experience. E-learning may be text centered, but interactive tools make it easy to swap stories of action, work on simulations, and even engage in virtual activities. Face-to-face training is often based on application activities with feedback. And at the extreme of the action continuum are adventure training, ropes courses, games, and other kinds of experience-centered activities typically linked to self-insight and application debriefs.

We cannot intend to settle, once and for all, what may be a fruitless debate about "the gold standard" in AL.[5] But it should be helpful to look at several different ways in which AL has been defined and understood in order to lay the groundwork for a road map that practitioners can use to make choices about how to design and implement AL in their own settings.

How Did the Process of Action Learning Come to Be?

AL is not a fad, a passing wave, but a process with a long and rich history. A review of that history can help a practitioner better understand the decisions and choices that may need to be made to use AL in an organization. We start our discussion of AL with Reginald Revans.

Reg Revans, recognized in many circles outside of the United States as the father of AL, was first exposed to AL concepts as he was studying for his doctoral dissertation under J. J. Thomson, the father of the electron and Nobel Prize winner at the Cavendish Laboratories. Thomson held weekly meetings with more than a dozen current and future Nobel laureates in which they would share both successes and failures—what Revans called "struggling with the unknown."[6] But Revans's early life probably informed his penchant for learning through action. His mother worked as a volunteer in a local hospital and was interested in the then-revolutionary ideas of Florence Nightingale.

> His father worked as His Majesty's principal surveyor of mercantile shipping and was heavily involved in the sinking of Titanic. The family lived by the docks, and Revans recalled a steady stream of sailors coming to his home to report on their experiences aboard the ill-fated liner. Revans recalls asking his father which lesson was the most important to be learnt from the tragedy. His father eventually said that we must learn to distinguish between 'cleverness' and 'wisdom.' Perhaps this reply prompted the young Revans to discern the importance of asking 'why' questions that seek understanding, rather than 'what' questions that yield mere information.[7]

Revans's work with the coal mines and hospitals in England led him to recognize that the knowledge needed by these workers to solve their problems had to be a product of their action rather than just the study of books. Revans was considered a renegade by universities but was embraced by leaders of business and industry. It was clear that AL led to economic savings and increased productivity, results that spoke for themselves. The approach that Revans refined over many years emphasized fresh insight through questioning. He maintained that questions free up one's mind to think in new ways about a challenging problem about which reasonable people would disagree and which cannot easily be solved by a known expert solution.

In 1940, Revans served as Director of Education of the National Coal Board in England. In this position, he became an advocate for the interweaving of education and industry and the blending of theory and practice. He thought that since people who engaged in similar work tended to encounter similar difficulties, they could offer practical solutions to one another. He felt that the mine managers should learn with and from one another.[8]

He organized the managers of coal mines into small groups, meeting with them in the coal fields near their own pits. They worked on coal field problems, visited each other's pits, and worked as consultants to one another. There was an increase in output of up to 30 percent in mines with these prototype AL groups.[9]

Revans was also interested in the problems of the health services and hospitals in England. He designed a program in which staff from one hospital visited another in small groups to look at their operating systems. The program was called the Hospital Intercommunication Study and ended up addressing forty separate projects or problems.[10] The program placed staff in a position of visiting a new environment, examining systems removed from their own expertise. Recommendations from the study resulted in a major drop in the mortality rate, shorter hospital stays, and improved employee morale.[11] Revans and his associates carried this concept he eventually referred to as AL to many other countries during the 70s and 80s.

While Revans and his associates were spreading his AL concept, similar but separate work was being carried out in Lund, Sweden. Lennart Rohlin was equally disgruntled with the limits of conventional management training in his country. In 1976, he led a group of academics and consultants who were dissatisfied with management and leadership development in Sweden to create their own brand of AL through the Management Institute in Lund (MiL). The group developed an open-ended process that came to be named Action Reflection Learning™[12] A hallmark of MiL's approach has been experiences that jolt people outside of their typical ways of understanding the world. Arts, sports, outdoor treks, or adventure training can be central to MiL's programs, as are journeys to other countries where the unexpected is turned into fertile territory for questioning one's own values, beliefs, and ways of working. The mindset of MiL involves using all the senses to interrupt mental models that prevent managers from seeing the world, and their problems, with fresh eyes and innovative solutions.

MiL's approach developed concurrently with that of Revans, and so, too, did AL approaches in other Scandinavian countries. Where was the United States when this ferment of AL was growing? Early efforts to introduce AL were not successful. Raelin suspected two reasons for the early resistance.

First, it may well be that this country's corporate directors are not willing to have someone poke around in critical problems in their organizations; it's a resistance to culture change. Second, action learning is not a product or an outcome; it's a process. And we tend to be outcome-oriented rather than process-oriented.[13]

A group known as Leadership in International Management (LIM) tried to introduce companies to the MiL model of AL but successful adoption of this approach did not come until the 1990s.[14] As globalization pushed U.S. organizations into new ways of working that demanded new kinds of leadership, companies experimented with their own approaches to AL. General Electric is among the best known of these companies. GE's financial success led other companies to adopt GE's approach to AL, shaped by consultant Noel Tichy, who advocates for managers developing other managers by taking advantage of teachable moments.[15]

How Has Action Learning Been Defined?

Although it is said that Revans never offered a specific definition of AL and always maintained that there was no one way "to do" AL,[16] he did provide the following description.

> Action learning is a means of development, intellectual, emotional or physical that requires its subjects, through responsible involvement in some real, complex and stressful problem, to achieve intended change to improve his observable behavior henceforth in the problem field."[17]

Willis has identified some twenty-four principles of AL that she describes as Revans's gold standard.[18] Revans himself never compiled such a list, but Pedler, Burgoyne, and Brook—in a review of AL programs in British business schools—examine findings in light of what they call "the notion of Revans's 'classical principles' (RCP)" or "a construct, a shorthand for the consistencies in reading of his considerable writings over more than fifty years" that includes:

- the requirement for action as the basis for learning
- profound personal development resulting from reflection upon action

- working with problems (no right answers) not puzzles (susceptible to expert knowledge)
- problems being sponsored and aimed at organizational as well as personal development
- action learners working in sets of peers ('comrades in adversity') to support and challenge each other
- the search for fresh questions and 'q' (questioning insight) takes primacy over access to expert knowledge or 'p'.[19]

Definitions evolved based on practitioners' own use of AL, without a view or discussion of different or other approaches. This can lead to confusion for practitioners about what AL really is. Table 1 provides a view of some key definitions.

There are common principles underlying the various definitions of AL in Table 1. First there is the idea of working in small groups in order to take action on meaningful problems while seeking to learn from this action.[20] McGill and Beaty add the notion of a cyclical process of taking action, assessing that action through reflection, drawing conclusions, and taking subsequent action based on these conclusions. Marsick, Cederholm, Turner, and Pearson bring in the idea of critical reflection and advocate the use of learning coaches who help learners to question their actions, challenge their assumptions, and commit to meaningful action without offering specific advice. Dotlich and Noel take a simpler view of AL going back to the basics of "learning by doing."

It is from an analysis of these common principles, plus some of the additional thoughts of these various theorists and practitioners that we developed our definition of AL:

> An approach to working with and developing people that uses work on an actual project or problem as the way to learn. Participants work in small groups to take action to solve their problem and learn how to learn from that action. Often a learning coach works with the group in order to help the members learn how to balance their work with the learning from that work.[21]

Although there are some common threads to the definitions in Table 1, as the authors go on to discuss their various approaches, the differences that can be found are often quite baffling for the practitioner. This confusion is often compounded when authors use the term AL to include other types of experiential exercises such as outdoor ad-

TABLE 1 Action Learning Definitions

Definition	Theorist/Practitioner
Action Learning is a method for individual and organisational development. Working in small groups, people tackle important organisational issues or problems and learn from their attempts to change things.[1]	Pedler
Action learning is a continuous process of learning and reflection, supported by colleagues, with an intention of getting things done. Through action learning individuals learn with and from each other by working on real problems and reflecting on their own experiences.[2]	McGill and Beaty
Action Reflection Learning™ is described as: "…in an Action Reflection Learning program (a form of action learning) the "training" becomes a project in which learning takes place while participants try to solve a work-related problem….The basic characteristics of an Action Reflection Learning program are working in small groups to solve problems; learning how to learn and think critically; building skills to meet the training needs that emerge during a project/problem; developing a participant's own theory of management, leadership, or employee empowerment—a theory that is tested against real-world experiences as well as established tenets.[3]	Marsick, Cederholm, Turner, and Pearson
Action learning is nothing more than learning by doing in a controlled environment.[4]	Dotlich and Noel

[1] Pedler, *Action Learning for Managers,* 13.

[2] Ian McGill and Liz Beaty, *Action Learning: A Guide for Professional, Management and Educational Development* (London: Kogan Page, 1995), 21.

[3] Victoria J. Marsick, Lars Cederholm, Ernie Turner, and Tony Pearson, "Action-Reflection Learning," *Training & Development* (August 1992): 64.

[4] David L. Dotlich and James L. Noel, *Action Learning: How the World's Top Companies are Re-Creating their Leaders and Themselves* (San Francisco: Jossey-Bass, 1999), 1.

venture exercises or simulation exercises intended to develop specific skills.

What is AL and what is it *not?* Are all these authors talking about the same thing? The issue that needs to be addressed is making sense out of what has been written, not ideological purity.[22]

"One of the problems of describing action learning is that it means different things to different people."[23] One way to address these differences and bring order to the confusion is through the schools of AL.[24] These four schools are categorized by the way in which practitioners view that learning takes place during AL. These schools are created to understand core similarities and differences and are not intended to label practitioners in any way. The categories have been inductively derived, based on the literature and interviews with AL practitioners in the United States, England, and Sweden, so others may categorize them differently.[25] The different schools have much in common, as shown in our definition, but the key difference is in the view of how learning takes place, and this view impacts many aspects of how the author views the AL process.

These four schools are summarized in Table 2, Schools of Action Learning. In the Tacit school the focus is primarily on action and results through the project. The Tacit school assumes that learning will take place as long as carefully selected participants work together, some team building is done, and information is provided by experts from within and external to the company.[26] Explicit attention is not necessarily placed on the process of learning, which makes the learning primarily tacit and incidental.[27]

The Scientific school is rooted in the work of Revans, who described his method for achieving managerial objectives as consisting of systems Alpha, Beta and Gamma. Given his early background as a physicist, these systems have a basis in the scientific method.[28] Learning occurs through asking questions, which leads Revans to a learning formula, $L = P + Q$ (L = learning, P = programmed instruction, Q = questioning insight.)[29] "P," programmed instruction, is "the expert knowledge, knowledge in books, what we are told to do because that is how it has been done for decades."[30] "Q," questioning insight, has been described as "discriminating questions."[31]

As part of the Experiential school, many proponents of AL see Kolb's learning cycle as its theoretical learning base.[32] Kolb emphasizes the cognitive and whole-person learning dimensions of taking in information (through concrete experience of abstract conceptualization)

TABLE 2 Schools of Action Learning

School	Tacit	Scientific	Experiential	Critical Reflection
Theory	Incidental learning	Alpha, Beta, Gamma; P&Q=L	Learning from experience	Learning through critical reflection
Practitioners	Dotlich & Noel; Tichy	Revans; Boshyk	McGill and Beaty; Mumford	Marsick; O'Neil; Raelin

and transforming information into knowledge through learning (by some combination of reflective observation and active experimentation). Kolb's cycle emphasizes learning by first experiencing something (or bringing it to mind via a simulation of experience), reflecting on that experience and sharing perceptions of the experience, checking these perceptions against theory that helps to explain what happened, applying what is thus understood to practice, and experimenting with new ways of thinking and working and being that generate a new cycle of this kind of learning. AL enables learning in each stage of the experiential learning cycle.[33] As a result, action plus reflection on the action produces an increased awareness of how work is getting done, giving participants and the team more choices for expanded repertoires for working effectively.

Practitioners in the Critical Reflection school believe that AL needs to go beyond the simple reflection found in the Experiential school to focus on "critical reflection,"[34] on basic premises that underlie thinking. That is, people recognize that their perceptions may be flawed because they are filtered through uncritically accepted views, beliefs, attitudes, and feelings inherited from one's family, school, and society. Such flawed perceptions often distort one's understanding of problems and situations. Critical reflection can also go beyond the individual and can lead to the examination of taken-for-granted organizational norms.[35] Through this school, participants can learn to ask good questions rather than always thinking they need to provide answers, make better decisions when there is no one right answer, experiment with new ways of doing things, think more strategically, and work with different points of view.

For readers who would like additional explanation of the schools of AL, a more detailed description can be found in the Theory Appendix.

What Do All These Action Learning Programs Look Like?

To bring the discussion of AL from the theoretical to the practical, following are the descriptions of four actual programs that we think strongly emphasize key characteristics of each of the four schools.

Our first program, discussed by Chuck Williams from Pfizer, demonstrates many characteristics of the Tacit school. Managers work on real business problems, are provided with both new information and work procedures as they address those problems, and are assisted by experts in their work. The design provides explicit focus on task for learning rather than emphasis on reflection for learning. Williams additionally believes that there are elements of the Critical Reflection school because participants and projects are expected to challenge the way work is done in the organization.

Pfizer, Inc.'s Performance Leadership Projects
Chuck Williams

Pfizer, Inc. is a $50+ billion research-based pharmaceutical and healthcare company headquartered in New York. When Chuck Williams, a Chief Technology Officer (CTO), came on board in late 2002, he recognized the need to align the IT strategy and organization with Pfizer's Strategic Imperatives, and to accelerate the implementation of those strategies in a rapidly evolving business environment. A second, equally important need was to achieve these results in a way that accelerated the development of leadership skills among top IT talent at Pfizer. Finally, Pfizer was about to undertake its second multibillion dollar acquisition within a period of four years, and it needed a way to quickly integrate the new Pharmacia colleagues into a culture composed of "legacy Pfizer" and former Warner-Lambert employees.

In his role as Chief Information Officer at his previous company, Georgia-Pacific, Williams had used a *leaders developing leaders* methodology developed by Noel Tichy at the University of Michigan and at General Electric. This program had proven to deliver rapid results when attacking critical business issues, as well as developing leadership capabilities among participants. The CTO engaged the firm that had assisted him at Georgia-Pacific, Brimstone Consulting, to help implement the processes that had been successful at Georgia-Pacific, and to provide leadership coaching. The founders of the firm had worked with Dr. Tichy at Michigan and at GE.[36]

Step 1: Senior Team Alignment
The first stage of the program is called Senior Team Alignment. The CTO took senior IT leaders offsite for two workshops within a sixty-day window, where IT strategies and

organizational values were clearly shaped into a concise "strategic business framework," composed of key long-term strategies, critical metrics, and an annually refreshed set of short-term deliverables. Values were operationalized using existing articulation of the Pfizer values, called Pfizer's "leader behaviors." The third critical component of senior team alignment is the requirement that each leader develop a *teachable point-of-view*, to interact with colleagues in a personal way, getting feedback from other colleagues and eventually developing ownership of the "strategic business framework." The senior team alignment process was designed to be rich in description of critical business issues, the external and internal environment of the business, team building through collaborative problem solving, and robust feedback from superiors, subordinates, and peers. Between the first and second workshops, each senior team member was required to go back to his or her respective staff, present key components of the emerging "strategic business framework", and collect feedback and suggested changes to strategies, metrics, and deliverables. The final result of the senior team alignment process was a three-to-five year "strategic business framework" owned by more than sixty top leaders in the IT organization.

Step 2 : Performance Leadership Projects

The second key component of the program is execution of multiple iterations of Performance Leadership Projects (PLP). Key characteristics of these projects include:

- Each project addresses a critical business issue or problem where significant progress can be made in 90–120 days.
- Projects are scoped to produce tangible, measurable results in the 90–120 day timeframe.
- Projects are staffed with six to eight high-potential emerging leaders.
- Project teams are structured as balanced teams of "athletes." In theory, any team can perform any project. Teams typically include a cross-organizational, geographically diverse set of members with varying skills. Normally customer-facing, financial, subject matter, program management, risk management, and technical operations expertise will be present through different team members. A great deal of care is taken to create these well-balanced teams.
- Goals are to achieve business results, develop leadership competencies and maturity, and foster organizational transformation at an accelerated pace. Team members are not permitted to give up their normal jobs, but are encouraged to negotiate reasonable expectations early with their supervisors.

Roles:

- Team participant. A high performer in his/her current job, with high potential to develop rapidly into leadership roles. Should have exhibited good leader behaviors as measured by Pfizer's internal 360 leader behaviors survey.
- Team sponsor. Each team has one or two executive sponsors, whose major purpose is to provide resources and guidance to the team as it works on the business prob-

lem. Sponsors have normally been through a previous cycle of PLP as a participant. Many former participants make excellent sponsors.
- Leadership coaches. Each team has one external coach and may have an additional coach from Pfizer's HR organization. The external coaches are very familiar with the processes and mechanisms used in PLP and provide direct one-on-one coaching to sponsors and team members. Coaches play critical roles both during workshops and at weekly team meetings. The PLP processes do not specify a method of team organization, governance, or leadership. Team members must define for themselves how they want to accomplish the work.
- Executive owner. The Chief Technology Officer leads the program, coordinating the efforts to select projects, assign colleagues to teams, and clearly articulate goals and roles for the program. The executive owner and sponsors are the teachers at the workshops

The best example of the Scientific school is one of Revans's own programs. The program at GEC was one of the first that Revans managed for an organization and demonstrates the application of Systems Alpha, Beta and Gamma.[37]

General Electric Company

One of Revans's most written-about programs was at the General Electric Company (GE) in England. In the early 70s, the head of GEC, Sir Arnold Weinstock, saw a need to provide management development for his senior level business managers. At this same time, Weinstock saw Revans on television discussing AL and charged his personnel director to explore the applicability of setting up a management development program based on AL. In 1974, Developing Senior Managers' Programme (DSMP 1) was launched with the cooperation of three organizations—GEC; Action Learning Projects International (ALP) which assisted GEC in designing and operating the program with project advisors (similar to learning coaches); and Dunchurch Industrial Staff College (DISC), which administered two residential courses and provided other expert specialists.[38]

The first program involved twenty-one executives who were divided into four sets (teams) of four to six people in each set. To be selected for the program, each participant needed to have proved his worth in the job and to have the necessary potential for promotion to senior general management. He also needed to have the capacity to develop himself for his own advantage and that of GEC and be convinced that the program would significantly assist in this development. The sets worked with project advisors from both GEC and ALP.[39]

DSMP 1 lasted for eight months. Participants worked fulltime on their AL projects for three months. They attended two residential courses—one at the beginning of the program (two and a half weeks) and one partway through (one week) and workshops organized by participants. Each AL set met for one day a week throughout the program.[40]

Participants had four options for consideration for their projects.

Option 1: exchange between operating companies
Option 2: remain in own GEC operating company (to allow senior managers to retain control of their participants)
Option 3: remain in own job (use own job as the project)
Option 4: exchange with a non-GEC company.[41]

Each participant had his own project—a common design for AL outside of the United States, rather than team projects. Once the project was chosen or assigned, the participant diagnosed the problem, proposed a solution, and persuaded members of the organization, and the client, to accept the diagnosis and act on the proposal. Sometimes the action involved the participant himself. In the weekly meeting with the set, participants reviewed members' progress, argued over the diagnosis, and discussed how to find needed information.[42]

The results of the program have been examined and discussed by all players. Some of the organizational impacts that have been discussed include unlocking underutilized resources within GEC to work on projects,[43] revealing where communications from and to the top were not working properly, and improving communications between top and middle management.[44] Individual results included the development of more open minds and a less individualistic, more cooperative team approach to management[45] and participants increased ability and willingness to deal with wider corporate issues as they went through the program.[46]

The PSE&G Leadership is Real Work program is a good example of the Experiential school. The main client, Bob Browning, recognized the need to create change in the organization, but also felt, based on the conservative past of a public utility, that an overtly Critical Reflection program wouldn't fit the culture. The co-design incorporated many elements of the Experiential school, including the use of a Learning Styles Questionnaire. Once the program had been in place for some time and had achieved a level of change, elements of Critical Reflection were more easily accepted.

PSE&G LIRW

Judy O'Neil, President, Partners for Learning and Leadership

In 1996, an AL program was co-designed for Public Service Electric & Gas Company (PSE&G), a major subsidiary of Public Service Enterprise Group, a Fortune 200 global energy services company. At this time, PSE&G was being challenged to transform a primarily regulated monopoly with a command-and-control hierarchy into an organization that would be successful in a competitive environment. The organization had made attempts toward the needed change with some training initiatives—particularly Quality training initiatives. While they felt some learning was taking place as a result of these initiatives, there was little transfer of the learning from the classroom to the workplace.[47]

At this point, the field organization, in the person of Vice President Pete Cistaro turned to the Leadership and Professional Development group for help. The manager of that group, Bob Browning, in turn engaged Partners for Learning and Leadership[48] to help co-design an AL program. Bob was familiar with AL and saw its potential value in this situation, particularly as a breakthrough change intervention with the ability to pick up where training left off. Partners and PSE&G co-designed an AL program called Leadership is Real Work (LIRW). The objectives for the program were:

- Enhance the way people communicate and interact with one another.
- Weave quality tools and behaviors into the fabric of the organization.
- Develop and use problem solving and coaching skills.
- Develop an environment of openness and trust and get conflict out on the table.

Based on the needs and current readiness of the organization, Partners recommended a design that placed LIRW primarily in the Experiential school, although as the program progressed elements were added that supported learning through critical reflection as well.[49]

The LIRW AL program ran from 1996 through 2000 and included two pilot sessions, one for senior leaders, and nine regular sessions with a total of over 250 participants. There were usually four teams in each program. Each team was made up of five to seven participants. The participants represented a diverse mix from the organization, and were not to be experts on the project. The teams met together as a community for six and a half days of sessions; spread over six weeks, which combined work in the large community with learning and project work in teams. Each team worked with a learning coach during the sessions and often met to work on the problem between the formal sessions without the learning coach. There was a presentation of learnings and project recommendations on the last day to the community, senior leadership team, and project sponsors.[50]

Each team worked on a single business project. In addition to the project, each team member chose one or two personal learning goals that they worked on both with the team and back on the job throughout the program. Each project had a sponsor who was a higher level manager in the organization, had an interest in the project, and had the ability to support implementation of the recommendations. Partners' agreement with the organization was that the role of the sponsor was a developmental role as well, so the learning coach contracted with them for development of their own personal learning goals.[51]

The learning coach helped the team by creating situations in which the balance and tension between work on the project, and learning from the project, could take place. Some of the design elements used by the learning coaches that helped to create situations for experiential learning were the use of a learning style inventory for an understanding of learning from experience and frequent reflection breaks during the team meetings.[52]

The Berlex program, described by Robert Ward, captures the most important characteristic of the Critical Reflection school, reflection that enables participants to surface, examine and challenge their own perspectives and beliefs and the norms of the organization. This is particularly true in the work participants did in connection with their personal learning goals.

Berlex Corporate Development Program
Robert Ward, President, Leadership Bridge, LLC

The Berlex Corporate Development Program is a six-month AL program that was designed as part of a global strategy for the development of high-potential leaders within the Schering AG organization. Berlex Laboratories is the US division of Schering AG, a global pharmaceutical organization that employs 21,000 people in ninety-four countries.

In 2001 the Schering AG organization embarked on creating a global organization with a matrix structure. Driving this change was a major emphasis on developing the U S. business as a strategy for growth. As part of a long-term strategy, the global organization identified the need to improve management and leadership development programs for the purpose of driving a performance culture and developing the capability needed for global success. To address this goal Berlex Laboratories chose to implement an AL program as part of their overall leadership development strategy.

The purpose of the program was to develop a bench of qualified leaders within the Berlex organization. The program objectives included helping participants:

- develop leadership skills that enable them to work above their current level
- move more easily from debate to decision making and implementation
- hone interpersonal and consulting skills to improve their ability to influence others
- develop self-insight and self-development capability
- learn more effectively from and through experience.

The program featured ten face-to-face sessions over a six-month period of time. Sessions were spaced one month apart with the first session being three days and the last being two days. The program had fourteen participants divided into two equal project teams. Each of the teams had a project that was of strategic importance to the organization and outside the scope of their typical responsibility and capability. There was a learning coach for each project team, and each project was sponsored by a top-level executive.

The AL projects selected by the Executive Committee were the following:

1. How can we do a better job of succession planning, i.e., creating the needed bench strength at all levels in our organization?

2. What role would e-detailing play in an overall marketing strategy? E-detailing is the digital equivalent of a pharmaceutical sales rep visit, using technology to supplement and reinforce traditional marketing investments, as well as tailoring a marketing approach for each customer.

The program design was structured to allow participants time to work on the projects between scheduled sessions and to collect additional data and information.

Several programmed learning sessions were built into the design to facilitate and provide opportunities for learning. First, each participant came in to the program with a personal learning goal developed from a multi-rater assessment and discussions with their manager and learning coach. Second, several learning sessions were developed to include critical thinking, meeting management, decision making, strategic thinking, and conflict management, primarily on a just-in-time basis. Finally, the Myers-Briggs Type Indicator and Learning Style Inventory was administered to all participants to gain an understanding of their own and others' style.

While content was an important component, the actual process for learning was accomplished primarily through the use of questioning and reflection on the projects and personal learning goals. The Berlex Corporate Development Program's theoretical approach focused on critical reflection, but as a matter of course shifted between the Critical Reflection and Experiential schools of AL. Hence the methodology for learning from experience involved extensive use of questioning insight to promote reflection and/or critical reflection on participants' thinking about the projects, personal learning goals, and experience in the program. The learning coach was key to this process. By asking questions, the learning coach helped participants reflect on their thinking and actions and provided observations and feedback on how the group was working together.

How Can We Decide Whether or Not to Use Action Learning in Our Organization?

As we look at this variety of AL programs, it starts to become obvious that the decision about whether or not AL is the right intervention for an organization is not necessarily an easy one. The decision is actually a two step process. First, decide if AL is the right intervention for the organization's needs. If the answer to that question is 'yes', then secondly, decide which of the schools will best fit the needs and culture of the organization.

To help with these decisions, we offer some help. First, we provide a questionnaire, "When Would an Organization Benefit from Using Action Learning?" (Table 3).[53] If your organization would indeed benefit from AL, the Action Learning Pyramid (Figure 2)[54] will help to determine the appropriate school. All organizations have problems that

TABLE 3 When Would an Organization Benefit from Using Action Learning Questionnaire

Are your organization's problems:	YES	NO
1. Problems for which no one knows the solution?	☐	☐
2. Critical business imperatives?	☐	☐
3. Problems that could have an impact on your business results?	☐	☐
4. Compelling, unstructured questions?	☐	☐
5. Problems no one knows how to solve, but about which many people have an opinion?	☐	☐
6. Problems for which regular problem-solving techniques would find an acceptable answer?	☐	☐
7. Problems that can be solved through systematic analysis?	☐	☐
8. Does your organization believe there is a need for leaders to learn how to learn?	☐	☐
9. Are change and possible transformation needed in your organization?	☐	☐
10. Do members of your organization generally accept the need for improved organizational learning?	☐	☐
11. Are members of your organization rewarded for asking good questions?	☐	☐
12. Are members of your organization encouraged to take time out to reflect on their experiences?	☐	☐
13. Is there a free flow of communication between management and employees; across business divisions or groups?	☐	☐
14. Is conflict surfaced and dealt with rather than suppressed?	☐	☐
15. Does your organization want to develop leadership skills in managers and executives?	☐	☐

FIGURE 2 Action Learning Pyramid

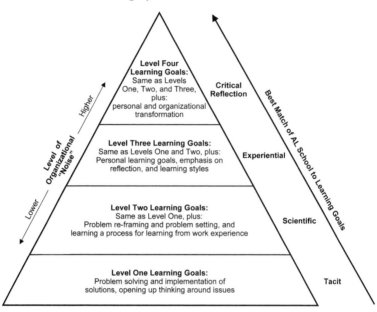

need to be solved and there are many ways to develop leaders. To find out if AL might be an intervention that would help your organization solve its problems and develop its leaders, answer the questions in Table 3.

If you responded "yes" to any of questions 1–5, AL might be an appropriate intervention to help address your organization's problems. If your "yes" answers were to questions 6 or 7 instead, a more traditional problem-solving approach might be a better fit.

For AL to be successful as a problem-solving and/or develop-ment intervention there has to be a certain degree of readiness in the organization. Some important elements of readiness are explored in questions 8–15.[55] If you responded "yes" to at least half of these ques-tions, you and your organization are probably ready to explore which AL school will be a fit through the Action Learning Pyramid.[56]

Yorks, O'Neil, and Marsick built the Action Learning Pyramid to help practitioners make choices among different AL schools and pro-grams based on readiness and desired outcomes. To effectively use the pyramid, it's important to consider three elements. First, consider the organization's readiness for AL. Second, identify the learning outcomes desired for the program, participants, and the organization. Third, determine the organizational impacts wanted from the program outcomes. The pyramid orders the schools in terms of kinds of learning and program outcomes desired. In short, as one goes from the bottom of the pyramid to the top, the learning and program outcomes that can be achieved become more complex, critical, and contextual. This kind of learning produces more *noise* in the system, and therefore, potentially both more leverage for organizational change as well as more resistance to the process. *Noise* can be thought of as comments challenging the program made by participants as they are asked to reflect on deeply held assumptions, mental models, and issues that the organization would not have previously treated as items for discussion. The more potential *noise* produced by a program, the more important readiness for AL and change in the organization becomes.

At the first level of the pyramid are found learning goals centered on problem solving and implementation of solutions for the task or problem. The focus is on strategic issues and developing a strategic business perspective. All four schools seek to provide this type of learning and appear capable of producing it. However, if this is the primary goal of the program, the Tacit approach is probably the best one, especially if management seeks to reinforce a strong existing culture. Some theorists and practitioners whom we believe fit in this school—Jim Noel, David Dotlich, and Noel Tichy—developed a popular AL approach at GE. Managers are brought together to work on real business problems. People are assumed to learn because they are working together on new challenges. As needed, they are provided with new information and may use new work procedures. Experts may guide the process. But more explicit attention is given to task and problem solving than to reflection on what one is learning.[57]

The second level of the pyramid reflects learning goals around the task, and places emphasis on problem framing and problem posing in addition to problem solving and implementation. It is also expected that participants will gain and subsequently apply skills in learning from their work. The Scientific, Experiential, and Critical Reflection schools can all deliver this kind of learning. If the goals of the program are limited to this kind of learning, a program approximating Revans's scientific approach may be the best fit.

Although he differentiates himself from the traditionalist Revans approach, the work of Boshyk, which he refers to as Business Driven Action Learning, has several elements that appear to fit with the approach in this school. Boshyk discusses five elements key to Business Driven Action Learning, three of which appear to approximate Revans' thoughts. First, the use of what he calls action research—an equivalent of the scientific method espoused by Revans. Second, an emphasis on implementation that Revans also considered critical and is not a part of all AL programs. Third, Boshyk talks about development through teamwork and coaching. Although Revans doesn't advocate for the learning coach role, and it doesn't appear that Boshyk uses learning coaches per se, Revans does believe that individual development happens through the team.[58]

At the third level of the pyramid, we add explicit goals and outcomes related to personal development, self-knowledge, and learning styles to goals already described of problem framing, posing, and solving. The Experiential and Critical Reflection schools are more likely than the other two to foster this kind of learning because of the added value of learning coaches and explicit reflection on learning goals around both the task and personal development. Experience has shown that in the absence of a learning coach who explicitly reinforces the goals of the program, learning tends to get driven by the task focus.[59] Our work that falls into this school, for example, programs co-designed for PSE&G and VNU, is discussed in later chapters. Another practitioner and theorist with a significant body of work that fits this school is Alan Mumford. He believes that AL programs are designed to help create the ability not only to learn, but also to learn *how* to learn. His Learning Styles Questionnaire, created with Peter Honey, is used in many AL programs in this school.[60]

In addition to learning goals around the task, at the fourth level of the pyramid goals and outcomes include transformational learning both for individuals and for changing the culture of the organization. The Critical Reflection school best provides for this kind of learning and culture change. The learning coach fosters a climate in these programs in which participants feel comfortable in examining their beliefs, practices, and norms. Much of our writing and work falls into the concepts of this school. We believe that taking time to reflect can be powerful and critical reflection even more powerful because it is directed at the root of the problem. Through this type of reflection, reframing of the presenting problem commonly occurs because people uncover misperceptions, norms and expectations that were often hidden.[61]

Raelin argues that public collective reflection is at the heart of AL's impact. He finds it important to develop the capability to reflect for several reasons. First, managers are often not aware of the consequences of their actions and therefore they cannot alter them. Second, without reflection, managers cannot close the gap between what they espouse and what they actually do. Third, biases in the way people work lead to errors that cannot easily be detected and corrected without reflection. And finally, new situations often present new contexts that require new ways of thinking about what worked in the past. Reflection is essential for such re-consideration. Private reflection is helpful but thoughts are not fully developed without conversation. AL provides a vehicle for questioning insight and conversations that help managers reframe their thinking.[62]

Conger and Benjamin have studied AL programs and agree that reflection is a critical ingredient that is also frequently missing in sufficient quantity or depth from many programs. They point out that reflection in many programs they researched was typically confined to one session on the last day of the program when participants presented the results of their work. They recommend, instead, "daily opportunities where participants reflect on learnings to that point in the program or on that day's work." In so doing, people learn more from what they do in each session and, more importantly, the program models the reflective practice that will stand them in good stead back on the job after the program.[63]

There are some caveats to the concepts in the pyramid. Because of the differences in program assumptions and design, we believe the potential for fostering transformational learning of a personal nature is greatest in a Critical Reflection program. However, this kind of learning is in no way insured. Learning of this developmental kind is not totally predicable or controllable by formula or technique. It is also possible for some people to experience personally transformational learning in programs designed in any of the other schools.

Success in achieving transformational outcomes depends to a good extent on the readiness of the learner to confront, rather than resist, the learning experience as well as the readiness in the organization for the program and the subsequent support offered to the participants. In any case, our own research demonstrates a range of learning outcomes from AL programs using Critical Reflection, including resistance. That being said, we also believe that changes in an organizational culture are more likely to be triggered by programs toward the top of the pyramid rather than the bottom, even though such results are no means assured. With this analysis in mind, we can turn to co-designing a successful AL program.

CHAPTER TWO

Co-Designing an Action Learning Program to Ensure Results

"If one learns but does not think, one will be bewildered. If one thinks but does not learn from others, one will be imperiled."
　　—Confucius
"The best learning happens in real life with real problems and real people and not in classrooms."
　　—Charles Handy

C o-design in Action Learning (AL) means that an AL consultant, either external or internal, the human resource or organizational development client within the organization, and the field organization are all involved in bringing specific knowledge and support to the design of the AL program. There are seventeen steps in the co-design process that we'll discuss in this chapter although not all the steps are needed for each program.

　　The Berlex Corporate Development Program demonstrates the importance of the involvement of the three key player groups in the co-design process.

Berlex Corporate Development Program
Bob Ward, President, Leadership Bridge

The program was developed jointly with Partners for Learning and Leadership, Berlex HR Department, and the CEO and Executive Committee members. Several critical success factors occurred during the development of the program that proved to be essential in setting the stage for its overall effectiveness. First was the involvement of the

22

CEO and several members of the Executive Committee in the design, selection of participants, and sponsorship of the program. Additionally, this group engaged in their own modified Action Learning program to fully understand how the program works and to "walk the talk" regarding leadership development. This level of support from the CEO and Executive Committee set the stage for a successful program.

A second success factor was the selection of organizational problems and participants by the CEO and Executive Committee members. Several criteria were used for the selection of the organizational problems: 1) it was a problem typically decided on at the executive level, 2) the problem crossed organizational boundaries and functions, 3) it was a complex problem with no known solution, 4) action could be taken within the program time frame, and 5) that reasonable people could disagree about the solution. This last criterion was evident in the executive's discussion regarding the selection and definition of the organizational problems. Selecting meaningful "real time" projects important to the organization was the end result of this process.

Of equal importance was the selection of the program participants. The selection criteria were based on maximizing a diverse mix of participants in background, work experience, age and gender; high potentials as identified by leadership; employed at the company for at least one year; and not considered a subject matter expert. While both the selection of the problems and participants evoked much debate, in the end there was buy-in from the entire Executive Committee.

A third success factor was the significant up-front time taken in the co-design and organization of the program by the Director of Human Resources and the AL consultants from Partners for Learning and Leadership.[1]

What Do We Mean by Co-Design?

Most change and development interventions are carried out by a consultant, either external or internal, acting upon the organization. Schein refers to this as "The Purchase of Expertise Model" in which someone within an organization defines a need, decides it cannot be handled by the organization itself, and looks for a consultant to provide the information or service.[2] Co-design of an intervention, particularly an intervention like AL which has the potential for transformative change, involves basically the same players, but in a much different dynamic, as seen in Figure 3.

Each AL program should be co-designed to be unique to the needs and capacity of the organization. The design produced must match with both the corporate culture and the issues and objectives of the program.[3] Since AL is intended to create change and sometimes transformation, it is important that the organization, through both the HR/OD client and the field organization, is involved in decisions regarding what and how

FIGURE 3 Co-Design Process

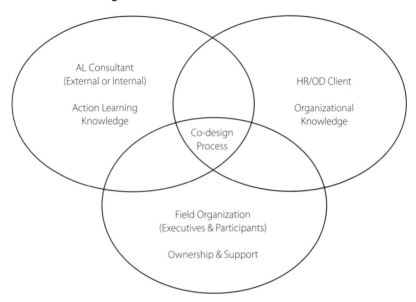

this is accomplished. Through this involvement, the field organization also begins to build the participant ownership necessary for the success of the program. Co-design also enables the AL consultant to ensure the design will stretch the organization, but not to the breaking point.[4]

To illustrate the importance of co-design, let's return to the Berlex example at the beginning of this chapter. As Ward stresses, critical to the success of the program was the early and systematic involvement of the CEO and Executive Team members who were from all parts of the business. That involvement was balanced by significant work by him in the HR role and the input and work of the AL consultants to round out the co-design effort.

The VNU Explorers Program shows how the involvement of the field organizations helped to co-design elements into the program that supported its acceptance and success.

VNU Explorers Program
Holly O'Grady, VNU

In 2003 VNU, parent company of ACNielsen and Nielsen Media Research, launched the Explorers Program to develop emerging leaders in its North American businesses.

The program, co-designed with Partners for Learning and Leadership,[5] supported VNU's organizational goal to develop future executives with a broader understanding of all of its businesses as well as to identify future leaders earlier in their careers. Since AL was a new development process for the organization, Partners for Learning and Leadership played an instrumental role in helping VNU determine a number of important factors in the design such as the length of the program, team development, and the coaching role.

As of 2006, three classes have graduated from the Explorers Program. Each class had twenty-two participants who attended four modules over a nine to twelve month period. The participants were nominated from their business units both for their leadership capabilities as well as for their consistently strong performance records. Although the final approvals resided with the business leaders, an advisory committee of human resource leaders offered recommendations to ensure that a cross section of job roles, diversity, and companies would be represented in each class.

We positioned Action Learning as the hub of the program because the projects allowed the participants to gain more in-depth knowledge about VNU's assets while working on their project. Action Learning also created a venue for the participants to learn about their leadership styles since they all had a chance to facilitate team meetings as well as take personal accountability for their contributions to the project.

The agenda for each of the modules was a balance between presentations from senior executives and other subject matter experts on topics relating to the Action Learning projects and time for the teams to work on their projects. Each session also included a component on team feedback with the learning coach as well as individual assessments and one-on-one coaching.

Prior to the launch of the first program, the head of Human Resources for VNU expressed some concern that the agenda seemed to have a lot of time blocked out for team meetings without much indication as to how the teams would actually use that time. To address this concern we developed a workbook, which served as a guide for introducing participants and others to the Action Learning process and a resource for just-in-time interventions that were used throughout the program. Topics covered in the workbook included:

- contracting/establishing ground rules for effective team work
- the Action Planning Cycle
- working in teams and possible team roles
- consensus and tools for decision making
- guide for conducting research interviews.

PSE&G also serves as a good example. In moving to an AL approach for organizational transformation and leadership development, PSE&G went through various stages. The initial design was created primarily between the external consultants and internal HR. After the pilot, HR and line management provided input for a re-design and established corporate processes to support the initiative, with top management articulating and leading the effort with strong external consultant support.

An advisory team was formed at PSE&G consisting of associates from different groups within the organization. Their responsibilities included recommending projects and sponsors. They kept the program "a work in progress", through use of program evaluation data, and by planning future strategy and direction of the program.[6]

To co-design effectively, collaboration has to be the watchword. Table 4 illustrates some of the many ways that this collaboration can take place among the three players in a co-design process.

What's Involved in Co-Designing and Implementing an Action Learning Program?

No matter which school is determined appropriate for the organization, there are some similar initial steps in the co-design process. There are some steps particular to some schools and not to others. There are also some steps particular to each certain school. Table 5 shows the co-design steps we usually use. There are seventeen steps in the table, but not all steps are needed all the time, especially when decisions pertain to either the team-based or individual project-based program designs. We'll go through them one at a time.

Why, and How Do We Secure and Maintain Top Management Support?

Step 1 is to secure top management support, a step needed for many learning and development interventions. As a result of their research, Conger and Benjamin came to the conclusion that the importance of top management involvement cannot be overemphasized.[7] As illustrated earlier with the pyramid, AL can create *noise* in the organization that can be seen as both an opportunity and a threat for changing the status quo. As a result, an AL program can be used as a wedge to stimulate changes around issues that surface in carrying out projects. At the same time, the program can become particularly vulnerable to criticism and political maneuvering. Working with top management, gaining what is often called a champion, is important in being able to handle potential resistance and help ensure success.

TABLE 4 Collaboration in Co-Design

Company	Key Stakeholders	Internal Resources	Role of External Consultant
VNU	CEO Top Business Heads HR Heads	Project Manager	Collaborated with project manager to co-design program to fit needs of organization Collaborated with sponsors to define appropriate AL projects Attended debrief meetings as SME
Berlex	CEO Executive Committee	HR Director	Collaborated with project manager to co-design program to fit needs of organization Collaborated with sponsors to define appropriate AL projects Co-coached senior leadership enrollment session with HR Director Attended debrief meetings as SME
PSE&G	Vice President Senior Leadership Team	OD Director	Collaborated with project manager to co-design program to fit needs of organization Collaborated with sponsors to define appropriate AL projects Attended debrief meetings as SME Co-coached Advisory Team with OD Director

Some of the questions that Marquardt suggests answering to be sure top management support is in place are:

- Is top management committed to AL?
- Do they understand the benefits and expectations?
- Will they support the AL teams with time and resources?
- Are they aware and supportive of the potential cultural changes created by AL?
- Have they discussed the program and its objectives with potential participants and their managers?
- How will the recommendations and actions of the AL teams be handled?[8]

TABLE 5 Co-Design Steps

1. Secure top management support

2. Establish the strategic mandate

3. Determine the primary focus

4. Decide on team projects or individual problems

5. Determine the role of learning coaches

6. Select the participants

Team Projects	Individual Problems
7. Recruit sponsors	
8. Choose projects	
9. Determine program length	9. Determine program length
10. Co-design strategies for success	10. Co-design strategies for success
11. Determine "P" learning	11. Determine "P" learning
	12. Choose problems
13. Choose personal learning goals	13. Choose personal learning goals
14. Provide orientation/introductory workshop	
15. Ensure alignment and integration with HR system	
16. Implement cascading rollout	
17. Co-design evaluation	

One way to gain the needed top management support is through a Senior Leader Enrollment Session (see Table 6). This type of enrollment session accomplishes a number of important steps with the top management of the organization. It enables them to become familiar with AL both through participation in an AL activity as well as lecture and discussion, that is, through action and learning. Learning about the successful experience of a peer can be useful to hear when senior leaders are about to begin to provide support for a program that will potentially create *noise* and change in their organization. Finally, the session

---

TABLE 6 Senior Leader Enrollment Session

Day 1
Overview of AL
• Description of the process
• Examples of projects and outcomes, etc

Discussion with Senior Leader from another organization about his/her experience with AL in his/her organization
• Pre-determine areas of interest/concern, questions
• Can be set-up via teleconference

Work as an AL team on problem, "How should we rollout AL within the organization?"
• Contract with learning coach
• Use of Action Planning Cycle (See chapter 3)
• Reflection (See chapter 3)

Day 2
Continue work as AL team

Just-in-time learning on appropriate subjects; for example
• TALK model (See chapter 3)
• Decision-making tools
• Dialogue

---

enables the senior leaders to spend some focused, reflective time on considering how they will rollout AL within their organization.

What Do We Mean by a Strategic Mandate?

Step 2 involves establishing the strategic mandate or critical business imperative of the organization that can drive the AL program. Although the program should be aligned with the HR system of the organization, it should not be positioned as an HR initiative. Development is a critical part of an AL program, but it is not an end to itself. AL is a balance between project and development—work and learning—as illustrated by Figure 4. Some examples of strategic mandates include those in Table 7.

Understanding the strategic mandate for the program is a necessity for the co-design process. A good illustration of how the strategic mandate can influence the AL design is shown in the Chubb Growth Leader Program.

FIGURE 4 Balance Work and Learning

Rather than:

TABLE 7 Strategic Mandates

PSE&G	The need to transform a primarily regulated monopoly, with a command-and-control hierarchy, into an organization that could be successful in a competitive environment.[1]
VNU	Development of future executives with a broader understanding of all of its businesses as well as identify future leaders earlier in their careers.
Pfizer	The need to: • align the IT strategy and organization with Pfizer's strategic imperatives • accelerate the implementation of those strategies in a rapidly evolving business environment • accelerate the development of leadership skills among top IT talent • integrate the new Pharmacia colleagues into a culture composed of "legacy Pfizer" and former Warner-Lambert employees.
General Electric	Turn a company of domestic-minded engineers into aggressive, global thinkers and marketers.[2]
Johnson & Johnson	Focus on human resources as a competitive strategy; rapidly disseminate strategic knowledge on the corporation's high priority business issues; proactively understand changing business environments; reinforce the corporation's values and culture.[3]

---

[1]Marsick and Watkins, *Facilitating Learning Organizations,* 121.

[2]Stephen Mercer,"General Electric's Executive Action Learning Programmes" in *Business Driven Action Learning: Global Best Practices,* ed. Yury Boshyk, 42 (London: Macmillan, 2000).

[3]Ron Bossert,"Johnson & Johnson: Executive Development and Strategic Business Solutions Through Action Learning" in *Business Driven Action Learning: Global Best Practices,* ed. Yury Boshyk, 91 (London: Macmillan, 2000).

The Chubb Growth Leader Program
Jeffrey S. Kuhn, VP of Leadership and Learning at Peer Insight

The Chubb Growth Leader Program is a three-session Action Learning program de-signed to turbo charge Chubb's high-potential Vice President and Senior Vice President business leaders in the areas of strategic innovation, organic growth (revenue growth derived from internal sources), and breakthrough leadership. The program is part of a multiyear initiative designed to build enterprise-wide strategic capability via a series of growth and innovation-oriented Action Learning programs. Chubb's Chief Operating Officer was the executive sponsor of the program.

The program was co-designed and co-facilitated by Jeffrey Kuhn, CEO of Growth Leaders, and Eileen Mathews, Vice President of Leadership Development at Chubb. Kuhn and Mathews also served as learning coaches, each working with two project teams.

FIGURE 5 Chubb Growth Leader Model

Founded in 1882, the Chubb Corporation is a holding company for a family of specialty property and casualty (P&C) insurance carriers headquartered in New Jersey. The firm has 12,000 employees serving customers in some 130 field offices throughout the Americas, Europe, and Asia. Core offerings include both off-the-shelf and customized risk management solutions for middle-market commercial and high-net-worth personal customers. The company has three core Strategic Business Units (SBUs): Chubb Commercial Insurance (CCI), Chubb Specialty Insurance (CSI), and Chubb Personal Insurance (CPI). Annual revenues are US$13 billion.

As a specialty insurance carrier, Chubb competes on a differentiated, value-added basis. The company's business model is predicated upon strategic innovation to drive organic growth and maintain healthy margins in a mature, relatively commoditized industry.

The program is premised on the notion that growth leaders think differently about the business. They look at markets expansively and conceptualize new sources of customer value that will catalyze new businesses and revenue streams.

Accordingly, the purpose of the program is to develop a cadre of growth leaders with the individual and collective capability to conceptualize new sources of customer value and create new revenue streams via new businesses, new offerings, new customers, and new markets. The program has a dual mission of leadership development *and* business impact. Program objectives included:

* develop strategic leadership capabilities in the areas of business acumen, strategic mindset, and transformational leadership
* cultivate a common language, mindset, and processes around innovation and organic growth among Chubb's high-potential SVP and VP level leadership talent
* infuse new thinking into the organization, generate new business models, new sources of customer value, and new revenue streams.

There are several areas in the co-design process that are directly influenced by the strategic mandate. For example, whether or not the primary focus of the program is to be organizational change or individual development—as in the PSE&G program that focused on the organization versus the VNU program that focused on individual development through working in teams. As will be seen in subsequent steps in the co-design process, the strategic mandate will also guide:

- nature of the project—as discussed below, team projects impact organizational change, whereas individual problems impact individual development
- selection of participants
- selection of the team projects themselves and the kind of "P" learning that might be introduced in the program.

We turn first to decisions about a primary focus on individual or organization development, Steps 3 and 4 in the co-design process.

How Do We Decide If the Primary Focus Needs to Be Organizational Change or Individual Development and If the Teams Will Focus on Team Projects or Individual Problems?

The strategic mandate for the program drives decisions about balance of focus on individual or organization development (Step 3). Once the decision is made for organizational change or individual development, that decision leads to a choice of team projects or individual problems (Step 4). As mentioned earlier, team projects usually fit with organizational change and individual problems help with individual development. This is not the only criterion that is used for the choice, however. Since either team projects or individual problems can be used in most of the schools and have a number of similarities, other issues need to be considered as well (see Table 8).[9]

Some criteria for individual or team project choice are similar, as can be seen in Table 8, so the decision is often based on other advantages and/or disadvantages of each focus. A team project can be part of the design in any of the schools and is frequently found in

---

TABLE 8 Team Project vs. Individual Problem[1]

Team Project	Individual Problem
Problem Criteria:	**Problem Criteria:**
• Real work that is meaningful to everyone in the team • A complex project that crosses boundaries/functions • A project with no known solution • A project about which reasonable people would disagree on the solution • A sponsor who is interested in and willing to support the outcome	• Real work of the participant • A problem with no known solution with which the participant has been struggling • A problem about which reasonable people would disagree on the solution • A sponsor/manager who is interested in and willing to support the outcome
Advantages:	**Advantages:**
• Greater focus on organizational change • An opportunity to meet and work in a cross-functional team • Often an opportunity to visit other company locations • Work on a project that has the potential of significant organizational impact	• Greater focus on individual development • Participant gets to focus on current work problem with which s/he is dealing • If working in intact teams, team building will also take place • If working in cross-functional teams, will have the opportunity to gain in-depth knowledge of other parts of the company • Easier to implement solutions
Disadvantages:	**Disadvantages:**
• Diminish the opportunity to have team building with intact team • Participants could view the project not as real work, but created for the program	• Lose the opportunity to work on an organizational problem with a cross-functional team • Divide time among several different problems rather than focusing on one

---

[1]O'Neil and Dilworth, "Issues in Design and Implementation," 24. Some of the criteria have been adapted from this chapter.

the Critical Reflection and Tacit schools. Individual problems can also be part of the design for any of the schools, although less frequently found in the Tacit, which usually centers on team projects sponsored by executives who are primarily seeking answers to the project questions.[10]

Should We Use Learning Coaches?

The presence, and the role of learning coaches, is a concept that has been debated in some of the AL literature.[11] From a co-design perspective, it is important to make a decision early on about if, and how, learning coaches will be used (Step 5) since their role can have a great influence on subsequent co-design decisions such as sponsor roles, program length, "P" learning subjects, team processes, and work on personal learning goals. The roles a coach can play are illustrated in many of the vignettes in this chapter and chapter 3. The aforementioned debate, how to make a decision about the learning coach role, and how to choose learning coaches is discussed in some detail in chapter 4.

Who Should Participate in the Action Learning Program?

As with the choice between team projects and individual problems, there are some guiding criteria to help select participants, which is Step 6 in the co-design process. Participants are described as "comrades in adversity" by Revans,[12] or "fellows in opportunity" by Mumford.[13] Participants are first chosen based on the strategic intent of the program. So, for example, participants were chosen from the ranks of upper management in Grace Cocoa for an AL program based on the need to create a global organization.[14] At PSE&G, the intent was to develop all levels of management to successfully function in a competitive environment, so participants were chosen from supervisors through senior level, and also included some bargaining unit employees depending on the project.

Once the type of participant has been established, project groups or teams can be formed. Research and experience dictate that teams be based on the greatest diversity possible. A greater mix of participants enhances learning, helps overcome narrow mindsets, and leads to more creative problem solutions. Diversity includes differences in background, work experience, age, gender, nationality, and where known, learning style differences and personality mix. Choices should be made to reflect the whole system under consideration. Included in this diversity mix should be an effort not to include people who would be considered subject matter experts on the project. This helps to avoid the expert solution that Revans warns about.[15] When experts are part of the problem solving groups, members look to them for solutions rather than learning and discovering fresh solutions on their own.

It's important that thought goes into the diversity mix. Consider the Berlex program.

Berlex Corporate Development Program
Bob Ward, President, Leadership Bridge

The selection of the program participants was important to the program. The selection criteria were based on maximizing a diverse mix of participants in background, work experience, age, and gender; high potentials as identified by leadership; employment at the company for at least one year; and not considered a subject matter expert. It is important that the participant selection process not be solely a human resource activity. Executive involvement in the selection process was just as important as in the development of the program because executives think differently from human resource professionals. While most of the selection criteria were adhered to, the "high-potential" term was largely defined by the eye of the beholder. In the end, most of the participants chosen met the HR definition of high potential, while others were selected based on executive choice. Don't discount this type of intuitive selection; at least one participant selected this way has since had the most career growth.

There are several aspects of selection to keep in mind. One is to keep the group size to no larger than seven participants; five or six is ideal. Because of group dynamics and time, having more than six participants begins to detract from both the learning and work on the organizational problem. Another take-away was to have at least two groups. This was important so they could provide critique to each other at different stages of the program. Last is the role of HR in the selection process, which needs to be facilitative. While HR provided guardrails, it was the Executive Committee who made all participant selections. While both the selection of the problems and participants evoked much debate, in the end there was buy-in from the entire Executive Committee. This was time well spent.

Invensys, a global engineering firm, co-designed Leadership in Action with Partners for Learning and Leadership.[16] In the process for choosing participants, we decided to incorporate even additional diversity elements that included looking outside the organization at the participants' background to ensure a real diversity of experience.

Invensys Leadership in Action
Kate Hoepfner-Karle, KHK Human Capital Consulting

Invensys is a 2.5 billion dollar global engineering firm headquartered in London, England. As part of a strategic business transformation the CEO placed a strong emphasis on developing global leaders. To enable this long-term strategy we defined a Leadership Lifecycle approach to identifying, assessing, developing, and evaluating leaders of the future. Specifically this meant that at different stages in a leader's career they required unique development opportunities to support them through their career transitions. In addition, as with all companies the market for talent is fierce and Invensys needed to accelerate the development of the talent it attracted and ensure that this talent believed it was the right place to stay. A critical component of the Leadership Life-cycle focused on Key Talent, high potential individuals with room to grow into senior leadership positions with the right development opportunities. For this population Leadership in Action, a development initiative using Action Learning was designed and delivered.

The first Leadership in Action initiative was structured for two teams of seven Key Talent leaders over a six-month period. Our goal for selecting team membership was to have highly diverse, global teams representing the following diversity selection criteria:

- identified in the Talent Reviews (Succession Plans) as Key Talent
- diversity of experience and background inside and outside of Invensys
- broad gender, race, age and nationality mix
- participation across all business membership.

The final roster of participants was submitted for approval to the CEO from the SVP of HR and the VP of Learning and Development.

The ideal team size is considered to be five to seven participants. This provides for diversity of perspectives and yet permits full participation on the part of everyone. In team projects, this size provides for meaningful team dynamics. With individual problems, each participant has a reasonable amount of time to address his/her problem within a one-day meeting time.

A final consideration in choosing participants is the issue of whether participation should be voluntary. Many AL practitioners believe that participants should be volunteers. Some initiatives use an introductory session to educate potential participants on the AL process. An example of such a session will be discussed shortly. However, the philosophy of volunteers only can run into problems when the organization is using the initiative for development or change, and therefore feels that it is necessary for certain employees to attend. In these cases, the design may need to address the issues of uncertainty and resistance that can arise.[17]

In the PSE&G program, the objective was to help all supervisors and managers change and transform the way they did their work, so the organization decided not to make the program voluntary. The design of the program included strong sponsor support for both the projects and the learning that participants gained from the project. Sponsors chose participants for their teams and called each participant in advance to explain why he or she was chosen and what he or she would bring to the team. In that initial telephone call and throughout the program, they stressed the importance of both the task and learning from the task.[18]

Generally non-voluntary programs are initiated in response to specific organizational needs around organizational change and management development. To be excluded from programs that have this type of strategic mandate could be considered career limiting; therefore, as long as the program is perceived by members of the organization as strongly supported by top management, participants will want to be selected.[19]

Once participants are chosen, it's important that clear expectations are set with both that person and his/her organization. The organization needs to decide if the participant will be:

- full-time in the program
- part-time in the program and part-time on the job, which usually means delegating part of his/her duties to someone else for the duration of the program
- full-time on the job as well as participating in the program.

Based on that decision, the participant and his/her manager need to understand the time commitment and the type of support the manager and organization need to provide the participant.

Who Exactly Is a Sponsor?

Recruiting and preparing sponsors is Step 7 in the co-design process. Sponsors might be involved in programs where the focus is on individual problems, but they are always involved in team-project programs. For team projects there is usually a high-level manager or executive outside the team who takes on the responsibility of supporting the work on the project, the participants' learning, and implementation of the results of the team's work. The role of a sponsor will be discussed more in the next chapter, but a good model is shown in PSE&G's LIRW program.

The sponsors for the LIRW program were first chosen from the Senior Leadership Team (SLT) of the organization. In their role as sponsors, they worked with the co-design team, and learning coaches, to choose and support participants, and to get help and feedback on their own development. The entire SLT attended the final session of each LIRW program to demonstrate interest and support in both the learning taking place and the project recommendations.[20] As lower level executives in the organization went through LIRW, the role of sponsor was eventually passed down to them to continue their development.

There are a number of ways in which sponsors are chosen or recruited. At Volvo Truck (VTC), past and present members of the executive management team were involved in the co-design of the program. This included final selection of the project sponsors, or hosts as they were called, and matching them with the right projects to move VTC towards becoming a global learning organization.[21]

The VNU program demonstrates another value of the sponsor role—helping to ensure organizational support for the program and discussing a way to help orient sponsors to their important role in the AL program.

VNU Explorers Program
Holly O'Grady, VNU

The sponsors for the Explorers Program at VNU tended to be either direct reports of the business unit presidents or one level below. Involving high-level executives turned out to be beneficial for the program as well as the participants. Since these executives had considerable influence in the organization, their active involvement helped build interest in the program as well as recruit other leaders for subsequent programs. Because of their position and internal networks, they were able to assist the participants in gaining access to other leaders and generate organizational interest in the outcome of their projects.

In the first program the human resource heads and business leaders were largely responsible for selecting the first sponsors. However, in the subsequent programs sponsors recommended other colleagues. In the last program, we also recruited a sponsor from one of our regional leadership programs.

The executives who accepted the role of sponsor in the first program were initially skeptical about participating because they were not familiar with the concept of Action Learning. In addition, they were concerned about the time commitment. To address their concerns, we developed a short overview that included a description of their role as well as a calendar. In subsequent programs, a brief orientation call was set up to review their role as well as to start them thinking about a problem that their business was facing that could be developed into an appropriate project.

As shown in the PSE&G and Pfizer examples, the role of sponsor can be passed down to executives who have been through previous AL programs. Since it is not always possible for a sponsor to have had this

---

TABLE 9 Sponsor Development Session

Introductions
- Learning coach
- Potential sponsors
- Additional members of executive team

Contracting between learning coach, potential sponsors, and executive team for day's events

The sponsor's role
- Surface and challenge assumptions
- Review and adapt best practices

Model Action Learning process with first sponsor using proposed project
- Use of challenging questions to deepen understanding of issues around the project and mandate of the team
- Surface and challenge assumptions about the project and mandate of the team

Reflection

Lunch

Model Action Learning process with second sponsor using proposed project
- Use of challenging questions to deepen understanding of issues around the project and mandate of the team
- Surface and challenge assumptions about the project and mandate of the team

Reflection

Q&A about the program design

Final Dialogue

---

experience, potential sponsors can get some exposure to AL through briefing on the role, contracting with the learning coach for development, and specifically designed workshops. An example of one such workshop is in Table 9.

How Do You Choose an Action Learning Team Project?

Step 8 involves choosing projects in a team-based program design. Choosing individual problems in non-team programs does not take place until after other decisions have been made, but team projects require more planning, discussion, and agreement among several stakeholders.

As was discussed earlier, a team project can be part of the design of a program in any of the four schools. There are certain criteria that should be considered when framing a project no matter which school is guiding the co-design. The project should be selected by senior leadership to help reinforce top management support. In the design where the project is chosen by the sponsor, it should be approved by senior leadership. It should link to the strategic mandate of the program or the strategic business plan or goals of the organization. As a result, it will be meaningful to both the organization and everyone on the team. After their pilot program, PSE&G's SLT decided that all their projects would be work required by the actual business plan.[22] Conger and Benjamin found, however, that it's important that the project focus on learning as well as the business imperative.[23]

For most programs, particularly global ones, the projects should be complex and cross-functional to expose the participants to many parts of the organization.[24] Projects should be structured so that action can be taken by the team during the period of the program. Some proponents of AL advocate that some projects in a program should be structured so they could result in profit to the organization.[25] In this way, the AL program could help pay for itself.

In a program that is trying to accomplish organizational change or transformation, such as one usually co-designed in the Experiential or Critical Reflection school, a project should be complex with no obvious, or known, solution. Reasonable people could disagree about the solution,[26] so the participants would be empowered to think outside-the-box and pursue different paths toward solution. These criteria could also be applicable in a Scientific or Tacit design, depending on the goals and strategic mandate.

The Chubb Growth Leader Program had projects that tied directly to the strategic mandate and provided complex projects that had no known solutions for Chubb.

The Chubb Growth Leader Program
Jeffrey S. Kuhn, VP of Leadership and Learning at Peer Insight

The program included an integrative growth project (i.e., Action Learning project) that provided a vehicle for participants to master the principles of innovation and organic growth by developing a strategic blueprint and implementation roadmap for a new growth engine. The projects emphasized the identification and development of new sources of organic growth, ranging from core business growth, to growth via adjacent businesses, to growth via new ventures. As such, this is an opportunity-oriented (as opposed to problem-solving) Action Learning program.

Four growth projects were chartered for the program:

Chubb Personal Insurance (CPI): Riding the Baby Boomer Retirement Wave
The CPI team was charged with examining the unique characteristics, customer needs, and market potential for baby boomers in the United States and developing a prototype portfolio of branded/differentiated offerings that address the unique needs of these customers.

Chubb Personal Insurance (CPI): Broadening the Pond
The second CPI team was charged with conducting a market analysis and identifying a portfolio of ancillary/adjacent offerings (both proprietary and third-party) that would complement and strengthen CPI's core business, enhance the total customer experience and expand its footprint, and provide a platform for market leadership and sustained revenue growth.

Chubb Commercial Insurance (CCI): Identifying a New Customer Segment
The CCI team was charged with conducting a robust scan of the external environment and identifying a new customer segment that would be the next big thing to drive sustained growth for CCI.

Chubb Specialty Insurance (CSI): Winning in the Small Business Space
The CSI team was charged with developing a breakthrough strategy for accessing, generating demand, and accelerating profitable revenue growth among customers in the private small business space.

In some programs, it is important that the solutions can be implemented by the team, while other programs require recommendations to the sponsor that will be carried out by others in the organization, sometimes with the help and support of the AL team. Having the project posed as a question provides a starting point for the team.

Some examples of project questions that fit the criteria discussed include those in Table 10.

One other consideration for project choice is the dichotomy of familiar or unfamiliar, that is, whether the project is chosen from areas with which the participants may or may not be familiar. This dichotomy, referred to as "Exchange Options," can also be considered for the setting for the program itself.[27]

Table 10 Project Questions

PSE&G	How can we take advantage of gas and electric synergy in the area of mark outs (i.e., indication of work that needs to be done)?
	How can we reduce the unit cost of overhead engineering and construction by 10 to 20 percent?
	What role can Distribution play in the communities we live in and serve?
Berlex	How do we assure a pool of people who are ready to assume leadership positions in accordance with the needs of our future growth?
	How can we improve the gross to net ratio while maximizing net sales?
Invensys	How do we organize resources around markets in Mexico?
VTC	What can we do about standstills (unplanned stops of the truck on the road)?[1]

[1]O'Neil, Arnell, and Turner, "Earning While Learning," 157.

Since research has shown that the objectives and outcomes of a project should be as clear as possible,[28] as a guide for the team in some programs, the sponsor sets out what are called Success Criteria for the project and for the team's learning. These guidelines stress the equal importance of the project and learning from the project work, and just as with the project, they can be questioned and challenged by the team. Some examples from various programs follow:

Project Success Criteria
- Investigate/conduct external research.
- Identify resource requirements.
- Develop and initiate a plan that has support and commitment from all team members.
- Identify most effective contact points and mechanisms to ensure effective dissemination of relevant data across divisions.
- Understand the barriers and resistance to organizational and individual change so you can incorporate steps to overcome any anticipated barriers and resistance to your project recommendations.
- Understand corporate legal implications of any recommendation.

Learning Success Criteria
- Build an environment of openness and trust across departments.
- Learn and demonstrate systems thinking and planning.
- Learn how to operate as a virtual team.

In the VNU program, the process for selecting projects evolved throughout the three programs based on the needs of the organization. As the sponsors better understood the process of AL and their role, they became more adept at developing criteria for their selected projects.

VNU Explorers Program
Holly O'Grady, VNU

In the first class the head of HR requested that the theme of the projects address how the VNU businesses could work more collaboratively. Given the business need, the project theme was timely. However, in subsequent classes the projects became more focused on specific business unit issues rather than on enterprise-wide problems. Part of this change was driven by a shorter time period for the project work; therefore, large open-ended problems could not be realistically addressed in that time period. Also, projects that were slightly more tactical in nature proved to be more productive because the sponsors could more readily take action on their recommendations. As a result, the participants could see how their recommendations were being utilized.

In the guidelines to the sponsors regarding their project question, we asked them to consider a problem for which they did not have a preconceived answer. In some cases this criterion proved to be challenging because many of the executives built successful careers by finding solutions to the hard-to-answer questions. However, one of the sponsors who did have a strong opinion understood that he and his organization could benefit if he did not share his views on the problem. While he fully supported the team, he did not interject his own opinion. Only at the end of the project did he share his views with the team. In my experience, the integrity and self-restraint that this particular sponsor demonstrated was exceptional. At the beginning of the program, the feedback we most often gave the sponsors focused on asking them to avoid sharing their views about the project and outcome. The team members, especially in the early stages of their work, were often very quick to pick up on what they thought the sponsor wanted. Fortunately most of the sponsors were receptive to our coaching and, in the end, they found watching the work unfold was far more engaging than what they had previously imagined. Once the problem had been identified, we assisted the sponsors in developing the problem as a question and provided suggestions on what might be included as project criteria. More important, our role at this point was also to suggest that learning criteria be included. We gave the sponsors a few suggestions for learning criteria, which included the following points:

- active and equal participation by each team member
- learn and demonstrate how to give open and honest feedback
- learn and demonstrate how to use reflection to improve team results
- how to effectively collaborate in conducting your research
- how to apply what you have learned while working on the project to your current position.

Initially, some of the sponsors saw the learning criteria as a soft skill requirement but agreed to include it in their project overview. However, a few of the sponsors began to bring up issues around change management. Based on these conversations, we invited them to include other types of criteria that would address becoming aware of dealing with change. Here are a few examples of the learning criteria developed by the sponsors:

- learn about and apply organizational and people influencing skills to help ensure your project recommendations will be accepted.
- learn to work with and manage differing points of view from senior leaders.

How Long Should an Action Learning Program Last?

In the last two co-design steps (Steps 7 and 8), the focus has been on team projects. For either team projects, or individual problems, the next step, Step 9, is to determine the length of the program. Length can differ by the school and the ideal balance between the time needed for project work and development, and organizational capacity. Organizational capacity includes readiness for the program within the organization and the ability to sustain the program needs.

The amount of time for an AL initiative varies widely. In some designs, participants meet one day at a time over the course of several months.[29] In other designs teams meet for several days at a time, spread out over several months;[30] and in yet other designs the teams meet for several days, but just once.[31] Tables 11 through 14 provide examples of designs of the programs discussed in chapter 1 for each of the schools.

The Pfizer PLP, Table 11, which has characteristics of the Tacit school, has a mandate that includes the need for alignment with the organization's Strategic Imperatives and integration into the existing culture, both key elements for a program at Level 1 in the pyramid, as well as the development of leadership skills. Well-balanced teams were put together to solve critical business issues. The teams worked on the projects for three to four months, making specific, structured recommendations and carrying some projects through to implementation. They were assisted by external, and sometimes internal coaches, who helped the team use processes for working through the project and developing leadership competencies.

The GEC Programme, Table 12, which can be considered in the Scientific school, emphasized the learning goals of problem framing and

TABLE 11 Design for Tacit School

Pfizer's Performance Leadership Project

Timing	Content
3 days	**Kick-off Workshop** • Team introduction and project assignment • Team building designed to rapidly begin to develop successful team dynamics • Project scope definition • Education around opportunities for benchmarking of best practices, inside and outside of Pfizer • Team role definition • An initial plan of scheduled meetings and processes designed to bring the team to the mid-course workshop
	Interim team meetings
2–3 days	**Mid-Course Workshop** • Presentation of project recommendation hypotheses • Feedback from sponsors and other teams • Training in stakeholder management • Team-on-team intense feedback, including forced ranking of team members • Final scope definition, including deliverables • Clear action planning to prepare for the final workshop • Development of key messages and work on team members' teachable points-of-view on their project and the leadership processes
	Interim team meetings
1 day	**Commitment Workshop** • Concise presentations of team recommendations, following thorough pre-read of materials distributed prior to the workshop in time for others to understand recommendations • Clear demonstration of successful stakeholder management by each team • A clear business case supporting each team's recommendations • Clear decision making by senior executives, including clear acceptance, rejection, or modification of recommendations, and adequate allocation of resources to produce project outcomes • Another round of serious team-to-team and team-on-team feedback, including feedback to sponsors and to the executive owner on the entire PLP program • Key messages and more work on the teachable point-of-view of each team member and sponsor

---

TABLE 12 Design for Scientific School

GEC's Developing Senior Managers' Programme[1]

Timing	Content
October	Residential session at Dunchurch Industrial Staff College • Two-and-a-half weeks • Formal classes • Start of individual problem work in AL sets (teams)
November–January	Full time work on problems • Diagnosis phase • Four days each week at client (sponsor) location • One day in AL set
February	Residential session at Dunchurch Industrial Staff College • One week
March–May	Full time work on problems • Implementation phase • Four days each week at client (sponsor) location or own company • One day in AL set

---

[1]Casey, "Programme Outline," 11.

reframing. Participants chose, or were assigned, individual problems/projects that were 'owned' by clients or sponsors. They worked full-time on their assigned problems for seven to nine months and carried them through to implementation. Their AL sets (teams) were assisted by internal and external learning coaches.[32]

LIRW, Table 13, was designed as an Experiential program so there was emphasis on personal development through the establishment and work on personal learning goals. Personal learning goals will be discussed shortly. Each team had an organizational team project and each participant had his/her own learning goal. Since this program lasted six weeks, as opposed to the lengthier Scientific program, and participation was part-time, not full-time, the learning coach who worked with each team used interventions and just-in-time learning to create situations that would help participants learn how to learn. Reflection was used throughout the sessions as well.

The Berlex Corporate Development Program, Table 14, in the Critical Reflection school, stressed personal and organizational transformation. The process for developing the personal learning goals of

---

TABLE 13 Design for Experiential School

PSE&G's Leadership Is Real Work

Timing	Content
Week 1 Half day	Orientation • Presentation by senior leader • What is Action Learning? • Sponsors present projects • Panel of former participants • Action Learning team meeting for introductions and norms
Week 2 2 days	Jump Start session • Action Learning team meeting with focus on project work • Sponsor meeting with team • Action Learning team meeting with focus on personal learning goals • Just-in-time learning sessions 　◦ Feedback • "P" learning sessions 　◦ Learning styles
	Interim work on projects and personal learning goals
Week 4 2 days	Interim session • Action Learning team meeting with focus on project work • Sponsor meeting with team • Action Learning team meeting with focus on personal learning goals • Just-in-time learning sessions 　◦ TALK model • "P" learning sessions 　◦ Conflict management
	Interim work on projects and personal learning goals
Week 6 2 days	Final session • Action Learning team meeting with focus on project work • Action Learning team meeting with focus on personal learning goals • Just-in-time learning sessions • Presentation of project and learning to Sponsors and Senior Leadership Team

---

the participants emphasized critical questioning and self-awareness. Dialog and other "P" learning subjects focused on organizational transformation. As in the Experiential program illustrated, each team had an organizational project, each participant had his/her own learning goal, and each team was supported by a learning coach. Reflection and critical reflection were used during the sessions.

Although the amount of time and spacing of days of initiatives vary, research does show that groups need to meet often enough to en-

TABLE 14 Design for Critical Reflection School

Berlex's Corporate Development Program

Timing	Content
Month 1 Three days	Presentation by CEO and sponsors Sponsors present projects Action Learning team meetings • Introductions and norms • Focus on project work Sponsor meeting with team Action Learning team meetings • Review of 360-degree feedback • Focus on personal learning goals Just-in-time learning sessions • Meeting management • Feedback "P" learning sessions during day and in evening • Myers-Briggs Type Indicator (MBTI) • Influencing Community team-building session Dialog **Interim work on projects and personal learning goals**
Month 2 One day	"P" learning session Action Learning team meeting • Focus on project work • Focus on personal learning goals Just-in-time learning sessions Dialog **Interim work on projects and personal learning goals**
Month 3 One day	Action Learning team meeting • Focus on project work • Focus on personal learning goals Community team building session **Interim work on projects and personal learning goals**
Month 4 One day	Action Learning team meeting • Focus on project work • Update with CEO and sponsors Dialog **Interim work on projects and personal learning goals**
Month 5 One day	Action Learning team meeting • Focus on project work • Focus on personal learning goals Dialog

continued

TABLE 14 *Continued*

	Interim work on projects and personal learning goals
Month 6 Two days	Action Learning team meeting • Focus on project work • Focus on personal learning goals • Team assessment Presentation to CEO and sponsors Dialog

---

sure continuation of the process. McNamara[33] found that if groups met less frequently than once a month, the participants tended to lose momentum and trust. Evaluation data from PSE&G showed that teams needed to meet for two consecutive days each time they convened in order to be able to address both projects and personal development.[34]

Having team work extend over a period of time can be important in all schools, but is particularly important in the Experiential and Critical Reflection schools for a couple of different reasons. First, having an extended time to meet is linked with the importance of having the time to take action, and therefore bringing about cycles of action and reflection. Second, as discussed further in chapter 4, most learning coaches try to work themselves out of a job by transferring the skills they use with a team to the participants. The extended time is needed to be able to achieve at least some measure of transfer of learning coach skills to the team. When a program has a time span of several months, or requires full-time participation, as in many designs in the Scientific school for example, the ability of the coach to make him/herself redundant is greatly increased.[35]

These time demands seemingly run counter to pressures in organizations for shorter training designs and problem-solving time frames. All things being equal, any program must be run as efficiently as possible in terms of time and resources without sacrificing effectiveness. However, two factors must be kept in mind relative to the issue of the time demands of AL. First, AL programs are generally targeted toward intensive development along a number of dimensions while working on relatively difficult projects and problems. They are not put in place to meet relatively routine, though important, needs in these areas. It is by no means clear that this level of development and problem solving is achieved as effectively by shorter investments in time. In practice, many of the problems worked on in AL programs are highly challenging ones that the organization has not been able to resolve through alternative means.

Second, generally the purpose of AL is accomplishing both problem resolution and development. Meeting both needs is a task more complex than attempting either in isolation of the other. The argument for AL is that dealing with this complexity is worth the investment, of time and resources, because it is a highly effective means of accomplishing both objectives.[36]

What Kinds of Strategies
Lend Themselves to Success?

The strategies and practices (Step 10) that can most help an AL program achieve success are those that are based in the school that's been chosen and those that help address the primary focus of the program. Table 15 illustrates how choices can connect with schools.

If the focus is on individual development, the co-design could include a process to help participants pursue personal learning goals or give and receive cycles of feedback. An organizational change focus could call for a co-design that helped teams challenge organizational norms and assumptions. These types of practices, and others, are discussed in chapter 3.

TABLE 15 Schools and Strategies

School	Organization	Strategy
Tacit	Pfizer	Team building to rapidly develop team dynamics
Scientific	GEC	Full time work on projects to allow use of Systems Alpha, Beta, and Gamma
Experiential	PSE&G	Consistent use of reflection to promote cycles of learning
Critical Reflection	Invensys	Process for questioning insight to provide challenge and support to participants

What Is "P" Learning?

Step 11 in the co-design process is determining appropriate content or "P" learning. Any programmed, "P", learning is determined based on the school and what the organization wants to achieve as a result of the initiative.[37] It is often established during the co-design, but is also introduced during the program as the need for a particular subject becomes apparent or is requested by participants. The designs in Tables 11 through 14 give some examples of "P" learning for each of the schools.

In the Tacit school program, "P" learning was included, such as benchmarking and stakeholder management to support the project focus, and team building and "teachable points-of-view" to help with team and individual development.

In the Scientific example, the residential sessions at the College were comprised of pre-set classes that were taught by either the College staff or outside experts.[38]

In the Experiential school there are samples of the kind of learning provided. For example, the Learning Style questionnaire and Conflict Management was provided in a lecture and/or experiential format and methods for providing Feedback were given on a just-in-time learning basis. In the Berlex program in the Critical Reflection school, the Myers-Briggs Type Indicator (MBTI) and Influencing were delivered to participants in a lecture and experiential format; and meeting management and methods for providing feedback were provided in project team meetings in a just-in-time format. Since the duration of the Berlex program was longer than LIRW, there was an opportunity for learning coaches to recognize, and participants to request, "P" learning that wasn't preplanned, such as Strategic Learning.

How Do Participants Choose Individual Problems?

As mentioned earlier, individual problems can be used in an AL program in any school. They are most often used in the Experiential and Scientific schools. When participants have their own problems, there is a greater focus on personal development and a greater chance for implementation of any solutions.[39] Preparing participants to choose individual problems on which to work is Step 12 of the co-design process when this is the focus of the program.

Many of the criteria discussed for the team projects are also applicable for individual problems. Of particular importance is:

- linking the problem to the strategic mandate of the program or strategic goals of the organization
- choosing a problem with which the participant has been struggling, that is complex and about which reasonable people could disagree regarding a solution[40]
- structuring the problem so that action can be taken during the period of the program.

Although the problems are often determined by the participants, they are usually discussed with senior management. Sometimes the participant's manager acts as a sponsor for the problem. While the participant usually comes to the AL program with an idea of the problem he/she is to work on, problems are often clarified during the first team meeting. In order to provide guidance in advance, a Problem Clarification Form (Table 16) can be used. The use of this type of form helps the participants focus and reflect on the problem from a number of different perspectives. The criteria set out on the form can vary depending upon the needs determined through the co-design process. Participants use the completed form when they first introduce their problem to the team.

Some examples of the types of problems that participants have addressed in programs are in Table 17.

What's the Difference Between a Personal Learning Goal and a Team Project or Individual Problem?

If in the co-design work it is determined that additional emphasis needs to be placed upon personal development, personal learning goals can be chosen. This is Step 13 in the co-design process. A personal learning goal is a behavior/attitude the participant chooses, usually with the help of his/her manager and the learning coach, to work on with the team during the AL program. Although it is a goal different from and separate from the team project or individual problem, it is often integrated into the work done on the individual problem during work in the team. A useful process for this work is discussed in chapter 3. Personal learning

---

TABLE 16 Problem Clarification Form

Problem Clarification Form

1. Identify your most pressing problem in your work right now that fits the following criteria:
   • it is a problem with which you have been struggling and for which you have no solution;
   • it is a complex problem that has no obvious, or known solution;
   • reasonable people could disagree about the solution to the problem;
   • it is a problem that crosses boundaries beyond your immediate work situation.

State your problem in the form of a question.

2. What is the background to this problem? Note important events which led to it. What solutions have you already tried and how did they turn out?

3. Who are the key stakeholders? What is your role?

4. What are the barriers you must consider in coming to a solution? (Time, resources, attitudes, politics, personalities, structure, etc.)

---

goals are often used in the Experiential and Critical Reflection schools. Data for choosing a personal learning goal might come from a 360-degree process, the participant's appraisal process, or personal insight. The Berlex program illustrates the use of personal learning goals in a program with team projects.

Berlex Corporate Development Program
Bob Ward, President, Leadership Bridge

The overall goal of the Berlex Corporate Development Program is leadership development. Development in the program is realized through a continuous process of action and reflection on real business problems, as well as individual, team, and organizational

TABLE 17 Individual Problems

Global Pharmaceutical Organization	How can I change the culture in sales and marketing (go from telling to selling because we lost patent) and accelerate buy-in at all levels? How do we become the employer of choice in country X? How do I get the X department to embrace the value of financial analysis in decision making?
Global Financial Organization	How will I identify and prepare an adequate number of facilitators for change events? How can I transition off a project and feel good about it? How can I best deal with a stressful relationship between my supervisor and her boss?
Other examples[1]	Reorganize a production line Increase profitability of a small engineering firm Change from autocratic to facilitative style of management

[1]Weinstein, Action Learning, 132.

learning goals. To make the most of this opportunity, participants will identify their own personal learning goal so that the real business problem and team activities can become a practice field for individual as well as team development. These personal learning goals can represent: 1) critical new competencies that the individual sees as important to his/her growth and development; or 2) current competencies that need updating or improvement; or 3) problem areas that are inhibiting effectiveness and need to be changed.

Personal learning goals identify observable behaviors that an individual wants to develop or improve. The learning coach and other team members observe and then provide feedback to the individual. If, for example, your personal learning goal is to foster open communication, there must be an observable applicability to the project or the team interaction. The application of fostering open communication would then be obvious to the team, i.e., the ability to convey the message that every idea is worthy of consideration.

Personal learning goals are shared with other team members and one's learning coach who can provide feedback based on observation and reflection. In addition, personal learning goals:

- focus the individual's attention during team interactions
- become a yardstick for the individual to measure his/her personal development
- are included in individual reflections at various point during the program.

A company with which we worked as learning coaches that we'll refer to as the Global Pharmaceutical Organization provides a good example of how a personal learning goal can be integrated into the individual problem during work in the team.

Global Pharmaceutical Organization

In one team, a technology executive learned from his 360-degree feedback that his people felt he could improve in the way he *painted the big picture,* so he chose a personal learning goal of "working on developing my ability to communicate vision and strategy." When the time came to decide on a problem, he explained that he had recently inherited an organization. The former leader had a completely different view of technology than he did and was not a very good leader. As a result, the organization and people were not performing very well. This executive felt that his problem was to find a way to both develop and communicate a new way of doing business—a new strategy—in order to turn the business around. He recognized that his 360-degree feedback from his old group was connected with his new problem, so he asked the team to help him with the problem—"How do I develop and communicate a new strategy for technology?"

When Do We Need an Orientation or Introductory Workshop?

Step 14 is to provide an orientation or introductory workshop, if and when it is needed, before an AL program is started. Even if not essential, there are times when a workshop can be useful. For example, top management may be supportive of using the process in the organization, but the rest of the organization now needs to be brought on-board.[41] Or HR may feel that AL is the appropriate choice for an intervention, but they now need to expose and/or convince other stakeholders in the organization. A third possibility is when, in the co-design process, it has been decided that the participants should be volunteers. As discussed earlier, although participants are often chosen for organizational programs based on the objectives of the program, if the decision is made instead to look for volunteers, a workshop enables those volunteers to make an informed choice.

McGill and Brockbank[42] provide some comprehensive guidelines for an introductory workshop useful for AL programs that use individual problems. With some adaptation, this process can also be used as an orientation or introductory/workshop for a program co-designed for team projects. The workshop consists of four kinds of activities:

1) introduction to AL through triads
2) AL in concentric circles
3) simulating AL
4) process review.

The first activity allows potential participants to be exposed to parts of the AL process in the safe environment of a triad. After a debrief the next activity has a team, forming the center concentric circle, demonstrate the AL process and receive feedback from observers in the outer circle. In the third activity, everyone gets to practice AL; the last activity enables a final debrief and processing of the experience.

A workshop can be formatted to last from one-and-a-half hours up to a full day. The benefits of a workshop with these elements include:

- enabling participants to experiment before committing
- conveying more accurately the "how" of AL rather than simply explaining the process
- providing a means for self-screening if the co-design of the program calls for volunteers
- being cost-effective.

An example of a workshop we co-designed with a diversified financial services client is found in Table 18.

How Do We Achieve Alignment with the HR Systems in an Organization?

Although AL is an effective intervention, it becomes more powerful in achieving development and organizational change when it works in coordination with other systems or interventions in the organization. One of the most important is the human resource system. Step 15 is ensuring alignment and integration.

There are a number of different ways an AL program might work with, or integrate, pieces of the HR system. For example, the Global Pharmaceutical Organization mentioned earlier used AL to help its global executives better understand one another and work together after a major merger. As an integral part of the co-design, their Global Leadership Capabilities were used to shape the "P" parts of the pro-

TABLE 18 Orientation/Introductory Workshop

Activity	Approximate time in minutes
Set-up AL activity with large group • Participants with projects • Concentric circle/fishbowl set-up • How AL teams will help the project owner • Contract as a learning coach • Provide learning journals	10
Project owner gives brief description of project to enable participants to choose teams Criteria for team selection • Need to be evenly divided • Members of team need to be as diverse as possible • Don't join team if you are "expert" in project area	10
Explain concept of a learning partner • Team members choose learning partner and decide on learning goals	10
First AL team • Discuss and establish ground rules • Project owner presents project • Team uses AL process including helping to clarify project; surfacing assumptions; questioning • Project owner commits to action	40
Reflection for all participants framed by questions from learning coach Learning partners provide individual feedback	20
Second AL team	40
Final reflection	20

gram. In this way, they helped ensure that executives from both merged companies were getting the same message about leadership.

Another example of the integration of organizational leadership models and AL is the PSE&G program.

PSE&G Leadership is Real Work[43]
Judy O'Neil, President, Partners for Learning and Leadership

"It was about this time, 1995, that Pete Cistaro moved from his role in the Quality initiative work to take the job of Vice President of Gas Distribution. He was now able to see, and hear, close up the disconnect between his supervisors and managers and the vision of the future he held for his organization. I asked Pete what it would be like if he achieved the changes that he wanted in the organization. Pete described this vision:

> It would be a lot quicker. We would get rid of the forms, we'd get rid of the paperwork and all the other bureaucracy that tends to hold us up. We would have this desire. Everybody would have this desire to really get things done faster, especially as it pertains to customers. So that when a question came in, there would be an intense effort to get that answer back, and to get the job done as quickly as possible. There would be a greater sense of urgency. That to me is, I believe, very important. That's one.
>
> People would take the initiative themselves rather than waiting for somebody else to either approve or give them the answer. And I think we would have a very clearly defined, aligned, and recognizable common set of goals, objectives, so that everybody clearly understood where we were going, everybody clearly understood how we knew when we got there, and everybody clearly understood their role in helping us to get there. And that they were consciously, on a daily basis, working to achieve those things, as opposed to getting there by accident.

I asked Pete if he thought people would also interact differently if his vision were reality. He replied that indeed they would:

> I think the respect for people would be a lot greater. That we would value people's thoughts and ideas, and that we would go out of our way to get more people's thoughts and ideas. That when we had information to exchange, that it would be based upon data and measures or information, as opposed to just "well, this is what I think" type of thing. And that people really would appreciate what other people do, and would appreciate how they're not holding their end of the bargain up. Or they're not being accountable for, and taking responsibility for, what they're supposed to do. How that impacts other people, and how that frustrates those other people, and how that's really not being respectful of those other people.
>
> So a little bit of that sounds like, and I suspect I could be accused from time to time of sounding like a philosopher, or a lot of soft stuff, and why is this guy talking about this stuff? You know, this concept of caring for other people, which, again, some people find difficult to hold onto, but I think that's very important. And I think a lot of the results, and I think a lot of the lack of results, and I think a lot of the success, or lack of success, that we have is really based upon the relationships that exist between different individuals. Whether they be peer to peer, whether they be department to department, whether they be subordinate to the boss, whether they be employees to customers, to suppliers, to whoever, it's all built on relationships. Because the company … when you say "the company" … and we all like to say "the company"… who is the company? It's us. I mean there's no entity. There's no body. There's no mind. There's no spirit. It's the spirit, the body, the mind of everybody in the organization.

In order to bring this vision even closer to home, Pete developed a model of leadership behavior that showed the balance between new behaviors and results that he felt would be necessary for the continued success of the organization and the individuals in the organization. In order to disseminate knowledge about his vision within the organization, Pete again tied in what he calls the soft stuff with the running of the organization and continued to draw upon what he saw as important for a leader—involving people. Pete described the way he did this through developing the business plan.

> I feel, again, because of my need for involving people, is that it's got to be done by more than just two people putting a business plan together, or three people, or ten people. There's got to be more people involved. So how do we do that? We've kind of experimented with different ways, and this past Spring we did it where we had two days of maybe eighty people working together to start to develop it, and get input from all those folks. I think that's key. And team work. How do you get people working together?

Pete also recognized the need for teamwork as he explored ways to solve the problem of how to engage his supervisors and managers fully in his vision of a changed organization. 'It's hard for me to do it alone. But if I know I've got somebody else who's with me, and trying to do the same thing, and helping me, and giving me some tools and some advice, that makes it easier for me.' In 1996, Pete turned to Bob Browning, the Manager of the Leadership and Professional Development group for that help. After additional analysis of the organizational needs, Bob proposed that the Gas and Electric Distribution divisions try Action Learning to bring about the desired changes."

A program co-designed with Grace Cocoa, the Global Forum, illustrates how AL can work with and be supported by other interventions. The HR vice-president had the charge of transforming a disjointed company into one company with one culture. He started with a search conference that began to create the vision of the organization as a global industrial cocoa and chocolate company, but lacked the follow-up that was needed. He next created a companywide organization development task force who gathered the necessary data and came back with seven dimensions that were lacking in management. The VP decided that AL would best develop these dimensions and create the kind of transformative change needed in the organization.[44] Pfizer's program design also built in their Senior Team Alignment workshop during which the IT leaders created their Strategic Business Framework that eventually helped shape PLP.

How Does a Cascading Rollout Work?

If AL is to be a repeated intervention, Step 16 in the co-design process is needed to design a cascading rollout. Since the process of AL is different from most other development programs, it is best for the executives of an organization to participate first. This way they are better able to appreciate the experience and to support future participants. The co-design can be modified for executive participants—often shortened—to ensure their participation. Special programs—like the Senior Leader Enrollment session and the Sponsor Development session described earlier in this chapter—are also used to start the cascade with senior executives.

Before the cascade within the organization begins, particularly depending upon the school used as the basis for co-design, it is a good idea to run a pilot of the program. As discussed earlier, the PSE&G LIRW program was co-designed based on the Experiential school, but had elements of the Critical Reflection school as well. As we co-design up the AL pyramid, we can end up with a program that can create more *noise* in the organization. A pilot is a good way to determine how well the capacity of the organization can handle this noise and what modifications might be needed to the program to better meet the needs of the organization.

PSE&G LIRW[45]
Judy O'Neil, President, Partners for Learning and Leadership

The pilot experiment took place over a three-month period. Through its process of creating ambiguity and challenging participants' concepts and beliefs, AL can create a lot of anxiety and discomfort at first on the part of participants. The AL design concept of a cycle of work in the team that helps the participant look at and think about the problem in new ways; action in the workplace; reflection on that action; more work in the team; and so on allowed that anxiety and discomfort to be manifested in the workplace. As this was happening, we found out that we had not sufficiently prepared the leaders in the organization, including Pete, for this manifestation. We had indeed succeeded in setting people's nerves on edge.

We, the participants, and the organization were fortunate that we had change agents in Pete and Bob, who were courageous enough to withstand the anxiety in the organization. We reassured them to *trust the process,* but it was not until the final session that the transformative learning that many had undergone became apparent. Participants spoke about changes in their work and personal life, how they were able to break away from preconceived boundaries, and the importance of understanding that there really were shared values in the organization. Based on what had been heard in the previous three months, the impact of the report of participants' learning and their project results was stunning to many at the session. We took the feedback, and lessons, from the pilot very seriously. We held several debriefing sessions with participants and significantly altered the pilot design before beginning the cascading rollout.

In the course of the PSE&G rollout—eleven programs; almost three hundred participants; over two years—there were a number of lessons learned. Despite the organization's desire to have all participants attend LIRW as quickly as possible, we decided to run just one program at a time for a number of reasons:

- Strategic projects have a significant impact on the organization, so having more than four projects—since there were four teams in each program—would have exceeded the capacity of the organization in supporting the projects and the teams.
- Each team averaged seven participants, so one program was staffed with at least twenty-eight participants. Although the program was part-time, the participants dedicated a significant amount of time to the team and project work, which meant the organization needed to provide some backfill for their work.
- Each team had an executive project sponsor who was required to devote time and resources in support of the team. It would have been difficult to engage more than four sponsors at a time.
- From the positive side of the equation, running one program at a time, and therefore allowing LIRW to be part of the organization for over two years, enabled the assimilation of AL concepts into the fabric of the organization.

How Do You Evaluate an Action Learning Program?

The final step, Step 17, in the co-design of a program is the decision if, and how, to evaluate the program. Some of the approaches to evaluating more traditional training, for example, Kirkpatrick's model[46], can also be used for AL to look for impact at various levels, ranging from satisfaction and learning of participants to impact on the job and perhaps even in the organization. There are additional evaluation and research methodologies that can also be used. Evaluation and research of AL programs will be discussed in detail in chapter 5. Now that we've looked at the key co-design issues, chapter 3 provides the detail needed to co-design a truly effective AL program.

CHAPTER THREE

Implementation Strategies for Success

"If in the last few years you haven't discarded a major opinion or acquired a new one, check your pulse. You may be dead."
    —Gelett Burgess
"We learn more by looking for the answer to a question and not finding it than we do from learning the answer itself."
    —Lloyd Alexander

W
e've looked at the concept of co-design and have introduced seventeen steps in the co-design process. We provided relevant examples to illustrate how the co-design process helps to ensure that the program will meet the needs and capacity of the organization and participants. But what differentiates a successful Action Learning (AL) program, that is, one that achieves or surpasses the objectives of the co-design? One of the strategies that can help to make a program successful is to ensure that there are co-design elements that support the chosen AL school. In the case of the Global Pharmaceutical Organization's AL program, co-design elements that provided both challenge and support, such as the use of *good* questions and the identification of assumptions, helped the program be successful within the Critical Reflection school.

Global Pharmaceutical Organization

The Global Pharmaceutical Organization used individual problems in their co-design. In the first session of one of the programs, the Executive Vice President of HR for the business in a European country presented the following problem to his team:"How can

63

I develop my senior management team to manage their learning better?" He went on to explain that his senior team of seven people, which included the marketing company President and himself, had achieved good results in the last year but weren't good at sharing their knowledge and expertise with others in the company. He had shared his concerns with some of his peers but was afraid to raise the issue publicly. Complicating the issue was the fact that some of the directors didn't get along. "The Marketing Director hates the other directors." He felt they all needed to cooperate in order to ensure that the business would continue to be successful.

The team and learning coach began their challenge and support with questioning insight. Some of the questions included:

- Where did the success last year come from if there was this lack of cooperation?
- Do all the directors behave this way? Do they behave this way all the time?
- What is your evidence this behavior is not good?
- Is the behavior open or hidden?
- Have you figured out how you're contributing to the problem?

Some of the assumptions raised were, "I assume personal ambition is a factor"; "I assume this is considered to be an acceptable way of working." Based on reflection on the questions, assumptions and reframes offered, the Vice President reframed his problem to "How can I help the senior management team recognize that their dysfunctional behavior will eventually harm the marketing company?" He decided that he needed to take the explicit action he had been avoiding and discuss the issues with the President and the management team.

Conger and Benjamin identified design factors through their research on AL programs that were discussed in the last chapter: choice of learning projects, clarity of objectives and outcomes, multiple opportunities for reflective learning, active involvement of senior management, and strong, clear buy-in from all affected operating units to team projects. Expert coaching and facilitation (which we address in chapter 4) and follow up, i.e., transfer of learning, (which we address in chapter 5) were also identified.[1] Our research and experience also suggest critical success factors associated with execution related to critical roles and strategies to help people learn.

In this chapter, we'll look at the elements and strategies that grow out of execution that help to make a successful AL program. We'll look at the critical roles of sponsor, participant, and learning coach (we'll also discuss the learning coach role in more detail in chapter 4). We'll examine strategies to prepare participants upfront for their experience and to help them better learn during the program. We'll describe methods for programs focused on team projects, guidelines for individual problem programs, processes for personal learning goals, and the use of learning journals to support the various types of programs. We'll close this chapter with a look at other execution factors that support success or contribute to failure in an AL program.

We will draw on examples from the VNU Explorers program and PSE&G's LIRW (Experiential school) and the Berlex Corporate Development program (Experiential and Critical Reflection schools). There are some additional programs we'd like to introduce as well.

First, a hybrid AL program in which an AL team was embedded within an action research[2] project. The action research process is very similar to ways in which Revans describes AL, so this program has elements that place it in the Scientific school and others that straddle the Critical Reflection school.

U.S. Department of Veteran Affairs Action Research Project Team[3]
Janet Reid-Hector and Lyle Yorks

The VA Stress and Aggression project emerged as a result of a mid-level HR manager in the VA Headquarters initiating inquiry and conversations about the problem of aggression in the workplace. The stimulus for his inquiry was his realization that many of the disciplinary cases that he and his colleagues dealt with appeared to be connected with reactions to stress that were manifested in the form of aggressive behavior. Disciplinary penalties seemed to be addressing symptoms but did little to address the underlying problems. His conversations with colleagues inside the VA and with academic researchers on the problem of workplace stress and aggression eventually led to the formation of a group of academic faculty members, VA human resource specialists, and other stakeholders into a research project team. Awarded a grant by the National Science Foundation (NSF), which supplemented budgetary support from various VA Departments, the project evolved, finally adopting three foci:

- the creation of an instrument for measuring stress and aggression
- the development of quantitative models for developing and testing a business case for reducing stress and aggression in the VA
- the adoption of a practice-grounded action research model for the process.

With the aforementioned funding in place the project team, consisting of three academics from three different universities (two psychologists, and a human resource expert) and several HR and VA professionals, embarked on a formal three-year project that included eleven field sites, each with its on local action team, and the identification of comparison (control sites).[4]

The AL project team was embedded within this larger action research project, using both quantitative and qualitative data to understand both the profile of stress and aggression within the VA, and the process that was unfolding, with the intention of creating a new framework for improving organizational performance that could be diffused throughout the organization. The formal project took place over a three-year period, late 2000 to 2003. The phases of the project involved organizing the field site action teams, data gathering from the field sites and control sites and feedback to the field sites, creating site specific interventions, visiting sites to discuss the experience of the site-based action teams, and sharing learning across sites. The project team worked with the field action teams on the design and implementation of the survey instrument that was created, fed the data back to the sites, and relied on the action teams to create actions in response to their site data.

As described above, the project was initiated by the mid-level HR manager who was a member of the project team. He was a catalyst, bringing together the network of people who formed the project team, eliciting financial support from various VA departments such as the Office of Resolution Management and the VA Learning University, and regularly making presentations on the project and the learning that emerged at various VA symposiums and senior meetings. His immediate supervisors provided him with the flexibility of coordinating the project. Additionally, a senior VA executive became active in the project and provided access to some of the field sites.

With the adoption of a practice-grounded action research model for the project, and a strong intention to initiate change in the organization, the academic working in an HRM research center and who was familiar with the organizational learning literature and research convinced the members of the project team to experiment with explicit learning practices. This led to the invitation of the fourth academic researcher with a background in adult learning to visit the team and introduce some learning practices. He subsequently was invited to join the team and became a regular participant in the project. His prior research and field work involved AL and collaborative inquiry in a range of organizational settings. Through his help, the team recognized they would have to learn their way into the process and develop new ways of looking at conventional problems. At several points along the way, its members had to reframe their understanding of the problem and their own role. They were functioning as an AL team.

Next, in the Experiential school, we co-designed a program that used individual problems. We'll refer to the organization as the Global Financial Organization.

Global Financial Organization

This program was co-designed in the late 1990s for relatively new managers who had either been promoted into a management position or were directly hired into the company as a manager. The goals of the program were to:

- learn to learn through challenge
- define your role in creating value

- build capacity for managerial judgment
- improve tactical leadership skills.

During a two-day start-up event, senior management discussed the vision of the company and its management staff, lectures were held on the theory and practice of management skills and responsibilities, and the participants engaged in various experiential learning activities. This event was followed up by three one-day AL workshops spread over three months. Prior to the first workshop, participants chose a challenge (problem) to address with their AL team using a Challenge Clarification Form for guidance. This challenge was chosen in consultation with their current Engagement Director. Guidelines were provided to help in choosing an appropriate challenge. These included:

- part of your current real work
- actionable within the scope of your responsibilities
- challenge-oriented, that is, with no simple, obvious or merely technical solution
- potential solution about which reasonable people might disagree
- compelling interest in the outcome.

Each AL team was comprised of four to eight participants who worked with a learning coach each workshop day. During the workshop, each participant was given approximately one hour of *airtime* during which the team used a number of different AL processes to help the challenge holder work on his/her challenge. Some of these processes will be discussed later in the chapter.

Another program that was mentioned earlier was the Volvo Truck Management Program (VTM). This program was co-designed in the Critical Reflection school and used the AL process developed by MiL called Action Reflection Learning™.

Volvo Truck Management Program
Dr. Sharon Lamm-Hartmann, CEO, Inside Out Learning, Inc

One of the leading companies in the truck manufacturing business, Volvo Truck Corporation (VTC) was a bit ahead of the game when in 1990 it realized that significant changes were taking place in its business environment. These changes included recognition of a new global competition. VTC was becoming part of a global community with interrelated, economic, political, cultural and ecological interests. At the same time, the company reorganized to a decentralized structure. The formula that brought it success in the past—one that stressed production, manufacturing excellence, and rapid decision making—had changed.

The VTC executive team realized that the changing business environment required a transformation in their leaders' mindsets from the old manufacturing-focused, directive boss toward a global leader who: 1) understands cultural differences and can work cross-functionally and cross-regionally in high performing teams, and 2) has a coaching style focused on customer satisfaction, developing his people and himself. In effect VTC wanted to transform their leaders' mindsets from a "power over" to a "power with" paradigm. VTC needed an approach for developing the type of leader who would have the skills and abilities to thrive on the challenges the company was facing. Co-designing with Management in Lund (MiL) and Leadership in International Management (LIM), VTC proved that it was possible for a leadership development program to help foster this type of transformation and develop leaders to more effectively address twenty-first-century challenges.

Eva Arnell, responsible for leadership and competence development in VTC, had participated in a MiL program and was inspired to create a similar program for VTC, using the ARL leadership development philosophy. VTC called this program the Volvo Truck Management Program (VTM).

An ARL program places an equal emphasis on both action (through project team-work on strategically important business problems) and reflection (separate, specifically designed opportunities to think about what took place to learn from each other and from theory).[5]

By 1997, VTC had conducted six programs, one program per year. These programs engaged nearly 100 managers from sixteen different countries in the completion of twenty-eight strategic business projects. Two examples of such projects were: 1) When and why should VTC use supplier partnerships? and 2) What are the major areas VTC should explore to extend its scope of business operations?

Each program involved sixteen to twenty managers and ran for four five-day sessions spread over six months. The four sessions were split between residential seminars and project work. Participants were divided into four project teams of four to six people each. To encourage cross-functional and cross-cultural communication, project teams were mixed to maximize diversity (i.e., of functions, cultures, and personality). Cross-cultural communication was also fostered in that each program session took place in a different part of the globe.

Participants learned as they worked with real projects that were of strategic importance to VTC but were outside the normal scope of their professional skills. A key design premise is that the greatest opportunities for learning often occur when people are placed in unfamiliar territory with unfamiliar and complex tasks and relationships.[6] With no experts around, leaders can no longer rely on previous knowledge. Creativity, innovation, courage and judgment become necessities.

Table 19 shows the program design for VTM program 2 (1992). Over time, from program 2 through 6, minor design changes occurred. It appears that what changed was mostly the repositioning of lectures and activities to different program weeks, the shortening or lengthening of some segments, and the experimenting with some new activities.

TABLE 19 The VTM Program Design

Program 2	Main design components for Program Two
Session one (1992) (Brugge, Belgium)	• Welcome/get to know each other: involved top management, project sponsor presentations, and project preparations • Total group interactive lectures (26.5 hours): lecturers included top management, learning coaches, and external presenters. Topics included scenario planning, the global environment of business, high performing teams, cultural differences with Belgians, strategies within the truck industry, and global competition. • Total group activities: cultural evening (visit the local culture in teams) and beginning of business game (one day) • Project work: approximately two days • Total group reflection and dialogue sessions: two hours
Session two (Greensboro, North Carolina)	• Project work: (almost three days interspersed with lectures and activities • Total group lectures: topics included cultural difference, business control, leader/manager skills, high performing teams, completion of Myers-Briggs Type Instrument (MBTI) • Total group reflection and dialogue: two hours • Total group activities: business game and cultural evening
Session three (London, England)	• Project work: one-and-one half days • Total group lectures: topics included—MBTI, 360-degree feedback instrument, project team feedback, high performing team instrument and skill development • Total group activities: cultural evening and business game • Total group reflection and dialogue: two hours
Session four (Gothenburg, Sweden)	• Total group lectures: global management and internal company presenters • Total group activities: completion of business game, outdoor activities • Project team presentation preparation • Total group reflection and dialogue: two hours • Project presentations to executive sponsors: one day and ending ceremony

What Does a Sponsor Need to Do to Help the Program Be Successful?

The first critical role we'll examine in more detail is that of the sponsor. The role of sponsor usually exists when the co-design of the program calls for team projects. In this case, the project *belongs* to this individual, who is usually a high-level manager or executive outside of the team. As we'll see with the Global Financial Organization AL program, however, the role of sponsor can also be appropriate for an individual problem program. The sponsor almost always has some effect on the work of the learning coach and the team, as shown by a comment from one of the learning coaches in O'Neil's research.[7]

> My relationship (with the sponsor) was actually a very good relationship. He'd actually been through an AL program and he knew the rules of the game. So there was no problem. I think if you talk to X, what happened to her, she felt the guy, the sponsor, was too manipulative. So she had to be careful of that. There is a question of actually engaging them, but making it clear that it's actually the team's problem and it's the team's responsibility to work through to a solution they find satisfies them and not the solution that satisfies him. Hopefully it will, but it won't necessarily satisfy him. So he has to be kept sufficiently distant to be helpful but not to be dominating, and I think that's where the boundary lies.

One of the ways of helping a sponsor understand the rules of the game is by defining the roles and responsibilities he/she should play according to the needs of the program. These roles and responsibilities can be used for recruiting, as well as training or briefing the sponsor.

Some basic roles and responsibilities for the sponsor are applicable for any school, for example, "Lend support in the form of resources and commitments" and "Work toward creating and supporting the changes that will result from achieving the objectives of the initiative." Table 20 shows these two roles and responsibilities, as well as others that were used with sponsors in the Critical Reflection school program co-designed for Berlex.

In her description of the sponsors in Leadership in Action at Invensys, Hoepfner-Karle describes some of the ways they played out their roles.

Invensys Leadership in Action
Kate Hoepfner-Karle, KHK Human Capital Consulting

Each team was assigned a sponsor, a member of the Executive Team to offer support, guidance and required resources as needed. Sponsors were *not* to supply the answer but were to encourage the teams to find the answers. Each sponsor met during the first session with his/her team to brief the team on the definition of the project and the

TABLE 20   Sponsor Roles and Responsibilities—Team Project Programs

Berlex Action Learning Sponsor, Roles and Responsibilities

Lend support in the form of resources and commitments
- attend program launch to 'charge' your team with their project
- provide support for what your team needs
- be available to the team during the initiative, as they need you
- encourage your team to accept responsibility and authority for their actions
- ensure that the participants' managers and peers support the time commitment needed for project work and learning
- act as liaison between team and organization as needed
- attend final program presentations

Role model the behaviors taught in the program
- ask for feedback from teams, senior leaders and learning coaches about your behavior
- discuss situations in which you have recognized your own need to learn, and how you went about learning
- share mistakes you have made in trying to model new behaviors
- encourage your team to ask questions

Expect participants to accomplish both their team project and their personal learning goal
- reinforce the balance through development of a measure of success for your project that focuses on both project work and learning
- stress balance in all your interactions with the team
- explicitly inquire about learning and behaviors when talking with participants

Create an open, supportive, and challenging environment for the initiative
- be willing to challenge assumptions about the organization and culture
- encourage teams to examine what they think are the rules or culture of the organization
- encourage risk taking by being open to thoughts that may run contrary to your own
- treat mistakes made by participants as opportunities for learning

Work toward creating and supporting the changes that will result from achieving the objectives of the initiative
- hold participants accountable for, and reward progress with, the new behaviors
- work to develop and change your own behavior so that it is consistently supportive of the desired changes
- encourage participants to use their new behaviors in situations back on the job
- after initiative, help create opportunities for participants to continue developing skills and behaviors

Contract with learning coach
- establish an agreement with your team's learning coach to include how you will work to-gether to support your team and a schedule for communication during the program
- provide learning coach with explicit, visible support of the fact that learning is as important as the project (the team will be very focused on the project so the sponsor doesn't have to worry about insufficient concern with task in favor of learning)
- be open to the project/problem being reframed or solved in a different way than expected
- be committed to open, ongoing communication with the coach

Invensys expectations for the team. Sponsors would then check in with their team for updates and progress review at a minimum of three times prior to final review at the program's end.

The role of the sponsor in an individual problem is somewhat different from the sponsor's role in a team problem since the problem is *owned* by the participant. The sponsor is in more of a supportive, rather than an owner role. It became apparent during the co-design work in the Global Financial Organization Action Learning program that it was important for the participants' Engagement Directors to be involved in the choice of problem, so their role was cast as sponsor. The sponsor roles and responsibilities were co-designed/adapted to

---

TABLE 21 Sponsor Roles and Responsibilities—Individual Problem Program

---

Global Financial Organization Action Learning Program, Sponsor Roles and Responsibilities

Discuss your expectations with each participant prior to the start of the AL workshops to include
- participants getting help, ideas, support from AL team members toward work on/solution to their challenge
- participants taking all opportunities to learn
- participants learning about developing the ability to ask insightful questions to learn; questioning assumptions; reframing their challenge
- the importance of participant attendance at all AL workshops to help ensure all participants fully benefit from the experience

Provide assistance with selection of participant challenge
- discuss the participant's selected problem or assist with the selection
- ensure the problem meets the following criteria
  ◦ it is a part of the participant's real work
  ◦ it is a problem with no known solution
  ◦ it is a problem about which reasonable people could disagree with the outcome
  ◦ it is a problem about which the participant can take action toward resolution
  ◦ you, and the participant, have an interest in the outcome

Attend the first session of the AL workshop
- tie in participants' work and learning in the workshop with overall goals of the department
- demonstrate support of the work participants will do together
- assist with any questions from participants

Provide support and encouragement to try out different approaches/new behaviors back on the job
- meet/talk with AL participants after each session to discuss what commitments to action and learning they made with their team
- explicitly discuss what you can do to support them in their efforts
- provide participants with the opportunity to share their learning with the rest of the department

---

meet the needs of the organization as shown in Table 21, Sponsor Roles and Responsibilities—Individual Problem Program.

How Can We Prepare Participants Upfront to Be Successful?

In chapter 2, we talked about how the choice of participants was made; the importance of diversity in the mix of participants in an AL team and the ideal size of a team; and the issue of voluntary or non-voluntary participation in the program. Upfront preparation of the participant is crucial to his/her success.

This preparation can take place in different forms. For example, in the PSE&G LIRW program, sponsors personally called each participant to explain why the sponsor had chosen the individual for the team and what he/she felt the individual would contribute. This type of contact between the sponsor/executive and participants can be particularly crucial for a new AL program to reinforce with the participant the importance and value of the program.

Often a pre-program conversation takes place between each participant and the learning coach. This sets the stage for the participant to understand what his/her role will be in the AL program and the role the coach will play. Just as with the sponsor, many programs also provide a description of the participant's roles and responsibilities. An example from the Invensys program is shown in Table 22, Participant Roles and Responsibilities.

What Role Does a Learning Coach Play to Support a Successful Action Learning Program?

When learning coaches are used in programs, their role is critical to success. Coaches are always used in the Experiential and Critical Reflection schools. Early research by MiL based on feedback from participants in programs that did or did not have learning coaches showed that coaches helped managers step outside of taken-for-granted mental models and routines. Bourner and Weinsten's work has also shown that not having a learning coach can lead to certain problems or pitfalls for a team. First, when there is no learning coach to work with the group the "whole focus of the set tends to shift to the solution of the problems. . . ."[8]

TABLE 22 Participant Roles and Responsibilities

Invensys, Action Learning Participant—Roles and Responsibilities

Openness to learning
- being open to learning in general
- being open to learning how to think differently about your self, your day to day work, and your organization
- working toward balancing learning while solving the team's problem
- being open to thinking about the problem/project from a different point of view
- sharing your learning with others in the team
- using your new learning on the job

Personal commitment to the success of the team
- regular participation—showing up at every meeting (either in person or virtually) and staying for the entire meeting
- equal participation—allowing adequate time for everyone to express ideas and ask questions
- questioning and challenging—posing reflective and challenging questions to ensure the best outcome to the project
- reflection—examining their own assumptions and the quality of their own participation
- taking action—carrying out what was promised

Support other team members
- colleague support—build a supportive environment by listening and caring
- build trust and confidentiality
- balance talking, listening, observing and thinking
- recognize issues underlying the problem/project that has been presented

---

Second, there is a danger of the learning dimension getting lost and the group becoming simply another project group.[9]

In the Scientific school, the learning coach is primarily involved in initiating an AL team and in that role has responsibilities similar to those in the other two schools. The coach's role in the Tacit school varies. Sometimes coaches aren't used at all.[10] Sometimes, teams are helped by process consultants who manage the group's dynamics. Conger and Benjamin describe active expert facilitation—closer to their role in early GE programs and in Business Driven Action Learning—through which "facilitators and instructors can assist teams to consolidate and learn from information. . . . (and) provide needed structure and analytic frameworks early in the process."[11] Expert facilitation is not recommended by others for different reasons. Revans's advocates decry coaches who, by inserting their own expertise into the process, can "steal the learning" of participants. In our experience, learning coaches help hold the space for learning. But they are more successful in this role when they resist taking on expert facilitation roles that participants themselves should take. The more that participants do on their own, in this argument, the more likely that participants will fully internalize the learning and be better able to transfer that learning back on their jobs. Raelin points out that "ignorance (of subject matter expertise) implies a need to ask difficult questions that participants might find useful in framing the problem."[12]

Many programs provide written roles and responsibilities for the learning coach to begin to clarify and differentiate the role from other similar team roles the participants may have encountered. Table 23, Learning Coach Roles and Responsibilities, shows the roles and respon-

---

TABLE 23 Learning Coach Roles and Responsibilities

Team Intervener
- ask questions as the favored approach for interventions
- help participants learn to ask the right questions
- help the team balance task and learning
- help the team deal with emotions generated by balancing task and learning
- make the work of the team visible
- challenge the team
- enable learning
  - create a supportive environment
  - help rather than teach
  - create ways to think differently
- say nothing; be invisible
  - hold back on interventions
  - allow problem in team to continue so learning can occur

Team Reflector
- help the team reflect on its progress and process in solving their project
- help the team to learn how to reflect to diagnose team problems
- use reflection as an integral part of the intervention work
  - do at specific set times
  - use when the team is stuck or heading into difficulty
  - reflection is prompted by the use of questions

Team Periodic Trainer/Coach
- use the *just-in-time* learning philosophy and requests for help from the team to determine appropriate times to offer training and/or development
- share the role with team members
- help the team learn how to transfer learning from the program back to the job

continued

TABLE 23 *Continued*

- help the team to learn how to learn from work
- work with the team to transfer learning coach skills
- help participants to give and receive help and feedback to each other

Sponsor Liaison and Coach
- establish an agreement with the team's sponsor that includes how they will work together to support the team and a schedule for communication during the program to help ensure sponsor involvement and comfort with his/her role
- contract with sponsor for appropriate coaching role with the sponsor for program
- work with sponsor to help create understanding of balance between work and learning required in team and how to reinforce that balance
- help the sponsor to have his/her assumptions and ideas of the *right* solution questioned and challenged, so the wrong message isn't sent to the team

---

sibilities used as a starting point in VNU. The learning coach role will be discussed in more detail in chapter 4.

What Needs to Happen for an Action Learning Team Focused on a Team Project to Be Successful?

Although programs are co-designed with the aim to produce particular outcomes, because of the nature of AL and the potential resultant learning, the outcomes can't be guaranteed. That being said, our experience and research have shown that the use of certain methods in an AL program is more likely to lead to success than others.

To start, we offer some general guidelines based on our experience and review of practice in other programs that can apply to the overall process of the team. They are:

- meet in privacy and relative quiet, free from interruptions
- use whatever meeting guidelines the team establishes, for example, decide on agenda and time allocations; rotate leadership and other team roles; set action steps at the end of each meeting
- use planning tools for project work that build in opportunities for reframing, questioning, and learning, as well as work planning
- question task, process and learning
- reflect on task, process and learning
- reframe project, as appropriate

- solve problems and make decisions
- uncover and resolve conflict
- challenge self, others on the team, and the organization
- keep a written journal record.

As with any meeting in which a team wants to accomplish work, having a place set aside helps to ensure that interruptions, whether in person or by phone, are kept to a minimum. The additional element of privacy is also important for an AL meeting since the hope and expectation is that participants will feel free to question and challenge one another and the practices and norms of the organization.

The wording of the next bullet item is important, that is: "Use whatever meeting guidelines the team establishes". What if the team doesn't establish any meeting guidelines? Then a learning coach will let participants try to proceed without them, at least during the earlier meetings. Some expert facilitators might provide the team with planning tools in advance to do their work. But in many AL designs, a key general principal, which also guides how the learning coach works with the team, is to allow people to learn from their own mistakes and difficulties.[13] If the learning coach intervenes too early, the team will depend increasingly on the coach rather than taking charge of their own learning. AL believes that people learn best from their experience based on good questions, feedback, and opportunities to look at the consequences of choices in a relatively risk-free environment. So this kind of self-directed learning is preferred in many AL designs. The work of the learning coach with the team will be discussed in more detail in the next chapter.

AL teams may use a planning process for their tasks that the organization has blessed and wants people to learn to use. But what continues to differentiate an AL team from other types of project teams is use of a process to address their project that combines planning with opportunities for learning. Part of the initial role of the learning coach is to help the team select and use these different processes. One such differentiating process, used by some coaches in the Experiential and Critical Reflection schools, is the Action Planning Cycle (Table 24), a problem-posing, reframing, and solving process rather than simply a problem-solving process.[14] There are several steps that provide the team with the opportunity to examine the project from an AL perspective.

The opportunity starts with Step 1, Identify/reframe the project. This step is based on the premise that although the project, and probably related information, has just been presented/provided by the spon-

TABLE 24 The Action Planning Cycle

The Action Planning Cycle[1]

6. Decide
Are we ready to make a decision?
Do we have a process for making decisions?
Do we realize we just made a decision?
Or avoided making one?

5. Develop recommendations
What have we done to ensure we've explored
all the alternatives?
Are we aware of the implications of the
recommendations?
Do our recommendations address the needs?

7. Empower and involve
Will the right people be involved?
Do they have the adequate resources and
authority?

4. Gather information/benchmarking
What is the best way to get the information
necessary to address the needs?
Who should be involved in getting and
providing the data?
How should we analyze the data?

8. Implement
How will we determine what is working and
what needs to change?
How can we institute reviews during and
after action?

3. Determine needs
What needs emerge from our assumptions?
What needs do we already know how to
address?
To what needs do we not know the answer?

9. Assess results
What did we say we would do and did we
do it?
How can we ensure we learn from our
successes and mistakes?
Did we celebrate our success?

**2. Surface, examine and challenge
assumptions**
Have we listed all our facts, beliefs, feelings
and opinions/engaged in critical thinking?
Have we identified all the issues to do with the
people, the process and the organization?

10. Use assessment to feed new cycle
What do we need to do next/now?
How do we know what's changed,
improved, diminished?

1. Identify/reframe the project
Can we clearly clarify/identify the task?
If not, who can help us and how do we get that help?

[1]The Action Planning Cycle was derived from the Power Planning Cycle originally developed by Leadership in International Management (LIM).

sor, each participant on the team may not have heard the same message. As the participants listened, each heard what was being said through his/her own frame of reference, or meaning perspective, the structure of assumptions and expectations through which we filter incoming data.[15] Since many of our meaning perspectives are not necessarily in our conscious awareness, it is important that the AL team discuss what they heard from the sponsor to try to determine if they have indeed arrived at the same initial understanding of the project definition and delimitations. If not, additional information and discussion may be necessary.

A frame of reference is composed of two dimensions. The first is called a habit of mind, which is defined as a set of assumptions that act as a filter for interpreting the meaning of experience. The second is the point of view that results from this set of assumptions.[16] The first dimension often acts as a trigger for moving the team into Step 2 of the Action Planning Cycle because it becomes necessary to surface, examine, and challenge the assumptions that are part of each participant's frame of reference in order to try to come to a common understanding of the project and its parameters. A process that can be used for this step is in Table 25, Assumptions.

TABLE 25 Assumptions

What?
An assumption is any belief, idea, hunch, or thought you have about a subject. We use our assumptions to guide behavior.

Why?
We get into trouble when we start believing that our assumptions and inferences are fact. Since we all have different assumptions about a subject, it's important to clarify and challenge all of our assumptions before we begin to work together. If we do not, we may find that what we assume to be true is not shared and our approaches to the project will not mesh.

How?
1. Have the team agree on a statement of the project, as you now understand it.
2. Reflect and write down the assumptions you now hold.
   - *"I think I am right when I say ..."*
   - *"I assume that ...."*
3. Analyze assumptions
   - *As a team, record on easel sheets your assumptions until all assumptions have been listed.*
   - *How can you check out each of these assumptions? What difference would it make if your assumptions are incorrect? Not shared by others?*
   - *To what extent do you think that each of these key assumptions is challengeable?*
   - *After your discussion, how might you change these assumptions?*
4. Refer back to the project information to determine if the project has changed or been further clarified.

Once the team's assumptions have been surfaced, examined, challenged, and clarified, the team may determine that the project should be reframed. This process is more graphically illustrated in Figure 6, Where Learning Takes Place.

As the team continues to work, they continue to pose questions about the project and move toward eventual solutions. The needs that should be pursued start to become evident as illustrated in Step 3 of the Action Planning Cycle. Many of the needs emerge directly from the

FIGURE 6 Where Learning Takes Place

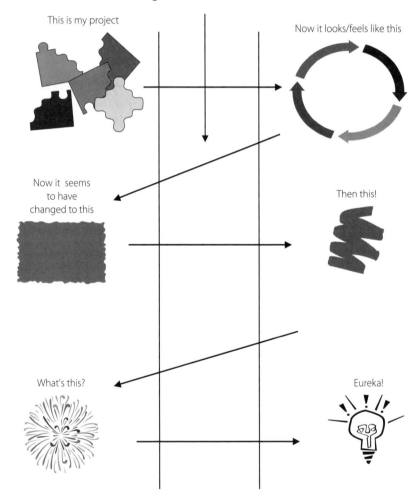

assumptions, and others surface through the ongoing questioning and reflection within the team.

What Else Is Going on with the Team?

As the team moves through other steps in the Action Planning Cycle throughout the course of the AL program, questions and reflection play an integral part of the AL project work. One of the principal ways learning occurs in AL is through asking questions or "questioning insight." Questioning insight has been described as "discriminating questions"[17] or "fresh questions."[18] Discriminating, fresh, naïve questions are important for reaching innovative solutions. The major difference between asking questions in AL work, as opposed to other project work, is that AL questions do not simply seek answers. Instead, questions are intended to go deeper and to enable better understanding. Asking questions is not only searching for answers but is also an opportunity to explore.[19] Marilee Goldberg Adams notes that "questions program the form and direction of answers." She has extensively researched differences between "learner" and "judger" mindsets that influence the nature of questions asked, which in turn influences whether questions open or close opportunities for fresh thinking.[20]

Just as with other new concepts, the skill and art of asking good questions is often first modeled by the learning coach. As will be discussed more in chapter 4, one of the aims of the learning coach is to first model new behaviors and then work to transfer them to the AL participants.

There are a number of ways to categorize what can be considered good questions. The end result should be questions that are challenging; questions that can generate reflection and learning; questions that will cause others to say, "I never thought about that". Some ways to think about this type of questioning are in Table 26, Action Learning Questions.

Some additional questions are found in each step of the Action Planning Cycle. These questions are intended to help guide the team through the process. The learning coach and sponsor also play a support and challenge role as the team moves through the cycle. Depending on the co-design elements of the program, the team may work through the entire cycle both implementing and assessing their recommendations. In other programs, the recommendation may be handed off to another team, or the impacted department, for implementation.

TABLE 26 Action Learning Questions[1]

Question Category	Sample Question
Objective	Who were the key people involved?
Reflective	What do you think would happen if we were to question why the organization continues to do X?
Affective	How would we feel if our recommendation caused people to lose their jobs?
Probing	Why is this happening?
Interpretive	What do we think is really going on?
Challenging	Why does it have to be that way?
Connecting	What would be the impact on the bottom line if we were to do X?
Decisional	How can we make the problem different?

[1]Some of the examples come from Marquardt, *Optimizing the Power of Action Learning,* 77.

The AL team often acts as consultants for their recommendation in those cases.

Reflection is also an integral part of how learning happens in AL. Multiple opportunities for reflection increase the likelihood of a successful program.[21] Reflection is intrinsically bound to questioning insight since it is often guided by good questions. "Reflection consists of those processes in which learners engage to recapture, notice and reevaluate their experience, to work with their experience to turn it into learning."[22] Reflection is not an end in itself. Some benefits of reflection may be lost if it is not linked to experience and action.

Similar to the concept of examining assumptions discussed earlier, critical reflection pertains to problem posing as distinct from problem solving.[23] In critical reflection, people recognize that their perceptions may be flawed because they are filtered through uncritically accepted views, beliefs, attitudes, and feelings inherited from one's family, school, and society. Such flawed perceptions often distort one's understanding of problems and situations. Taking time to reflect even in a surface fashion is powerful, and critical reflection is even more powerful because attention is directed to the root of the project.[24] Table 27 shows some

---

TABLE 27 Reflection Guidelines

What?
Pausing to think about what has just occurred in the team or about what lies ahead; thinking critically about what you or others on the team have done and said.

Why?
Reflection helps to make the work of the team more explicit and in doing so offers the team more choices in how they work together. It enables the team to better understand what has been done well as a team and by individuals, and what needs to be improved. It can prevent the team from jumping to the wrong conclusions and allows learning about alternatives.

How?
- Provide time in the agenda for the team to stop work in order to reflect.
- Ask appropriate probing and reflective questions to help focus the reflection.
- Ask team members to record their thoughts and feelings in their journals before speaking.
- Ask team members to share their reflections.

Guide team members in thinking about the implications of these reflections on the team project, process, and self.

---

guidelines that are useful for helping teams understand the process and rationale for reflection.[25]

There are other good ways of helping a team to integrate reflection into their ongoing teamwork as well as transferring the concepts, and benefits, of reflection into other aspects of work and life. The AL team at the Veteran Affairs' project demonstrates some examples.

U.S. Department of Veteran Affairs Action Research Project Team[26]
Janet Reid-Hector and Lyle Yorks

Different metaphors for stimulating reflection became regularly used by the project team. They were introduced to the field site teams as well. The learning window of what we know we know, what we think we know, what we know we don't know, and openness to the unexpected became a common framing for presentations at various academic meetings as well as in the team meetings. However, this acceptance came with experience. Initially, there was passive resistance. In the words of one team member:

> At the first meeting [the coach attended] he started to use the learning practices … I hated it … I was crawling out of my skin. All I kept thinking about … was we have a limited amount of time, we haven't gotten anywhere and now I've got to get into this touchy-feely crap … . It was just driving me nuts and I have to admit I really wasn't very forthcoming. I mean I'd stare at the piece of paper and I couldn't think

of anything then it would be my turn and I would just kind of echo what everybody else said.

With experience, over time, the practices became a valued part of the process. In the words of one member of the team, "The learning practices have seeped into the common language of the team without being viewed as a formal event." Another member of team states, "the learning practices ... have become part of our repertoire." Yet another member said, "introduction of the learning piece helped us to be able to talk to one another, ... because we are in a learning mode...."

As the team members became more comfortable with the learning practices they included more extensive learning practices for reflection on their actions. This included harvesting the learning exercises that permitted the team to visualize the interconnectedness of various roles within the team. One team member describes the first of these experiences:

> We did a project meeting in Washington ... [that included] ... harvesting learning. Everyone is asked to write on little Post-its significant events that occurred in the project and put them on these big sheets of paper that had time lines ... you could see different people remembered different things and forgot some things ... we had planned the harvesting the learning thing for 2 hours in the morning. In fact we decided to extend it almost 5 hours because it was so useful and we spent time talking about it.

Another team member stated, "With harvesting the learning experience, we could all hover over the project, look at it in a global way and then descend and come back again to look in a new perspective."

Later in the project, the team members used a similar format to examine connections between their process and the data (both quantitative and qualitative) from the field sites. They also used the learning window to classify findings from the data and to test the premises that they were attaching to the results.

Although we've been discussing questions and reflection from the perspective of learning about and understanding the project more deeply, both questioning insight and simple or critical reflection are also used in the AL team in connection with the processes the team uses in their work and in participants' self understanding and individual development. Some questions that can be used to guide reflection in these various areas are found in Table 28, Questions for Reflection.

Up to this point, we've discussed strategies for infusing learning into problem solving through questioning, reflection, and assumption identification. Following are some examples of the results of using these kinds of strategies.

TABLE 28 Questions for Reflection

Situation	Sample Reflection Questions
Understand what's happening/not happening within the team	How are we doing as a team? What did we learn about how we work together as a team? How well are we communicating with each other and why? What worked today? What didn't work today? What's the most important thing I've learned about the team?
Understand what's happening/not happening with the project	What is happening on the project? What is not happening? What can I do to influence the action? What is our comfort level with our progress on the project? What's the most important thing I've learned about the project?
Understand what should happen next	What can we do differently at our next meeting? What do we want to continue to do at our next meeting? Based on what we just did, what are our next steps?
Build on progress from previous meeting/call or prevent/avoid problems encountered during last meeting/call	What did we do at/on our last meeting/call that we want to be sure we do at/on this meeting/call? How did we feel about our last meeting/call? Why didn't we accomplish what we wanted to at/on our last meeting/call? What should we do differently now?
Help during a team meeting/call when the agenda or process has gotten off track	We've run over time on an agenda item again. What are we doing that is causing us not to keep to our time allotments and how can we correct it? We seem to revisit agenda items/discussion areas. Why aren't we clear about our decision making?
Help participants understand how they can transfer what they are learning to their day-to-day job	What have I learned about working on a team that can be useful to me in my current job? How can I improve how I make decisions based on how my Action Learning team makes decisions? What one thing have I changed about my leadership style based on my experience in my team?
Help participants provide feedback to teammates about what they contributed to the successful outcome of the meeting/call	What did each participant do to make it easier for me to contribute? Who added the most "above and beyond" to the meeting/call today? What feedback do I think is important to give to someone today?

Volvo Truck Management Program
Judy O'Neil, Eva Arnell, and Ernie Turner

Through questions, challenging organizational assumptions, and some eventual sponsor support, a team was able to reframe their initial project to one that had organizational implications. The team was originally asked to find a common definition of a "standstill," that is, a truck's unplanned stops, and then figure out how to handle it. It would seem that the concept should be a pretty simple one and would not take several months to figure out, but as the team started to study the subject, the scope of the project changed from just a definition to looking at the problem from a much more systemic basis.

Through identifying the reasons for standstills, the team went back through the service organization and warranty part of the business to the design and engineering departments. They came to realize that, through a lack of systemic communication, valuable information regarding manufacturing issues and servicing cycles was not reaching the right people in a timely fashion. Given the importance of servicing to a customer, what had started as a fairly straightforward question about standstills evolved into questions about relationships among customers, dealers, service centers, distributors, and manufacturers; and ended up improving communications throughout the chain.

The project team met with their sponsor in week three of their program and a rather heated conversation regarding the project ensued. The sponsor at that point was saying, "That's more than I want you to do. I just want to get a better system for accounting for standstills." The team said, "Anybody can do that. The people in your organization can do that. We need to look at this from more of a systemic perspective."

The team finally won out and some of the ensuing results were significant. One of their data gathering meetings was with a customer who said that since he wasn't getting the kind of help he needed in dealing with standstills, he intended to go to another company. Now here was a group of high-level managers sitting with a customer who was telling them he was leaving their company, and at that point in the project, they had no answer for him. What they did was go back to the CEO who responded by visiting the customer himself. The work of the team eventually helped develop a faster, more efficient way of identifying problems that caused standstills and getting information about those problems back to the appropriate source.[27]

Another example illustrates ways that a problem posing process, one of the most important steps in the Action Planning Cycle, rather than just a problem solving process, is more apt to get to the real cause of a problem. The team was assigned the project of finding ways to improve employee satisfaction. The results of the employee satisfaction survey indicated several areas that were problematic. They began with an investigation of extrinsic rewards, but an analysis of the Total Quality movement in the organization and its links to employee satisfaction led to questioning whether or not meaningful work in a true Quality culture might be a stronger motivator than extra pay or benefits. Further work in raising of assumptions led them to realize that a key characteristic of a Quality culture was respect.

As they began to question and challenge their assumptions about the organization's attitude toward respect, they realized that one indicator of a lack of respect in their culture was that employees were often interrupted, albeit with stated apologies, in the middle of phone calls or closed-door meetings by others who demanded immediate information or attention. Such behavior did not feel respectful, nor did it result in high quality work because attention was diverted to multiple uncompleted tasks. In this project work, problem posing began with extrinsic rewards, moved to meaningful work, and ended with the way in which the company could create a culture of respect and, as a result, improve employee satisfaction.[28]

The Pfizer PLP offers a different way for a team to work on their project. Although team members must define for themselves how they want to accomplish their work, they are provided with a guiding framework and a number of key processes.

Pfizer, Inc.'s Performance Leadership Projects
Chuck Williams

Every team meeting includes using the GRPI framework:

G—Are the goals clear?
R—Are the roles defined?
P—Are the processes clear?
I—Is the interpersonal interaction among team members appropriate?

Other key process components include:

- emotional journey-lines (i.e., life experiences that have shaped a member's work experiences)
- rules of engagement
- benchmarking techniques and best practices
- 360 feedback
- leadership assessment (behavioral styles)
- do more, do less, continue feedback
- team-building exercises (collaborative problem solving)

- change management lifecycle and leadership
- stakeholder mapping and management
- business case development and communication
- teachable point-of-view development and refinement
- executive "fishbowl" decision making processes.

The AL consultant provides many frameworks, processes, and mechanisms, and works with the teams and their sponsors to adapt and organize tools and the program as a whole. Their tool set has been developed over a period of several years working with many leadership teams in the United States and internationally.

How Does the Work of a Team Differ That Focuses on Individual Problems?

Although the general outcome of the work is the same, that is, the balance of solving the task and learning, the process that this team uses needs to be different since there are multiple problems to address, not just one. General guidelines that can apply to these teams include:

- Each participant has a particular time period in which to present/discuss his/her problem
- Each participant plays two roles: presenter and supportive member
- Participants do not provide solutions to the presenter, but help the presenter to derive his/her own action plan
- Presenter may use the time as s/he wishes (although the learning coach usually provides some guidelines from which s/he can choose).

One way that teams have worked together successfully on individual AL problems is shown in Table 29, Action Learning Individual Problem Process. Each participant has an allotted amount of time, preferably at least one hour, for focus on his/her problem. He/she first presents the problem with the background he/she feels is necessary for understanding. This time is usually kept to less than ten minutes. If in use in the program, the Problem Clarification Form (Table 16, shown in chapter 2) provides useful information for this initial presentation. The team next works with the participant to provide support and challenge regarding his/her thinking about the problem. Since the problem is an important problem with which the participant has been struggling, it

---

TABLE 29 Action Learning Individual Problem Process

When you have the floor ...
- Describe your problem and why it is important to you
- Discuss the result/outcome you are hoping for
- Describe what success would look like
- Focus the team on what help you would like from them
- Listen closely to the team's questions, assumptions and reframes
- Reflect and answer, or reflect and consider later
- Describe what action you plan to take

When someone else has the floor ...
- First ask 'objective', 'reflective', and 'interpretative' questions
- Ask 'decisional' questions last
- Avoid giving advice
- Don't interrupt
- Avoid taking over the floor
- Don't *bombard* the presenter with too many questions
- Provide your assumptions
- Help reframe the problem

---

can be assumed he/she has already thought about most ready solutions. So the intent of the work is not to offer solutions, but to help the participant think differently about the problem.

The team members and learning coach begin by posing questions that will help to start that process. Table 30, Action Learning Team Questioning Guide, provides some examples. These questions are intended as a starter guide to give the participants some examples of what AL considers questioning insight to be. As the team gains experience, and the learning coach models other *good* questions, the participants develop their own questions that are more particular to the problem at hand. Although the participant can be given the choice about answering questions in the moment, we usually suggest they write the questions down and not answer at the time so they can be receptive to new ideas the questions suggest. The participant will often reflect on the questions offered at a later time.

The next step in the process is similar to the second step in the Action Planning Cycle, that is, the participants surface and examine and challenge the problem holder's assumptions. Since the focus is on the individual's problem, the process is slightly different.

TABLE 30 Action Learning Team Questioning Guide

As a member of an Action Learning team, your role is to help the problem owner reflect on, and think about, his/her problem from a different perspective in order to be able to take some productive action. It is not your role to immediately offer advice or solutions.

Objective
What happened?
What did you do?
What exactly?
Can you tell us more about that?
Who were the key people involved? Everyone? Always?
Are you saying that …?
What else was happening?
And then what happened?
How can we/I best help you today?

Reflective
So what you're saying is …?
Have you thought about asking …? (questions you would have had in the situation)
Have you explored/thought of …?
What do you think would happen if …?
What were the highs? What were the lows?
What did you hope to achieve by doing …?
How does that make you feel?
Would it make any difference if it were a different person, time, place?
How do you think … needs to be altered?
How would you like … to respond?
What *could* you do?

Interpretive
What have you learned so far?
What do you think is really going on?
What solutions have you already tried and how did they turn out?
What were the implications?
What constraints do you have in trying to come to a solution?
What prompted you to do …?
How did you think … would help?
What would happen if you …?
Why is this a problem for you?
It sounds as though you are feeling …. How do you react to that?
How would you know if …?

Decisional
What will you do next?
What's stopping you from …?
How can you …?
What can you do to make the problem different?
Do you think that …?
Would … be of any use?

1. Have the team members reflect and write down the assumptions they have about the problem that they think may be different than those of the problem holder.
"I assume that . . ."
"I think I am right when I say . . ."
2. Tell the problem holder each team members' assumptions. Allow the problem holder to question, react or just listen so he/she can use the assumptions to help him/her think differently about the problem.
3. An alternative approach is to have the team reflect and write down those assumptions that they think the problem holder may have that he/she does not recognize he/she has.

If there is time, the problem holder is asked to choose one or two questions or assumptions that he/she thinks are most challenging or have helped him/her to think differently about the problem. Based on the problem holder's answers or reactions to the questions and assumptions, the team is able to get some additional information for their last step in the process—reframing the problem. Again, this step is similar to the team's activity in the Action Planning Cycle with the more direct focus on the individual and his/her problem. The process of reframing is explained in more detail in Table 31, Reframing the Problem.

Before the end of the allotted amount of time, the last step the problem holder takes is to decide upon and describe the action he/she plans to take on their problem. As a result of using good questioning insight, providing challenging assumptions, and offering insightful reframes, the intent of the team is to enable the problem holder to come up with some new paths for action, paths that he/she would never have thought about without the help and input of the team and learning coach. There are several additional/alternative processes that a problem holder might choose to use during their allotted amount of time. These will be discussed in chapter 4 as we describe the role of the learning coach in more detail.

When a team project-based program also incorporates personal learning goals, the process used for the latter can be similar to the one used to work on individual problems. The focus simply shifts to the personal learning goal. (See, for example, the Berlex program design in Table 14 in chapter 2, which incorporated both project work and personal learning goal work.) When the entire program is built around individual problems, participants may also have a personal learning goal in ad-

---

TABLE 31 Reframing the Problem

What?

One of the things that generally happens as we probe deeply into the root and underlying dynamics of a problem is that we begin to see that our original framing of the problem was incorrect. As a result, one of the most important steps in critical reflection is that of reframing the problem. This step is also one that may be iterative, with several possible takes on the problem offered, and explored, before the problem holder agrees the problem has been reframed.

How?

1. As a team, make sure you have sufficient information from the problem holder in order to help reframe the problem.
2. Each team member shares his/her theory on what he/she believes is the *real* problem. Explain why you think that is so.
3. The problem holder should question, react, and/or just listen to each potential reframe of the problem.
4. The problem holder should indicate which understanding—the original or one of the newly reframed approaches—he/she would like to use going forward.

---

dition to their focus on a particular problem. In that case, it works best to choose a personal learning goal that will help in addressing the individual problem—as illustrated in chapter 2 with the Global Pharmaceutical Organization Technology Executive. The integration of the two makes it easier to manage the focus of one's learning. If that isn't possible, separate time is set aside for the personal learning goal work as well.

How Do Participants Use a Learning Journal to Support Their Work and Eventual Success?

A learning journal—a book for recording one's thoughts and feelings as one tackles a problem and experiences the program, responses during reflection opportunities, and thoughts on project work—is a useful tool to help support both the task work and the learning of each participant. MiL typically presents managers in their AL programs with a blank book entitled something like "Leadership" to emphasize that managers must write their own theory. They should develop their own view of leadership based on their own experience as well as what they learn from colleagues and from experts on the topic.

Minimally, a learning journal provides an ongoing record of the project and work of the team. Maximally, it's a tool to help learn from that work. When we increase our awareness of our thoughts, intentions and actions, we increase our understanding and learning. Use of a learning journal, particularly to record thoughts during reflection, is an opportunity to stop and think about what's been done in order to learn from action. It's a place to record significant events so a participant, or team, can plan more effectively for future activities. Raelin points out that journals record personal reflections that can then be examined with others more publicly in AL groups:

> The journal can serve as a vehicle to integrate the information and experiences that run counter to preexisting viewpoints. It can also help participants more deeply understand their current reasoning and associated behavior or spur their consideration of new methods or skills introduced in the program.[29]

Table 32, Use of a Learning Journal, provides guidance for keeping a journal during an AL program.

TABLE 32 Use of a Learning Journal

---

1. Record your own and your teams' responses to reflection questions
It is important to take time to record your own thoughts before sharing with the team. That is the way you develop your ability to become self-aware and develop the ability to understand what is happening in the team. You are then better able to help yourself and the team.

2. Write about:
- the task itself, i.e., "the meeting showed that we didn't understand what the customer wanted."
- or interpersonal or team process, i.e., "I noticed that Susan was especially effective in the way in which she gave feedback to Joe because she…."
- or insight into yourself as a learner, i.e., "I realize that I like to learn by plunging in and trying out something, where Tom prefers to research the project very thoroughly before he is ready to take any action."

3. Record significant events
Identify experiences that for some reason are important to you. You may wish to write about experiences in advance, in order to better plan for them, or after an event takes place that you find has been significant.

4. Address your comments to yourself and your own needs.
Do not write for another reader, even though you may use your journal when you review your experiences with your learning partner and your action learning team. You only need share those portions of the journal that you wish to share.

continued

TABLE 32 *Continued*

---

5. **Include notes on:**
What happened, i.e., "I tried to do Y."
Your comments and conclusions, i.e., what you have learned.
Any action steps to increase your effectiveness in the future, i.e., "Next time I will make a plan before the meeting."
Reflection on results of action taken as a result of your learning.

6. **Use any format that you wish to use.**
There is no one *best* way to keep a learning journal. Some people prefer to write in a *stream of consciousness*. Others like a consistent set of headings under which to record their thinking. Others prefer pictures or mind maps. You may wish to record different kinds of information on the left and right sides of the journal. Do what best fits your learning style.

What Other Factors Can Help to Ensure the Success of an Action Learning Program or Contribute to Failure?

Since people work on real problems in an AL program, they inevitably bump up against practices and viewpoints in the organization that affect the resolution of their challenge over which they do not have full control. Sometimes the program provides a mandate for systemic change, but even when this is not so, participants have to consult with people elsewhere in the organization who are affected by their problem and may join with others to make some changes needed for effective resolution of the problem. Therefore, many of the factors that need to be in place to help contribute to success are the same as other kinds of systemic interventions. Strong top management support, as discussed earlier in this book, is crucial in any change intervention and a critical success factor for AL. There are other factors that are unique to AL that need to be considered—particularly for programs in the Experiential and Critical Reflection school, because of the *noise* these programs can generate in the system and the *waves* created in the organization.[30] Many of these factors are found in Table 33, Factors for Success or Failure.

The Invensys AL program offers an example of the integration of some crucial factors that helped to support the success of the program—"top management acting in accord with the vision and values of the program" and "the program being part of a larger strategic effort."

TABLE 33 Some Factors for Success or Failure

Factors That Support Success	Factors That Contribute to Failure
Top management acts in accord with the vision and values of the program	Top management is not committed
The environment is one of trust, not one of fear	Risks and mistakes are not tolerated
Co-design of the program involves HR, AL consultant, and field organization, including buy-in from the business units that are sponsoring projects	Design of the program takes place without involvement of all stakeholders
The program fully engages the participants	There is inconsistent, part-time participation
The program is part of a larger strategic change effort	The program is seen as a passing fad; that is, as "this too shall pass"
Projects are built around real tasks of importance to the organization	Projects are seen as make work or not important to the organization
Learning coach feedback is seen as vital to the process	The culture does not tolerate open, honest, and challenging feedback
A sponsor is seen as vital to the process	Sponsors are not intrinsically motivated; not engaged; don't understand their role in the process
The organization understands and expects *waves* and ongoing change in the program	The organization tolerates only the *status quo*
Participants understand their role and are open to learning and thinking differently	Participants are not adequately prepared or supported to learn and think differently resulting in closed mindsets and statements like: "We've tried that before." "I know how to fix it. The same thing happened five years ago." "This is not my job." "Let's not get emotional." "Let's get right down to the task." Dysfunctional team dynamics

TABLE 34 Practices for Success in AL Programs

	Top Management Support	Co-design Process	Good Sponsor Preparation	Good Participant Preparation
Berlex CDP	Chap. 2 pp. 26, 27	Chap. 2 pp. 22, 23, 27	Chap. 2 p. 38 Chap. 3 p. 71	Chap. 2 pp. 35, 36
Global Financial Organization		Chap. 2 p. 23 Chap. 3 p. 66	Chap. 2 p. 38 Chap. 3 p. 72	
Global Pharmaceutical Organization				
Invensys LIA	Chap. 2 p. 26 Chap. 3 pp. 94, 96–97	Chap. 2 p. 23	Chap. 2 p. 38 Chap. 3 p. 70	Chap. 2 pp. 35, 36 Chap. 3 p. 74
Pfizer PLP	Chap. 2 p. 26		Chap. 2 pp. 38, 39	Chap. 2 p. 35
PSE&G LIRW	Chap. 2 pp. 26, 27	Chap. 2 pp. 23, 25, 27	Chap. 2 p. 38	Chap. 2 pp. 35, 37 Chap. 3 p. 73
Veteran Affairs ARP	Chap. 3 p. 65			
Volvo Truck VTMP	Chap. 2 p. 26	Chap. 2 p. 23	Chap. 2 pp. 38, 39	
VNU Explorers	Chap. 2 pp. 26, 27	Chap. 2 pp. 23, 24, 27	Chap. 2 pp. 38, 39	Chap. 2 p. 35

Invensys Leadership in Action
Kate Hoepfner-Karle, KHK Human Capital Consulting

The senior leadership of each Invensys business was engaged in the participant nomination and selection process. Business leaders were given an overview of the business goals, a brief description of the method and approach to be used, and the requirements for their own support for the participants from their own business. It became immediately obvious at the first session how critical management buy-in and engagement was going to be for each participant. As a result additional communications for participant managers were delivered emphasizing the critical nature of the project, encouraging

Problem Posing/ Reframing Process (APC)	Individual Problem/ Personal Learning Goal Process	Questioning Insight Process	Reflection	Learning Journals
Chap. 3 p. 78	Chap. 1 p. 16 Chap. 3 p. 88	Chap. 1 p. 16 Chap. 3 p. 81	Chap. 1 p. 16 Chap. 3 p. 82	Chap. 3 p. 92
	Chap. 3 p. 88	Chap. 3 p. 81	Chap. 3 p. 82	Chap. 3 p. 92
	Chap. 3 pp. 63, 88	Chap. 3 p. 81	Chap. 3 p. 82	Chap. 3 p. 92
Chap. 3 p. 78	Chap. 3 p. 88	Chap. 3 p. 81	Chap. 3 p. 82	Chap. 3 p. 92
Chap. 3 p. 78	Chap. 3 p. 88	Chap. 3 p. 81	Chap. 3 p. 82	Chap. 3 p. 92
			Chap. 3 pp. 82, 83	
Chap. 3 p. 86		Chap. 3 p. 81	Chap. 3 p. 82	Chap. 3 p. 92
Chap. 3 p. 78	Chap. 3 p. 88	Chap. 3 p. 81	Chap. 3 p. 82	Chap. 3 p. 92

each manager to actively engage in the participant's learning goal work and ensuring that participants could devote time and energy to their project work, including travel and time away from the office. We also proposed a Strategic Learning Intervention, focusing on developing awareness in this population of the link with learning and business capability, for participant managers to be built into the program design for all subsequent Leadership in Action rollouts.

Based on our experience, and that of others, we've tried to provide some examples of the practices that we think best contribute to the success of AL programs. A summary of these practices and where they appear in this and previous chapters, is provided in Table 34, Practices for Success in Action Learning Programs.

Many of the strategies we've discussed in this chapter are initially taught, supported and eventually transferred to participants by the learning coach. In order to better understand the role played by learning coaches, we'll examine this role more closely in our next chapter.

CHAPTER FOUR

What Action Learning Coaches Do

"I never teach my pupils; I only attempt to provide the conditions in which they can learn."
—Albert Einstein
"Come to the edge, he said. They said, we are afraid. Come to the edge, he said. They came. He pushed them … and they flew."
—Guillaume Apollinaire

There are many factors that shape the roles and responsibilities of a learning coach. One of the most important to his/her practice appears to come from internal influences—a coach's background, values, and attitudes. These influences can be expressed as metaphors that reflect a belief system a coach holds that helps to shape his/her work (Table 35).[1]

Some of the additional topics that we'll examine in this chapter include how the role of learning coach is viewed in the various schools; how the role of the learning coach might change based on the co-design that best fits an organization's needs; the responsibilities of a learning coach including helping with group process and creating situations for learning; how coaches might work together; and finally a discussion of how to develop an individual to work as a learning coach.

TABLE 35 Learning Coach Metaphors

Metaphor	Description	Quote[1]
The Radical[2]	The coach enables participants to become empowered and use that empowerment to question and challenge authority.	"It's worked when the group has shown some courage to oppose authority. It's working well when I see people with the courage to do something unconventional."
Consecrated Self[3]	The coach submerges or subordinates his/her needs to those of the group and may have an underlying current of spirituality to his/her work.	"He talks about working in the context of grace.…We are servants seeking service."
Deep Diver[4]	The coach describes his/her work as going below the process level of the group to a deeper learning level.	"…the first level is the task itself, then below is the task process,… then the group process,…then the fourth level …the learning process."
The Legitimizer[5]	The coach conceives that one of his/her main roles is to just be there and be instrumental in creating an environment in which people are free to learn.	"You represent the whole idea of the program and just being there and seeing and listening to the group is sometimes enough."
The Sage[6]	The coach easily draws upon his/her own experience; is in contact with his/her own psychology; and has entered into the Socratarian world of humility by discovering what he/she doesn't know.	"Our sage would be operating at a distance from the set member… and be thinking of himself as another person. This way of thinking helps our sage be totally immersed in the processes.…At this stage of intimacy, he is …reminded of his own ignorance …."
The Wizard[7]	The coach, like Merlin of legend, points out unconscious contradictions; helps support people as they try to find the courage to face the contradictions; is present when things go awry; and creates a field of tension in which learning can happen.	"Merlin is an archetype …who alone opens up dimensions which are unseen. …to those around him. Thus he becomes a guide, a guardian, and a link to the spiritual realms …."

The Benedictine and the Jesuit[8]	In keeping with the religious orders, the coach needs to create an accepting, supportive environment for learning (Benedictine), but then needs to confront participants to help them break through the shell of their understanding (Jesuit).	"The (Benedictine) set adviser encourages members to give support; emotional support is often badly needed ....Only the (Jesuit) set adviser has the courage and skill to sharpen the pick and tell the chief executive just where to tap, if he is to begin the painful process of learning ...."
Mystery Maker[9]	A role that many coaches struggle to avoid and most often criticize—the coach creates a mystery about what he/she does and through this mystery brings the focus of the group on self and what he/she knows. The coach "steals" learning opportunities from the group.	"And you've got to watch out and use self control. Knowing that you've got this potential in you to devise a bully pulpit and come across as a sage/guru figure."

The quotes for The Radical, Consecrated Self, Deep Diver, The Legitimizer, and the Mystery Maker come from participants in the research found in O'Neil, "The Role of the Learning Advisor in Action Learning."

[1] The quotes for The Radical, Consecrated Self, Deep Diver, The Legitimizer, and the Mystery Maker come from participants in the research found in O'Neil, "The Role of the Learning Advisor in Action Learning."

[2] O'Neil, "The Role of the Learning Coach in Action Learning," 186; O'Neil, "A Study of the Role of Learning Advisors in Action Learning," 68–69; O'Neil, "The Role of the Learning Advisor in Action Learning," 183–189.

[3] Ibid.

[4] Ibid.

[5] Ibid.

[6] David Botham, "Discussion paper: Relationships Between" (Unpublished manuscript, Manchester Polytechnic, Department of Management, MSc Think Tank, England, January 1991), 3.

[7] Thomas Sewerin, "The MiL Learning Coach" (Unpublished manuscript, MiL Concepts, Lund, Sweden: MiL Institute, April 1997), 4–6.

[8] David Casey, "The Role of the Set Advisor" in *Action Learning in Practice 2d Ed.,* ed. Mike Pedler, 261–273 (Brookfield, VT: Gower 1991).

[9] O'Neil, "The Role of the Learning Coach in Action Learning," 186; O'Neil, "A Study of the Role of Learning Advisors in Action Learning," 68–69; O'Neil, "The Role of the Learning Advisor in Action Learning," 183–189.

How Is the Role of the Learning Coach Viewed in Each of the Four Schools?

While ideally each Action Learning (AL) program that is co-designed determines how the role of a learning coach might best meet the needs of a particular organization, there are some generalizations that can be made regarding the role as it might play out in a particular school.

In many Tacit school programs, there is no learning coach as part of the co-design since there is a working assumption that learning will take place so long as carefully selected participants work together, some team building takes place, and information is provided by experts from within and external to the company.[2] When learning coaches are part of the co-design, they often help the team with developing team process through interventions and team building. The goal is usually to accelerate learning about the project and the company.[3]

In the history of the Scientific school, Revans early on expressed concern about the use of experts and facilitators.[4] He stated that people who know about AL can help but should "not be allowed to solicit for recognition as 'set advisors' (learning coaches) . . . or other specialists in ensuring that the participant managers not be prevented from introducing spontaneous improvements to their own efforts at mutual support."[5]

However, Revans differentiated between the role of set advising and the role of set initiating.[6] He said that in the interest of effectiveness and to conserve managerial time, there may be a need when a set (team) first forms "for a supernumerary to help the set develop an initial trustworthy cohesion through orderly debate; a catalyst of this kind, brought in to speed the self-integration of the set, must contrive that it gains independence of him at the earliest possible moment . . . ."[7] So while the Scientific school philosophy cautions against an ongoing learning coach role based on concern about "stealing the learning," it does see a role at the start up of the AL program to help the team develop the kind of environment that best supports inquiry and learning.

In co-designs within the Experiential school, the role of a learning coach is usually an integral part of the design in order to help support the team's learning throughout the learning cycle. The role includes attention to both team process and learning. It differs from that of the traditional management trainer in that the role is not to teach, but to provide conditions under which AL participants might learn themselves from their project work and from each other.[8] The learning coach tries to primarily use questions as the way of working with the group in order to model questioning insight. Reflection is also key to helping ensure that what is learned through the experience of working on a real project is explicit and planned, rather than erratic and half-hearted.[9]

As in the Scientific school, the role in the Experiential school is considered particularly important in the beginning of the program. There may be some cases where the learning coach may be able to transfer skills so successfully that he or she will work him/herself out of a job.[10] This is most likely to happen when the team has some experienced AL participants who have gone through a program before or when participants have an "awareness and concern for group process and learning outcomes" and have the ability to deal with resultant issues.[11]

Since the co-design of a program in the Critical Reflection school is intended to go beyond the kind of reflection found in an Experiential school design, the learning coach role plays an important part in the creation of opportunities for critical reflection and fostering the potential resultant transformative learning.[12] Since a learning coach is not a team member, and often comes from outside the culture, he/she can be freer to ask questions from an outsider's perspective since he/she is not immersed in the organization's mores and norms and is not constrained by political issues.

When Yorks, O'Neil, Marsick, Nilson, and Kolodny studied the Grace Cocoa program—a program in the Critical Reflection school—they found that the role of the participant observer researcher in many ways mirrored the role of the learning coach. They described the role as a "sophisticated barbarian," who by his/her very outsider nature is intended to see the situation through fresh eyes and then use those insights to raise critical questions to help reframe the participants' understanding.[13]

In addition to the roles played in an Experiential school design, learning coaches in a Critical Reflection school program can help a team learn the following:

- how to frame, reframe or provide an alternative framing for the project/problem, since complex issues are seldom what they first seem
- how to identify, clarify, and test the participants' personal insights and theories about the project/problem
- how to reflect on the way in which the project/problem is formulated, tested, and solved.[14]

What's Different About the Way a Learning Coach in the Different Schools Might Interact with a Team?

Although there is no standard protocol for the work of a learning coach, how he/she might interact with a team in a given situation is influenced by a number of factors. At the beginning of the chapter, we looked at some metaphors expressed by practicing learning coaches that help to shape how they might interact. The AL schools, that is, how coaches think about how learning takes place within AL, also influence the interaction. In addition to these internal influences, there are external influences that could have an impact including the length of the program and the role of the sponsors. Before we discuss the possible impact of the external influences, let's look at an example of a possible situation within a team (Table 36) and how coaches from the various schools could support the team (Table 37).

We begin by considering what may have happened up to this point. Based on the co-design element of a team project, learning coaches in the Tacit school would probably have been providing information to the team, through lectures and exercises, about the culture of the organization. They would want to help the team operate effectively within that culture through a focus on team building. The learning coaches in the other three schools have probably been creating situations for learning in which the team has been looking at both its task and its team process. The task, since that is the team charge, and the process, since the team needs to work together well to produce good recommendations and particularly since the recommendations deal with team interaction. Any recommendations would be less credible if the team did not function well itself.

Based on the learning philosophy of the school, that is, how it is viewed that learning takes place, the learning coaches would probably vary their approach as shown in Table 37, Responses to the Hypothetical Case by Different Schools of Action Learning. A coach from the Tacit school would probably want to help the team better understand the expectations of the senior manager and the organization. The Scientific school coach might encourage the team to consider the encounter from the perspective of Systems Alpha, Beta and Gamma, that is, from a scientific perspective, while the Experiential school coach would probably focus on some aspect of personal development and how the individuals handled themselves during the interaction. In addition to the personal aspect, the coach in the Critical Reflection school might sug-

TABLE 36 The Manufacturing Manager Comes to Visit

Background: In a large high-technology company, a team of managers and supervisors were asked to work on a new project to achieve quality and cost improvement through empowerment and self-directed work teams. The senior manufacturing manager charged his staff with identifying individuals for this team, after which he signed off on the project. The team members were asked to learn more about the issues, take action to address problems that arose, and make recommendations about what the organization might do in the future. It has now been six months since the project started. The group has invited the senior manager to each of their meetings, but this is the first time they have met with him.

Thoughts and feelings	What was said
Whew, he finally came to a meeting. He's been invited to every session. Everyone is really nervous about this session.	Team leader (to senior manager): Our team has decided that our goal will be to identify ways that each of us can help eliminate non-value-added work in our area. Each of us will develop an individual project and implement it over the next year. The team will be our sounding board to improve the project, help us move forward and take additional steps, and so on.
What! You finally come to a meeting six months after we start and suddenly don't like what we've done?	Senior mgr.: That won't work. You were supposed to develop a precise plan for quality improvement to cut down on costs. We don't need a sounding board.
We should have known. This is what they really mean by empowered teams.	Team leader: We were told that you wanted us to be empowered and to identify our own work task. What gives?
Oh, great—we asked for it so now we got it.	Senior mgr.: You asked me to come to this meeting to hear a progress report and I am telling you what I think of what you've done.
You keep cutting us off at the knees—how do you expect us to get anywhere?	Team leader: Well, we have done as much as we could with the membership of the team changing every time we meet. You keep adding people, moving people to different jobs, and so on.
Can you believe this guy?	Senior mgr.: That's how things are now. Your team should be working to learn how to handle that changing team membership—people being moved, or demoted.
In a pig's eye.	Team leader: We need to discuss this and we will get back to you with our team's goals.

TABLE 37 Responses to the Hypothetical Case by Different Schools of Action Learning[1]

Point of Comparison	Tacit School	Scientific School	Experiential School	Critical Reflection School
Framing of the encounter by learning coach	Opportunity to better understand the organizational culture	Grist for the mill of situation analysis	Opportunity to learn from a mistake and grow personally in choices and skills	Focus on deep values and beliefs in individuals and system
Interventions with the team before the team meeting	Help the team role play the upcoming interaction	Reflect on steps he saw team take and suggest they look at gaps or needed data	Reflect on situation; encourage action to test understanding with manager; plan and role play	Help probe organizational assumptions; encourage questions regarding empowerment; plan and role play
Interventions with the team during the team meeting	Ask the manager what would be acceptable to him in order to help the team achieve that outcome	(1) No intervention (2) Ask the manager to join team in situation analysis	(1) No intervention (2) Ask everyone to think together about situation so they can learn from this	(1) No intervention (2) Put difficult issues on table; raise questions about system; share views
Interventions with the team and / or system after the team meeting	Help team figure out a way to meet senior manager's expectations	Reframe the problem and consider next steps for data collection in light of what was learned	Examine behavior and implications for personal growth and for understanding system; reframe the problem, next steps	Analyze data from team analysis of forces shaping own behavior and system's culture; reframe problem, next steps

[1] Marsick and O'Neil, "The Many Faces of Action Learning," 166. The discussion of the Tacit school has been added to the original table.

gest the team examine some of the underlying organizational issues that came into play.[15]

Turning to the external influences, one of the more significant on the work of a learning coach is the length of the program. Having an extended time with a team is important for a couple of reasons. First, having an extended time to meet ties in with the importance of having the time to take action. Second, since most coaches work to transfer their skills to the team, and possibly work themselves out of a job, an extended period of time is needed to achieve what they want to do. Third, over time people can build deep trust that often enables giving and receiving more frank, honest feedback from which to learn.

Time can also present constraints on how the learning coach does his/her work. In organizations, it is often the case that time is at a premium, and as a result the work of the learning coach is impacted in ways that are not preferred by the coach as evidenced by data from O'Neil's research.[16] "If I'm working in a program that lasts for only a short time, I'll step in more. That may seem like 'stealing learning.'"

As discussed in chapter 3, part of the role of a learning coach is interaction with the sponsor, particularly in co-designs that involve team projects. When sponsors are involved with a program, their presence is usually felt in the team—sometimes positively, sometimes otherwise—and will often have an impact on how the learning coach interacts with the team and the sponsor him/herself. The impact the sponsor can have is illustrated in the following:

> If you get into a relationship with the sponsor you can challenge him and intervene and he'll be personally involved. It's very good. On the other hand—you're working hard to engage with the sponsor, the sponsor doesn't care, but yet has an order to do the job. But you could try everything. It can help to have such a sponsor, to challenge the team, to motivate it, and to turn it to help them see, "why doesn't he have an interest? Why doesn't he have—and why was he ordered to take the job of sponsor. Yeah, it's part of the problem. Why did he take it?" And they (the team) have to be part of the problem.[17]

What Does a Learning Coach Actually Do with a Team?

There are many kinds of interventions that a learning coach may choose to make in order to help his/her team. Many of the interventions that we'll discuss are intended to help the participants and team to learn so fit best with the learning philosophy in the Scientific, Experiential, and Critical Reflection schools. Some of the learning coaches' intervention practice is similar to, and based in, work done by a process consultant—someone whose role is to help the team improve their interaction. Much of the work they do with their teams, however, goes beyond the level of a process consultant—goes beyond and deeper to a learning level. Table 38, Differences between Process Consultants and Learning Coaches, shows some ways in which the interaction of a process consultant and a learning coach with a team might differ.

In order to get to the deeper learning level, learning coaches try to create situations for learning rather than put themselves in a teaching role. There are a number of ways they try to create these situations. Table 39, Creating Situations for Learning, illustrates some of the ways coaches go about creating these situations.

Before learning can happen, it's necessary to create an environment in which there is sufficient trust for participants to feel they can

---

TABLE 38 Differences Between Process Consultants and Learning Coaches

Process consultants	Vs.	Learning coaches
Intervenes as problems arise		Allows problems to continue so learning can occur
Improves group interaction		Helps group change their own interaction
Helps to find or provides the right answer		Helps group learn how to ask the right question
Diagnoses the problem		Helps to learn to reflect to diagnose own problem
Helps improve process and task		Helps to learn how to learn
Recommends needed training		Provides just-in-time learning
Helps group to work well within existing paradigm		Helps to change the paradigm
Supports single loop learning		Supports single loop and double loop learning

---

TABLE 39 Creating Situations for Learning

Situations	Action Learning Intervention
Creating an environment for learning	Emphasis on confidentiality Create a supportive environment
Specific interventions for learning	Questioning Reflection Critical reflection Programmed knowledge and just-in-time learning Make work visible Create ways to help think differently Challenge the group
Transfer skills needed for learning	Help participants to give and receive help and feedback to each other Help to learn how to transfer learning Say nothing and be invisible

take risks like questioning themselves and others in the team; engaging in reflection; and challenging the organization. In Lamm's research on the Volvo Truck program, participants described an open, trusting, and supportive program environment where participants bonded and became friends and felt safe to share personal experiences and feedback as one of the program elements necessary to transformative learning. She noted that one of the key roles of the learning coach in the program was to develop this environment. In addition, informal time such as having drinks at the bar, sharing meals, and traveling together also helped foster this kind of environment for the program.[18]

Confidentiality about everything that goes on in the team and program—what other participants say about themselves, the content of personal learning goals, how participants feel about their work and goals, what action participants intend to take—is critical to establishing trust and a learning environment.[19] Confidentiality is one of the elements many learning coaches introduce in the process of contracting their role with the team.

Learning coaches typically contract first with their group to clarify their role and help the group understand how the learning process will take place. A process for contracting—for confidentiality as well as other ways in which the team and learning coach will work together—is found in Table 40, Contracting.

TABLE 40 Contracting

What?
Establishing the expectations of the role of the team members and the learning coach as you
  work together

Why?
Establishing expectations avoids confusion and makes expectations that are generally
  unspoken explicit

How?
The learning coach:
*   explains the rationale for contracting
*   requests team members' input
*   provides examples of what he / she thinks the learning coach role should be and how the
    team might interact
*   records ideas on an easel
*   checks for agreement
*   comes to final agreement

Elements of Contracting/ Establishing Ground Rules:
*   What are some of the ground rules for how we will work together in team meetings?
*   What has happened in some teams/meetings that has worked well?
*   What has happened in some teams/meetings that has not worked well?
*   What is each of our expectations, both about the role of the learning coach, and of the team?

The work of creating a supportive environment starts at the very
beginning of the time with the team and continues throughout the
program. Trust needs to be established, and continually reinforced, both
between the coach and participants and among the participants themselves. One way to begin establishing trust is through a willingness to
reveal some of oneself to others. This can be done through a variety of
processes or exercises. A simple, effective exercise is shown in Table 41,
Critical Incident Introductions.

Once work has begun on establishing the needed environment,
a learning coach looks for opportunities to continue to create situations in which learning may take place. Some of the ways in which this
is done is through questioning the team; using reflection and critical
reflection; using "P" or just-in-time learning; making the team's work
visible to them; creating ways to help the team think differently about
their work and themselves; and using processes that may serve to challenge the team.

TABLE 41 Critical Incident Introductions

Write the following questions on the board or easel.

What formed you?

What critical incidents brought you to where you are today?

What contributed to who you are today?
- family of origin
- present family
- school
- work experience
- society

Have the team take five to ten minutes of reflection time and write responses to the questions in their journal. Depending on time allowed for exercise, you may suggest that participants focus on one or two critical incident areas. Have each participant share their responses with the team. You as the learning coach should also participate. For a team of six, allow one to one-and-a-half hours for the exercise.

We discussed questions and questioning insight in chapter 3. Questions are one of the most used learning coach interventions. Questions that are asked by the learning coach need to be both supportive and challenging. They need to truly be questions, not advice framed as a question, and need to try to help participants think in new ways—particularly in a Critical Reflection school program.[20] In asking good questions, the learning coach is also modeling behavior that he/she intends to transfer to the participants for use in the AL program as well as back on the job.[21]

Reflection and critical reflection were also discussed in chapter 3. Reflection can be planned in advance or used when a team appears to be in difficulty or to be *stuck*. In either case, coaches frequently use questions as a way to help the team with learning through reflection. The establishment of a supportive environment contributes to the ability of the learning coach to use critical reflection. In such an environment, participants feel comfortable in examining their beliefs, practices, and norms and can *shine a spotlight* on taken-for-granted norms of behavior and thinking.[22] Lamm discusses how the coaches in the Volvo Truck program used questions, reflection, and critical reflection.

Volvo Truck Management Program
Dr. Sharon Lamm-Hartmann, CEO, Inside Out Learning, Inc.

A MiL or LIM learning coach helped each team to learn from their action and to balance action with reflection. Learning coaches are skilled in process facilitation, individual, and group coaching. They support learning around business processes, applying just-in-time teaching and constantly challenging the participants' mindsets and ways of working. Learning coaches help foster reflection on oneself, leadership, team, and company/business problems. Often the team reflects on questions posed by the learning coach and then discusses their reflections. Also, the coach works with tests, exercises, and theory during "reflection time" in order to problematise, challenge or support the team and the individuals in learning about themselves, teams, the business, and leadership.

I believe the learning coach is a critical component in maximizing the potential for transformative learning. While the learning coach was not specifically mentioned (by participants) as a key condition in fostering transformative learning, many activities that the learning coach facilitated were mentioned (i.e., reflection breaks). This could confirm that the learning coaches were doing their job. A good learning coach is one who makes him/herself invisible and creates an environment where the learning comes from the participants.

In chapter 2, we looked at various kinds of "P" or programmed learning—presentations, exercises, classes—that are part of the co-design of a program. Just-in-time learning is different. It can also be a mini presentation, an exercise, or a job-aid, but the learning coach offers it to the team at a point in their work when it would be most helpful. So just-in-time learning will vary from team to team and some subjects may not be used in a particular team at all. Many just-in-time learning options are anticipated based on the program co-design, but given the ambiguity of AL, the coach needs to be prepared for almost any eventuality.

Many times the coach will ask if the team is interested in a tool that might help them with the current dilemma or issue. This allows the team to proceed without the coach's help if they so decide. There may be other times when the coach identifies an issue and asks if anyone on the team has a way to help. In this way, he/she is continuing to transfer learning coach skills.

An example of a just-in-time learning opportunity that frequently comes up in a program is when the team first arrives at a time when a decision needs to be made. Sometimes the participants don't recognize that they are at this point, so the learning coach may need to ask a question to help make the situation *visible*. For example, "You've been discussing this issue for quite a while. Why do you keep going over the same ground?" Since most teams will not have identified a decision-making process in advance, once the team realizes a decision is called for, the coach can offer to teach them a process that works well in AL programs. One such process is shown in Table 42, Seeking Consensus.

Making the work of a team *visible* can catalyze learning because participants become aware of what they do not see, or see in only one way. It is easy for a team to get caught up in a focus on the task and be unaware of the dynamics of the team process. Learning coaches have

---

TABLE 42 Seeking Consensus

What?

Fist Five: A tool for consensus testing
Fist Five is a means of testing for consensus in which members use a visual means of indicating their degree of agreement with the decision. Each hand position signals a different position.

Why?

By using this method to visually test the potential for consensus, everyone can see where everyone else is on the decision continuum. The team leader can then get the people on opposite ends to exchange perspectives with the hope of uncovering new information and either coming to consensus or making a different and better decision.

How?

Team members hold up their hands to indicate the following positions:

Closed fist:	I cannot live with the decision; I will block it or leave the team.
One finger up:	I can live with the decision; I do not like it but I will not block it.
Two fingers:	I am not excited by the decision; I will do some work to support it.
Three fingers:	I think the decision is okay; I will get involved.
Four fingers:	I think the decision is good; I will work hard to support it.
Five fingers:	I think the decision is great; I may leave the team if it is not made.

---

different ways in which they try to make the work of the team *visible* in those situations. Some may use questions as in the example above. Others, based on their backgrounds or philosophies, might use other kinds of interventions like role plays or diagrams to illustrate the dynamics. One of the coaches from O'Neil's study[23] describes her intervention.

> I say, I see a lot now. Do you want me to tell you what I saw? And if they agree, I say, I'm going to say some of the things that you will not recognize. Then you have to say no, no, no that's not what happened. If you want to, you may see something in what I'm saying. Then I'm telling them. And that's sort of a guiding, because I take out things that they know that they do that they think no one else saw.

Particularly in the Critical Reflection school, it is important for the learning coach to look for opportunities to help participants to think differently. In chapter 3 we introduced a variety of processes that can be used for that purpose. Two other processes that we've used effectively with teams follow. When the co-design calls for individual problems or personal learning goals, a process that can be used by the team as the program progresses is called Fly on the Wall (Table 43). This process can be used in place of asking questions, making assumptions, and re-framing the problem or personal learning goal. In a team project program, teams might get stuck in seeing their project through the same cultural lens and/or not systemically. We've used an exercise called Make Dragons (Table 44) to try to help break that mindset. There are many other exercises, or ways of thinking creatively, that are also useful.

Challenging the team can often lead participants to think differently, but the process varies because the coach wants to push the team into looking deeper at their thought processes than they may be accustomed to looking. One way to operationalize this intervention is through the use of tools adapted from Action Science.[24] The learning coach in the Veteran Affairs program used some of these tools in his work with the team.

U.S. Department of Veteran Affairs Action Research Project Team
Janet Reid-Hector and Lyle Yorks

The learning coach introduced several learning practices, including reflection and dialogue, right-hand, left-hand column discussions, the ladder of inference, and the learn-

TABLE 43 Fly on the Wall

The member of the team updates the others on the action he/she has taken since the last time he/she spoke about the problem/personal learning goal; the results of that action; what he/she is currently thinking about the problem/personal learning goal; and any other relevant information. Based on that update, the team can first take a short time to ask questions for clarification and/or better understanding.

After that short interval, the team holds a conversation about what they have heard as if the person with the problem/personal learning goal was not there (he/she can be a *fly on the wall* to listen in and take notes). The conversation should be both supportive and challenging. The team should speak as though the person with the problem/personal learning goal was not actually there. Statements should be made and questions should be posed that would continue to help the person with the problem/personal learning goal consider the situation from various perspectives. It is okay to be provocative.

After the conversation, the person with the problem/personal learning goal is invited back into the conversation for response, clarification, and discussion. Based on that interaction, the team asks the person with the problem/personal learning goal to determine the action he/she will take.

TABLE 44 Make Dragons[1]

The ability to see relationships and patterns, and to make unfamiliar combinations and connections, is one of the basics to thinking differently. It is also a way to help thinking theoretically and systemically. The way to develop that ability in this exercise is to look at things that at first glance seem unrelated, and find different ways to link them.

For example, what connections can you make between:

A bullfrog and the Internet?
The frog's feet are webbed; the Internet links you to the World Wide Web.

An Oriental rug and psychotherapy?
Oriental rugs have complex repeating patterns and so does your psyche.

Get the idea? Try to generate three or four connections for each of the following. Have fun!

An oak leaf and the human hand
A porcupine and a computer
Samurai warriors and the game of chess
Gershwin's "Rhapsody in Blue" and rain
Juggling and your career
The global economy and a Portobello mushroom

[1] Adapted from Michel J. Gelb, *How to Think Like Leonardo da Vinci* (New York: Dell, 2000).

American Management Association

ing window as methods for surfacing and reflecting on the experiences of the groups and the premises held by individual members.

At the first project team meeting he attended, the learning coach gave a brief overview of the distinction between process facilitation and the role of learning coach. He then contracted with the team to observe the meeting and suggest a learning practice when he felt it would be useful. About an hour into the meeting it seemed that the group was wandering without focus across various topics and back again. He asked if he could suggest a learning practice. Describing the concept of the left-hand column and the process of stop, reflect, and dialogue, he asked the members of the team to take a few minutes to quietly reflect and note what was on their minds and not being stated. Then, without discussion, and going around the table, each person shared his or her left-hand column and what they thought the group should do next to make progress.

TABLE 45 The TALK Model

What?
A method for one-on-one communication that helps you
- become more aware of your own thinking and reasoning
- make your thinking and reasoning more visible to others
- ask about others' thinking and reasoning
A method that also helps you sort out the assumptions and inferences we make about a topic from what has actually happened

Why
- The outcome of the conversation is important to you
- You want to be sure that you are clearly understood and that you clearly understand the other person
- You have had difficulty communicating on this topic in the past

How?
Tell the person what you are thinking from the start.
　　—Illustrate your assumptions about the situation with examples that you have directly observed or heard that led you to your conclusions.

Ask whether he/she has the same interpretation of the situation.
　　—If not, ask that the person explain his/her alternative view of the situation.

Listen to his/her response.
　　—Listening refers to stating what was understood, checking to see if this is what was meant, exploring differences, and working to reach consensus on a joint meaning of the situation

Keep open to other's views.
　　—For talk or dialogue to be productive, all parties must acknowledge that theirs is only one interpretation of a situation; shared meaning can, therefore, come only from accepting and surfacing our multiple understandings.

There was a high level of consensus and the meeting gained focus. A few other such interventions were made, including a final reflection at the end of the meeting.

One tool that we have adapted and found particularly useful is from the concept of advocacy with inquiry. Our tool is called the TALK model (Table 45) and we help participants learn how to use it when they need to have a particularly difficult conversation either in the team or in the organization in connection with their project.

As we've mentioned several times in this chapter, as a part of their work, most learning coaches try to transfer their skills to the participants—work themselves out of a job. One of the useful ways that participants can learn some of the skills of a learning coach was discussed in chapter 3 in the AL individual problem process, which can be used for both problems and for personal learning goals. Since both the learning coach and participants take part in this process, the participants are able to learn from and model the coach as he/she asks *good* questions, offers and challenges assumptions, and reframes the problem or goal.

In addition, in many AL programs we suggest the use of feedback sessions as part of the co-design, so participants can learn from each other as well as the coach. The coach takes part in these sessions in providing and receiving feedback so that he/she is able to model both parts of the process. Guidelines for feedback and an exercise are found in Tables 46 and 47.

Another important skill that learning coaches want to turn over to participants is how to go about transferring what is learned in the program back to the job or life. In many co-designs a certain degree of transfer is built in and the learning coach helps to reinforce those elements. For example:

- Linking the general principle with the concept of the most teachable moment—just-in-time learning, modeled by the coach, demonstrates how an explicit link can be made between the principle and the team's experience.
- During periods of reflection, the coach can draw attention to how current issues in the team are similar in principle to those experienced earlier and those that may be encountered back in the organization.
- By spacing AL meetings over time, participants are able to try out new behaviors back on the job. These behaviors can then be dis-

---

TABLE 46 Principles of Good Feedback

Feedback is a way of helping another person to consider changing his/her behavior. It is communication to a person (or team) that gives that person information about how he or she affects others. As in a guided missile system, feedback helps individuals keep their behavior *on target* and thus better achieve their goals.

Some Criteria for Useful Feedback:

1. **Descriptive rather than evaluative.** By describing one's own reaction, it leaves the individual free to use it or not to use it as he or she sees fit. By avoiding evaluative language, it reduces the need for the individual to react defensively.

2. **Specific rather than general.** To be told that one is dominating will probably not be as useful as to be told that, "just now when we were deciding the issue, you did not listen to what others said, and I felt forced to accept your arguments or face attack from you."

3. **Directed toward changeable behavior.** Frustration is only increased when a person is reminded of some shortcoming over which s/he has no control.

4. **Solicited rather than imposed.** Feedback is most useful when the receiver has formulated the kind of question(s) that those observing him/her can answer.

5. **Well timed.** In general, feedback is most useful at the earliest opportunity after the given behavior (depending, of course, on the person's readiness to hear it, support available from others, etc.)

---

cussed and questioned by the coach and team to reinforce the transfer.[25]

The learning coaches in the Invensys program worked to try and create many of these situations for learning in the work they did with their teams.

Invensys Leadership in Action
Kate Hoepfner-Karle, KHK Human Capital Consulting

A learning coach was assigned to each team for the duration of the initiative. The role of the coaches was:

- co-design of the program with the VP of Learning and Development
- development and delivery of any "P" learning recommended in the design
- team and individual coaching during formal sessions and in-between sessions
- provision of opportunities for critical reflection

TABLE 47 Team Exercise for Giving and Receiving Good Feedback

---

Each participant will have time to provide personal feedback to each person on their team. This will be your main opportunity to formally discuss the experience of working together. Since good feedback takes some time to prepare, we wanted to give you some advance information to begin that preparation.

Please review the criteria as you prepare feedback for each person on your team. In accord with the criteria, use your journals to remind yourself of specific examples of behavior that you can cite to the individual. Try to provide feedback that accounts for his/her behavior since the beginning of the program, not just recent events.

In order to provide consistent feedback for the whole team, the feedback that you prepare for each person should try to answer the following questions:

- "What have you done that has been helpful to me?"
  or
  "What do I most appreciate?"
- "What should you do more of?"
- "What should you do less of?"

For example: "I appreciate that you demonstrated early leadership in our meetings. In the first session, before we even worked through roles, you helped us set the agenda and got us working on action items so we lost very little time. Your action-oriented manner has helped us right along. You need to be sure that you don't let that manner dominate, however. As the leader, you don't always check with the reflective people to be sure they are ready to move on. I've enjoyed your occasional joking e-mails. They helped to defuse tension in the team. Please use your sense of humor more."

- support of participants in developing and meeting their personal learning goals
- team evaluation and feedback
- identification of tools to help the team with project work.

The coaches proved to be an invaluable benefit to participants by providing:

- critical questions
- skill development, just-in-time learning
- individual observations and coaching
- team assessment and guidance
- sponsor support.

As stated earlier in the chapter in Lamm's vignette, "A good learning coach is one who makes him/herself invisible and creates an environment where the learning comes from the participants." The principle of "saying nothing and being invisible"[26] manifests itself in a number of ways. It involves holding back and helping the team to grow by letting them learn from their own mistakes and letting them produce their own good answers.[27] "The learning coach lets them get into trouble and even lets them stay in it for a while".[28] In this case, the coach wants the team to learn how to recognize the process issues or stop for reflection to sort things out. This is not as easy as it sounds, even when this role has been clarified and contracted early on. The group can put pressure on the coach to earn his/her keep by taking on an *expert role*—in contrast to using a different kind of expertise to help people learn through and from their own experience. People often learn better through trial-and-error accompanied by feedback. As one coach put it, "you need to get used to the fact that they're going to complain, well, why didn't you say that three hours ago?"

So in some cases, the coach decides to actually do nothing in order to let the team figure things out for themselves. For example, this principle is practiced when a learning coach makes an explicit decision not to intervene in order to see if the team is able to respond to a participant acting aggressively.[29] "They find it strange that there is somebody sitting there who is supposed to be a professional and is not actually doing anything."

How Do Learning Coaches Work with Other Learning Coaches?

Learning coaches work mostly alone and so have little experience in working cooperatively with other learning coaches. Even those who have worked in programs in which there was more than one coach have had little opportunity for interaction with one another since most of their focus, time, and primary interaction is with the AL team.[30] In many of the programs that we've talked about in this book, however, there has been more than one coach, so what has their interaction been like?

The VNU Explorer's program illustrates how the learning coach role can be played out in a flexible way to meet the needs of the program. In the program, we developed a method we called *collaborative coaching* to enable us to rotate among teams and allow the internal coach and program manager to gain better familiarity with all participants in ways that would not have happened if she had stayed with one team.

Since the work a learning coach does with a team is usually confidential, we needed to first get the permission from the three teams involved to share the necessary information that allowed us to rotate without disrupting the work of the team. Ongoing analysis of the notes we shared enabled us to use the results of the teams' reflection times to better understand the struggles and successes of the different teams.

VNU Explorers Program
Holly O'Grady, VNU

During the first program the external coach and I each had a team and I was able to recruit a third coach internally, a talented HR generalist. When I started to make plans for the next program, I was confronted with several issues. Having worked closely with one team, I realized that I had not had as much opportunity to know the participants on the other teams. The second issue was recruiting another coach internally. Because of changing business needs, those who might have been interested were involved in many other new initiatives and were not available.

As a result of these changes, we developed a collaborative approach to coaching by rotating among the three teams. To implement the collaborative process we needed to redesign the first face-to-face meeting so that we would be able to work with all the teams before they started working virtually. During these rotations the teams also got used to our styles as well. When the teams started to meet virtually, we kept notes for each other. Generally, the notes included discussion of the team roles, how the meetings were run, how decisions were made (or not) and, most important, team reflections at the end of the call. Although we did not have a prescribed approach to recording information in our notes, we were able to capture the critical events in each call, which enabled us to establish continuity as we moved among the teams. We also made it known to the teams that we would be exchanging notes so they would not have to backtrack when a new learning coach joined the call.

Looking back on our first venture with the *collaborative coaching* process, the use of reflection became a very important indicator to us of how well the teams were able to make progress on their projects. Early on we realized that one of the teams was very challenged due to a combination of personalities and time management skills. Relative to the other two teams, our notes revealed that this team struggled with the process of reflection. There was some resistance in the group to the process but, more often, poor management in running the meetings often led to them abandoning reflection altogether. By comparison the other two teams began to adopt the practice of reflecting without prompting by the learning coaches and effectively used the tool as a way to improve their work together and their understanding of the projects.

As a result of our documentation, we were able to analyze some of the factors that contributed to the challenges experienced by one of the teams. Because of our notes and subsequent discussions, we could more successfully intervene with a new team in the third program that initially exhibited some of the traits we saw in the more challenging team in the second program. In addition to encouraging the team to engage more in the process of reflection, we were also more adept at capturing other incidents that were early indicators of positive growth or possible derailment. Our notes in essence mirrored the process that the teams were going through in that we reflected on the team's experience and through that process arrived at new insights and approaches in working with each of the teams.

In general the process of rotating among teams worked very well based on evaluations from the participants. Because our notes tended to capture the significant points of the meetings, one of the participants noted that "It was impressive how each learning coach was able to keep up to speed with each project, even without being involved in every conversation."

Although it would have been easier in some respects to stay with one team throughout, I found the opportunity to coach all the teams to better help me coach each participant one on one. I had a stronger sense of each participant's capabilities based on their contributions to the team. I was able to reinforce and support what they had personally gained through the program.

The PSE&G LIRW program required even more flexibility and coordination on the part of the learning coaches and the external program manager. During the course of the more than nine programs over three years, a total of fourteen different learning coaches participated.

PSE&G LIRW
Judy O'Neil, President, Partners for Learning and Leadership

Prior to each session in the program, three learning coaches were hired to work in that session. They were hired based on diversity of background and experience, and availability. The fourth learning coach played the combined role of external program manager and learning coach throughout the program. These four coaches would work individually with an AL team and as a learning coach team. The coaches were prepared for the program first through an initial verbal and written orientation by the external program manager. Second, a meeting of the learning coach team was held. Since in many cases the members of the learning coach team did not know one another or had not worked together before, it was important for them to spend time to understand one another's backgrounds and the strengths they brought to the program, as well as their perspectives and assumptions about the work of a learning coach. They also met as a team with the sponsors and then individually with the sponsor for their team. These meetings were of importance to the learning coach team in that they mirrored the program design in which the learning coach team would work. The program design required them to work as a learning coach team in the learning community as a whole, as well as individually with their AL teams.

Since each learning coach was working independently with his/her team, consistency became problematic, particularly because of the emphasis on diversity in each team. In addition, the learning coach team needed to address the balance between the needs of the individual AL team and the needs of the program, which would not exist if a learning coach was working on his/her own. Consistency and balance were addressed in two ways; first through the combined role of the program manager/learning coach. This role helped in a number of ways. It provided continuity for the program, from session to session and between the various learning coach teams. It was also a checkpoint for the learning coaches in each learning coach team for their questions, issues, and concerns about the organization, the program in general, and their interaction with their individual AL teams. Finally, the role served as a pushback on individual learning coaches, as well as the learning coach team. It helped ensure that the work in the community and in the individual AL teams stayed within the broad parameters of the program, while still balancing the individual needs of the coaches and AL teams.

The second important element to the consistency and balance of work was the dedication of the learning coach teams to spending long hours in preparation, debrief, and acting as *sounding boards* for each other. These discussions enabled coaches to better understand what might be happening in their own team, especially in the context of other teams and the program as a whole; as well as to get helpful suggestions and support for dealing with difficult issues in their team.[31]

What's Involved in Training or Developing a Learning Coach?

As illustrated by the previous two vignettes, whether or not to use internal resources (within a company) or external resources (outside consultants, academics) to perform the learning coach role is one of the choices that organizations need to make. Unless experienced coaches are already members of the organization, initially there will often be a dependence on external resources to develop an internal capability. Long term, there are both advantages and disadvantages to each choice. Table 48, Using Internal and External Learning Coaches, summarizes the options.

Internal-positive: Depending on the organization, there may be readily available resources within the human resource organization who have some of the prerequisite skills for being a learning coach. If that's the case, they are already on the payroll and could be dedicated to the AL initiative. By having these existing resources learn and play the role of learning coach, the skills will be readily available for transference to others in the organization.

TABLE 48 Using Internal and External Learning Coaches

	Positive	Negative

Internal	May be easily available
	Less cost
	Ease in embedding skills
	  within organization
		Difficulty in operating 'outside the culture'
		Difficulty in confronting participants within own
		  culture
		Not easily available

External	Experience Outsider to the culture	More cost More difficult to embed learning skills within organization

---

Internal negative: One of the most important interventions in AL is that of asking questions. Being able to ask naïve, fresh questions cannot be underestimated, but the fact of being "within the culture" creates difficulty for the internal resource with this intervention. The learning coach needs to challenge the team. He or she needs to put a spotlight on taken-for-granted norms of behavior and thinking.[32] In addition to the difficulty in even recognizing your own taken-for-granted norms of behavior, the internal coach may need to confront others within his/her own organization in ways that may cause the participant to react negatively to the coach. Finally, not all organizations nowadays have readily available resources. Cutbacks in human resources and line departments may make this option not possible.

External-positive: There are a number of experienced practitioners of AL available to help organizations think through whether or not AL is the right intervention. If AL is right, an external practitioner can then help decide what school and co-design would best fit the needs and assist with the implementation of an initiative, including the learning coach role. Outside learning coaches do not encounter the same problems as those from inside the culture. They automatically operate outside the culture and do not run the same risks in challenging participants as someone who must return to work with them the next day.

External negative: External consultants, however, cost money. Budgets, as well as people, are also at a premium in many organizations, so cost is a consideration in this decision. Finally, as discussed earlier, most AL practitioners espouse the philosophy of transferring their skills to participants and the organization. So, with external resources doing most, if not all, of the learning coach work, specific attention has to be paid to how these skills will become embedded in the organization.[33]

There is general agreement in the literature about the basics of developing new learning coaches.[34] The first step is to have prospective coaches participate in an AL program. Unless an individual experiences the process as a participant, it is difficult for him or her to understand and support participants in the future. This is not always that easy to accomplish if the decision is made to use entirely internal resources. As a result, organizations opt to use external resources to help start a program, moving as expeditiously as possible to internal resources. Attendance as a participant can then be followed up by the new learning coach either *shadowing* an experienced coach in a program, working with a group with an experienced coach as a mentor, or plunging right in to work with a team.

Research suggests that some content training may also be appropriate depending on the background of a new coach.[35] In order to develop a theoretical base for their work, new learning coaches need to understand the background for forming that base. This should involve an introduction to the different approaches to AL and the assumptions about learning held by each.

The fundamentals of the adult learning theories, such as learning from experience and transformational learning, should be included as a part of learning coach development. Consistent with AL theory, this content learning should be reflected on in light of the new coach's experience as a participant in AL.

If new learning coaches do not have group process skills in their repertoire, a formal class or developmental opportunity should be incorporated. In any case it is important that the new coach understand the differences between process consultation and the learning coach role.[36]

After this look at the complex role of learning coach, we'll next turn our attention to the results of a well co-designed AL program and how the various elements we've discussed so far can contribute to those results.

CHAPTER FIVE

Evaluating Action Learning

"Even if you're on the right track, you'll get run over if you just sit there."
—Will Rogers
"Learning is not compulsory … neither is survival."
—W. Edwards Deming

A t this point we've examined ways in which you can tell if Action Learning (AL) can help your organization; provided information to decide what school of AL will best fit the organization's needs; looked at the concept of co-design and how to use it to design the best program; examined some of the elements and processes that will be most apt to produce good results; and explored the important role of learning coach and its connections to a successful program. Despite all of this work, how can you be sure the program you've co-designed and implemented was actually successful? How can you show the organization that their investment of time, talent, and resources is producing the intended results? One way is through the participants' voices we hear in Lamm-Hartmann's composite vignette.[1]

Volvo Truck Management Program
Dr. Sharon Lamm-Hartmann, CEO, Inside Out Learning, Inc.

Vignette of a Typical Participant's Program Experience
As I am flying to Brugge, Belgium, for program session one, I am thinking—How can they expect us to take care of our normal work and home life responsibilities when participating in this six-month program? I finally get to the program room and see fellow

126

participants from different cultures and functions; all different personalities. *Oh, no,* they have those chairs in a circle. This is going to be one of those *touchy feely* things. I want to go hide now.

According to the agenda, it looks like we'll have very little free time and the program goes until late in the evening. One night is a cultural evening where we will explore Brugge. I have never been outside the United States and I don't like not being able to speak the language. Where can I get a Pepsi?

We are now in our first project team meeting. We got our project and everyone is trying to get to work except for the French guy at the end of the table. I am wondering if he can even talk. This pesky learning coach just stopped our action and wants us to reflect and write in journals. We were making progress until he became involved!

Good, that it is over and now we are in the business game. I love competition and we will win. The other marketing guy and I are taking control and *Oh not again,* that learning coach stops us to reflect again. However, in the reflection, I learned that the French guy who hadn't said anything could not speak English that well and had no clue what was going on and felt left out and two other introverted team members also felt left out. It turns out that they had the best ideas if we would have stopped to listen. I don't like excluding others and I wonder if I have always done this? I am a pretty strong extrovert and probably have always talked over others. I want to start to change this.

We are back in the large group of twenty participants doing a reflection and dialogue session, and I can't believe what people are sharing. You mean I am not alone in having these problems? Maybe we all are just simply human? At the same time I am hearing completely new points of view from those that bring different backgrounds.

Between sessions one and two we met and were more productive because the learning coach was not slowing us down. Session two was in the United States, where we made reflecting on action a part of the way we work. I saw how taking pauses to reflect on what we were doing and how we were working together slowed us down in order to speed us up. We actually were more productive in the long run by slowing down to reflect on our action, so we decided to use this stopping and reflecting whenever we work as a team. And I am starting to use it back at work with my team.

I am now on my way to week three—in India. I am really glad that I got to know these guys because we are getting into some personal stuff—Myers-Briggs, 360 and team feedback, and the lifeline exercise where we share life experiences. All of these tools are giving me insights into who I am and walking down the streets of India seeing a woman with a dying baby ask me for small change really had an impact on me. What do I possibly have to complain about? What is the meaning of life anyway? How do I become a better husband, father, and member of the human race?

In the lifelines exercise one guy even broke down, telling us how burned out he was and how he sacrificed his entire personal life for work. I felt complete empathy for him and I saw myself heading down that road. We stayed up talking at the bar until 4:00 A.M.. His story helped me find renewed balance between home and work life, which surprisingly has made me more productive at work. I find if I am happier at home, I am happier and more productive at work.

Between sessions three and four we met to finish our project and prepared for and made our presentation to executive management during session 4 in Sweden. I found out that I got a new job and I think it will be really good for me to continue to practice what I have learned. I now have 100 additional employees, so I will have to continue to let go of control and delegate. I am sad this is ending. Funny when I started I thought this was going to be a royal pain—now I see it was one of the best personal experiences of my life.

As mentioned in chapter 2, an important part of co-design is determining how an AL program will be evaluated. This chapter will examine methods for evaluation and research and demonstrate some of the success stories that have been found from the evaluation and research on many of the programs we've been discussing, such as:

- PSE&G's LIRW
- Grace Cocoa's Global Forum
- Invensys' Leadership in Action
- Berlex's Corporate Development Program,
- Volvo Truck Corporation's Volvo Truck Management Program
- Global Financial Organization's Action Learning Program
- U.S. Department of Veteran Affairs Action Research Project Team
- Pfizer, Inc.'s Performance Leadership Projects.

How Can We Evaluate an Action Learning Program?

For many years, workplace educators have often turned to the Kirkpatrick hierarchy to check for learning and performance gains at different levels: satisfaction with the program, learning gains immediately after the program, impact on learning and performance back on the job, and at the most complicated level to assess, impact on the organization. Recent writers on evaluation have found problems with this approach. While it points to levels at which one should look for impact, the hierarchy in itself does not offer advice on how to do good or useful evaluations. And there is increasing recognition of how complicated it is to attribute results, other than satisfaction and individual learning, to training because of the complicated environment to which individuals have to transfer their learning. It is difficult, if not impossible, to link learning causally to impact.

As Raelin points out, one can "establish an intervening effect between the program and financial results" and then look at links between the intervention and the intervening effect, and between the intervening effect and other results, financial or otherwise. Raelin illustrates this approach with a study done at Sears by Boudreau and Ramstad that looked at relationships between leadership development and employee attitude change, which in turn could be linked to customer satisfaction. Raelin also suggests that one could look at links between reflective practices in programs, known to influence group development, and then examine links between products of AL groups that are effective and financial indicators.[2]

Various expansions of the Kirkpatrick hierarchy or alternatives to it have been suggested, some of which we discuss later in this chapter. But given reliance on this hierarchy, how has it been used in AL evaluation efforts?

AL co-designers using this framework typically begin by looking at the program itself. This first look is usually characterized as the participants' reaction to the program, a Level 1 evaluation according to Kirkpatrick, measured by a questionnaire.[3] Although the questions or items on the questionnaire usually try to assess participants' satisfaction with the program, AL programs also try to focus more on utility questions that are considered more effective in predicting impact.[4] An example of this type of questionnaire from the Berlex Corporate Development Program is shown in Table 49, Berlex Corporate Development Program Evaluation Form.

How Do We Know if Learning Is Being Transferred?

If we continued to use Kirkpatrick's model as a way to examine evaluation and research, we'd next look at methods to examine whether or not learning is happening in the program.[5] One way to attempt to measure and map team dynamics in AL teams was explored by Dilworth.[6] He worked with ITAP International to modify The Global Team Process Questionnaire (GTPQ), a diagnostic tool to measure process changes over time on global and distance teams for use in an academic AL program. His research showed that a modified version provided useful quantitative and qualitative feedback on the team process to both the researcher and the AL team. But, since most of the

TABLE 49 Berlex Program Evaluation Form

Berlex Corporate Development Program Evaluation Form

1. What part of the program was most effective for you? Least effective?

2. In terms of the learning coaches' role, what would you like them to do more of? Less of?

3. In what way was the personal learning goal activity effective for you? Not effective?

4. On which of the organizational learning goals were you able to gain some insight and in what way(s)?

5. What part of the program helped most to advance the project you are working on? Helped least?

6. What other feedback do you have?

strategic mandates for AL programs have to do with organizational and/or individual change and development, we're also interested in whether or not learning from the program is being transferred back to the workplace.

The theory and rhetoric of AL says that an AL program produces significant learning and that the appropriate co-design of the program can enhance transfer. The evaluation of that transfer involves looking at the initiation of subsequent action based on what was experienced in the program and the maintenance, or continuing application, of what was learned over time. The extent of transfer of learning depends on the degree to which changes in knowledge, insight, understanding, meaning, attitudes, competencies and/or behaviors are applied by the participant outside the program. Managers going through AL programs must engage in "far transfer," that is "the ability to think and take action in diverse, complex, and uncertain contexts," and "forward-reaching high road transfer," that is, the ability to apply "an explicitly known general principle to a new situation."[7]

Some data collection and evaluation methods and designs lend themselves more to measuring individual change and development. Other methods and designs are more often used to ascertain organizational support. We'll look at some of each.

The first data collection method we'll discuss is the use of critical incident questions in a relatively straightforward post-training evaluation where data were collected after participants had been in the program, but while the intervention was still going on.[8] This approach to evaluation was used during the LIRW program at PSE&G to show the organization that the developmental and behavioral objectives of the program were being met based on the examples of behavior change being cited by the participants as illustrated in the following.

PSE&G LIRW
Judy O'Neil, President, Partners for Learning and Leadership

In order to understand the impact LIRW was having on the participants and the organization, we did ongoing and follow-up evaluation and research. Some of the earlier evaluation made use of critical incident questions such as, "Can you think of a situation in which you found yourself using better, or different, communication skills to get better results?," to find out the impact of the program on participants and/or the organization. As discussed in chapter 1, the program was co-designed in the Experiential School, but as changes were made to the ongoing program, critical reflection also became evident. So in the evaluation, we looked for evidence of single-loop learning that improved ways of working and being in the organization based on the experiential learning cycle and double-loop learning that changed underlying ways of defining the problem or situation based on critical reflection and transformative learning, linked with the objectives of the program.[9] Some examples of what we found are in Table 50.

Critical incident evaluation supports the collection and analysis of "incidents," instances of actual behavior that are perceived to reflect either very effective or very ineffective performance with respect to the activity assessed. Not just any behavior occurring in the course of the activity is considered critical, only behavior where the purpose or intent of the act seems fairly clear and where its consequences are sufficiently defined to leave little doubt concerning its effect. The behavior can be self-reported or obtained from the observations of persons in a position to personally observe those performing the activity.[10]

Critical incident questions can be answered verbally or in writing and should:

- be as short as possible
- be clearly written
- address directly what information the evaluator is seeking to obtain
- be readily and easily understood by the participants or other interviewees
- state that a description of actual behavior is desired
- be designed to help respondents isolate the action/behavior of the individual from the situation preceding it and from its consequences
- tie down the selection of the incident to be reported in some way, i.e., most recent incident, in order to prevent the giving of only the more dramatic or vivid incidents or those which fit the interviewee's stereotype
- encompass the full range of behaviors relevant to the evaluation.[11]

A complete example of one of the questions used in the PSE&G evaluation is found in Table 51, PSE&G Critical Incident Question.

Other kinds of questions can also be used in evaluation. After the LIRW program had been running for about two years, a comprehensive study was done to help determine the perceived organizational

TABLE 50 Illustrative LIRW Participant Results

Objective	Single-Loop Learning Results	Double-Loop Learning Results
Enhance the way people communicate and interact with one another.	"One of my learning goals is to be a better listener.…What I do now is go over what I said again and again if necessary. I am much more patient with my associates. I am getting good results, much better results, and I have a good crew. I was short a guy this last week and they really busted their tails and got the job done. I am seeing a real improvement with the attitude of the team."	"One of my teammates asked me a question about my personal learning goal that made me rethink the action I was taking. I'd never thought about it from that perspective. I decided to act in response to the area opened up for me and got very positive feedback from my co-workers."
Weave quality tools and behaviors into the fabric of the organization.	"LIRW is the jump start that the quality process needs."	"The process works. I won't hesitate to use the tools. It's not rocket science, but if your eyes are closed it might as well be."
Develop an environment of openness and trust and get conflict out on the table.	"I had an incident occur where I used the conflict resolution model with two union employees. …I wanted this to be a win-win situation.…We both agreed and one of the union officials came up to me and said afterwards that it was a real good meeting."	"I guess as I get further way from the time spent in LIRW, I may not recognize the LIRW learnings, possibly because they are becoming more ingrained into my style of management.…So what I did was talk to each party separately that needed to be up on the plan to find out what would be more acceptable."

TABLE 51 PSE&G Critical Incident Question

"Think back since you started LIRW. Can you think of a time when it occurred to you to use the quality tools, or the ideas behind them, to get improved results?" (Pause until he/she indicates he/she has an incident in mind)

"Please tell me about the situation—where and when did it occur?"

"Who was involved?"

"What aspects of the situation caused you to react in that way?"

---

impact of any behavior change. Approximately 200 participants were contacted and the following questions asked by an outside researcher:

1. Have you found other people in Distribution are able to say things more openly with you and with others since the start of the LIRW program? Why do you think that is?
2. Do you see more teamwork (cooperation) with others inside and outside your department since the start of the LIRW program? Why is that?
3. Do you feel people are acting any differently when there is a disagreement now than before LIRW? What do you think the reason is for that?
4. Do you see the Quality tools, or the ideas behind them, being used more now than before LIRW? What is causing that?

Although data depended on perceptions obtained through self-report, the results were positive.[12] Depending on the objective being discussed, 65–79 percent of the interviewees responded that they had seen the desired changes in their day-to-day interactions. The negative responses—indicating that they had not seen the desired changes—ranged from a low of 6.5 percent to a high of 15.5 percent. The highest percentage of positive responses was on the Quality objective; the highest percentage of negative responses was on the communication objective.

Although Invensys experienced business changes that precluded a robust evaluation of their AL program, interviews showed the perceived impact of the personal learning goal work in the program as well as the impact of the team project work.

Invensys Leadership in Action
Kate Hoepfner-Karle, KHK Human Capital Consulting

For one participant, his personal learning goal(s) "were to develop a structured approach for strategic thinking / strategic planning and to develop what I will call corporate leadership—the kind of leadership that applies to corporate level." The results he reports having achieved:

> I consider I achieved a "90 percent+" on both goals. On the first one, I came back with tools to develop and maintain strategic thinking. To this day, I still refer to the literature we were given and to new literature in the same axis. I learned how to differentiate strategic thinking (which hill to take) versus tactical thinking (how to take it). Finally, scenario planning was very helpful. I still use this approach almost on a day-to-day basis.
>
> On the leadership side, I still work on this, as I think we never finish with this work. What I learned, especially from the 360° review, is still almost invaluable. It helped me to better understand … me! I realized I had weak points in communication. This, surprisingly, was more helpful in my personal life than the professional (although very helpful there as well).

What else did you learn or take away?

> I acquired much more self-esteem / self-confidence on my business capabilities. Before I thought I could do things. Now I know I can. I had followed many "executive training" (sessions) at McGill University, Queens University, Montreal University and to this day, it is by far, very far, the best training I ever (will ever?) got.

This feedback is consistent across each of the program participants. They report bringing a different level of leadership to their own organizations by differentiating the types of leadership required for their multiple responsibilities. In particular, all participants report greater emphasis on their strategic responsibilities using the tools and learning to restructure their own organizations, to enhance the strategic planning for their business and thereby improving the business results for the business they manage.

Pfizer gathered data through interviews from their participants' experience and also looked at the teams' project results in order to assess the benefits of their PLP AL program.

Pfizer, Inc.'s Performance Leadership Projects
Chuck Williams

Outcomes of Performance Leadership projects vary greatly. Sometimes teams far exceed original expectations and scope. On occasion teams fail to gel effectively and produce incomplete or inadequate results. Most often, teams achieve very good results on some of our most difficult business problems. They develop as leaders and establish relationships that often last for years, helping them on other cross-organizational assignments.

Individual benefits: Almost without exception, team members state that the 90 to 120-day period of the project is one of the most difficult times they have ever had in the workplace. They must find ways to delegate to subordinates and prioritize other work along with the project work, and they view the project as the ultimate *stretch* assignment. Almost without fail, they state that they are very happy to have participated, and feel that they have developed more quickly as a leader than they could have under more normal circumstances. They are particularly appreciative of the time and energy spent by the sponsors, coaches, and other team members. The most common leadership skills highlighted by participants are the development of:

- delegation and empowerment of subordinates
- trust of peers and team members
- ability to work across geographies, time zones, and cultures
- stakeholder management
- dramatic improvement in ability to give and receive high-quality feedback
- ability to develop and communicate business value
- ability to teach and interact with team and other colleagues
- relationships across the organization that make day-to-day work much more productive
- team-building techniques and skills.

Business results: Most often, these cross-functional teams produce excellent results on some of our most difficult business issues. Examples of outstanding results from the IT organization at Pfizer are as follows:

- A new global services model for support of shared IT infrastructure (i.e., computing, networks, desktop services, messaging, security operations). This model structures part of Pfizer's internal IT group as a competitive services organization with a clear services portfolio, customer and operational metrics, demand planning, and tiers of service. The model is currently being implemented consistently globally. Customer satisfaction has improved by 20 percent. Cost per unit of service has improved by 20 percent over three years, with another 15 percent targeted. Agility and speed have improved dramatically, allowing Pfizer to change its business rapidly through acquisition and divestiture. These changes are being driven by the colleagues who sponsored and participated in PLP projects to define these services.
- A radically different approach to successfully managing enterprise data. IT and business process leaders developed a data stewardship and ownership model that allows data sources inside and outside of Pfizer to be properly understood and managed. This master data management service supports the understanding of massive amounts of clinical, product, patient, colleague, and financial data, turning it into se-

cure and reliable information that can be shared inside and outside of Pfizer. This fundamental building block is vital to Pfizer's efforts to help redefine portions of its business and innovate around new healthcare services and products. In the clinical data space alone, this information saves tens of millions of dollars annually and months of valuable time in bringing new medicines to market.

· Dramatic improvements in talent development and other HR processes, including meaningful career ladders, management competencies, and workforce development planning tools for the IT function. The IT function will continue to be a leader at Pfizer in pioneering leading-edge HR practices, including use of technology to better integrate talent development tools and processes.

All teams have learned to articulate their project recommendations in terms of business value, whether it is measured as ROI, risk mitigation, new sources of revenue, or more rapid adaptation to a changing environment.

We view our Performance Leadership projects as a critical element of continuing to focus on colleague development at Pfizer. Although the program is demanding and difficult, our high-potential, emerging leaders are eager to participate and accelerate their personal learning. As a Pfizer business leader, it is exciting to see some of our most talented colleagues more rapidly solve some of our most pressing business problems and grow as leaders at the same time.

There are additional ways to collect data for evaluation of an AL program other than critical incidents or interviews using direct questions. One method is through observation during the program itself. Although the presence of an observer can be a difficult role to handle, through proper negotiation it can provide effective results and even assist in the program. This evaluation/research method is described by Yorks, O'Neil, Marsick, Nilson, and Kolodny.[13]

Although the organization, Grace Cocoa, was initially reluctant to allow researchers entry to the Global Forum program, they eventually allowed one observer-participant, who was backed up by a research team, to help with analysis of the data. The researcher attended the first residential week of the program with the understanding that his role would continue beyond that only with the concurrence of the participants.

During that week, he kept a low profile, interacting informally with the participants, learning coaches, and program director. He observed the teams; went on field trips and observed program activities; took notes and wrote up his reflections. He had agreed not to comment as part of the program process unless invited to by the learning coaches, but in the end, his authentic participation as a member of the total community was necessary for him to build and sustain the relationship he needed to do his work as a researcher. By the end of that first week, the researcher had succeeded in gaining the confidence of the community and was permitted to stay for the balance of the program. In addition, the program director allowed him to conduct interviews with non-participants in the organization who were affected by the program.[14]

Inductive analysis of data gathered through these observations, and the interviews the researcher was allowed to do as a result of the trust he gained from his role, provided evidence of both organizational change toward the objective of creating a global organization and individual change and development. Individual change was also measured by 360-degree assessment tools. For example, one of the European units had a problem with meeting the need for production of a certain powder and asked an American plant for help. As one Forum participant said, "Two years ago we would have said no, it's not our problem. Now we said sure, if we can help we will." In another, more personal situation, an individual described a meeting in which his boss, a Forum graduate, asked everyone to take the time for reflection prior to the meeting. "I thought to myself, What is this? But the meeting was very productive."[15]

A weakness of the Grace Cocoa study was a lack of baseline data against which to measure change. This was not the case in a multimethod study (still in process) done by Ward, who as the internal consultant in charge of the program at the time, also collected data as a participant observer. As seen in the following vignette, Ward has rich data through which to look at changes in both individuals and the company.

Berlex Corporate Development Program
Bob Ward, President, Leadership Bridge, LLC

The author of this vignette conducted research that assessed the extent to which individuals participating in an Action Learning leadership development program transfer what was learned back to their workplace setting and identified whether or not this learning resulted in perceived performance improvement. The learning methodologies of questioning insight, reflection, and critical reflection were specifically examined as well as the participants' personal learning goal for transfer. Additionally, did transfer of the above and participation in the program result in improved performance improvement?

Results of this research are based on interviews with participants (pre, post, and six-month post program), participants' managers and co-workers, as well as results of a pre and post multi-rater assessment.

Preliminary results from the interviews indicate quite a bit of transfer and application at the workplace post program that continued with only a slight decrease six-month post program. Performance improvement was also perceived for the majority of participants as measured by peer and manager interviews. The above findings were also confirmed in the results of the pre- and post-multi-rater assessment. It should be noted that the projects on which the participants worked were eventually implemented at the organization and that other Action Learning programs have since taken place.

Evaluation of the program was conducted one year after the program and the key lessons learned are:

- Action Learning is highly regarded by participants and executives for the learning.
- It was important to involve participants' boss prior to and during the program.
- Future programs need to have an executive who is the champion for the implementation phase for the projects.

Finally, Action Learning is a much different way of working together and solving major organizational problems or developing new growth-related opportunities. As such it can create *noise* in the organization. Executive support during the program, and particularly after, is critical to sustaining the projects as well as the program in the early years.

The results from the U.S. Department of Veteran Affairs Action Research Project Team are interesting because there are actually two components—the results of the AR work and the originally unintended personal learning from the learning practices introduced by the coach.

U.S. Department of Veteran Affairs Action Research Project Team
Janet Reid-Hector and Lyle Yorks

In 2003 results from the sites with action teams demonstrated significantly more improvements than the comparison facilities, including reductions in self-reported stress and in all forms of reported aggression, and a substantial increase in employee satisfaction. It also needs to be noted that each site has a unique story. Variation in both site factors and the extent that local teams took on the collaborative inquiry role and a posture of learning are associated with differences across the teams. Political legacy issues at the sites also played a role.

Additionally, following the end of the formal project, other VA locations have requested the establishment of action teams following a similar process. Various members of the project team, both academic and VA professionals, working together have formed sub-teams to meet these requests. Practices from the team have been adopted by other staff groups working on similar issues within the VA.

Further, the data from interviews with members of the project team, both academic and VA professionals, demonstrate profound personal learning from the learning practices that has transferred into other aspects of their work lives. One academic member who was quoted earlier stated:

I think that when I kind of opened up a little bit and stopped being so resistant to this notion, I started really paying very careful attention to [the learning coach] and what he was saying, and then more importantly what he wasn't saying, and then I started to see things that maybe I hadn't seen previously. So I really started paying attention in the meetings and I started doing something that I hadn't done previously. I started shutting my mouth. You know as an academic, you suffer from this thing...you want to just talk, you are always talking ....What I was trying to do now was really listen and not become as invested .... So anyway, the transition to the learning component and the learning practices was initially painful for me, and then I kind of opened up to the possibility that maybe this stuff actually had a purpose. ...I'm ready to sit back and listen more...entertain some other possibilities, be open to some other realities, try to understand that there are different lenses and that that really means something.

Lamm's research on the Volvo Truck Management Program was conducted after participants completed the program. It focused primarily on understanding transformative learning and the elements of the program that would have cast it into the Critical Reflection school. Since, as she states, there is little documentation that supports conclusions about whether or not transformative learning has resulted from a program, she had to develop her own framework for the research. Interviews were done with participants who had participated in different programs over a long period of time.

Volvo Truck Management Program
Dr. Sharon Lamm-Hartmann, CEO, Inside Out Learning, Inc.

It was clear that VTC wanted transformation in their leaders' mindsets as one outcome of the program, and this was the primary focus of my qualitative research study. Specifically I wanted to answer three research questions:

1. To what extent, if at all, did the program foster transformative learning?
2. Which, if any, leadership behaviors were most likely influenced by participation in the program?
3. In what ways did conditions foster or hinder transformative learning?

Transformative learning is very difficult to measure.[16] Even when leadership development programs are designed to achieve transformation, there is little documentation that supports conclusions about the resulting impact. I developed my own framework for studying transformative learning that you can find in my dissertation.[17] I think this framework could be very helpful to anyone who is interested in determining whether a leadership development or other educational program fostered transformative learning.

My research was a qualitative case study of the perceptions of people in VTC, MiL, and LIM. The research sample included twenty-four program participants (representing about 25 percent of the total population), twenty-four people who work with them (co-workers), three learning coaches, and one key executive. The participant sample was demographically comparative to the participant population and included participants from across six different cultures (Swedish, British, French, Belgian, Australian, and American) and five different programs (from 1992 through 1996).

I used a number of data collection methods including: 1) document analysis (staff documents, descriptive staff interviews, program evaluations and designs, population demographics), 2) pre-interview forms (demographic and descriptive data of learning experiences), 3) participant, executive, and learning coach interviews, 4) participant leadership reflection forms, and 5) co-worker critical incident questionnaires.[18] Five participant interviews then took place to pilot the approach. At least six weeks prior to the interview, each participant completed a pre-interview form. The five co-worker questionnaires were tailored based on the participant descriptions of personal change and then distributed. The pilot was successful. This process was repeated with the remaining nineteen participants. To help clarify questions raised (i.e., about program design), the learning coach and executive interviews were spread over time, taking place at the beginning, middle, and end of participant interviews.

Some sample results of the research follow. While VTM wanted to foster a transformation in their leaders' mindsets, they also wanted to achieve business results through the project teams' solving critical business problems. Many of these project solutions made and saved the company money. The following are examples of some of the business results that were achieved:

- save $7 million by designing an innovative distribution system that surpassed a #1 competitor
- save $3 million in raw material procurement costs through a well-developed internal benchmark study
- save millions in lost sales by recovering a dealer who had previously cancelled all orders.

However, the main focus of my research was to answer my three research questions to determine whether the leaders actually did experience transformative learning and what conditions helped them to do so. Below are reported some of the results that answered Research Question 1, that is, the extent to which, if at all, the program fostered transformative learning.

A total of twenty-two of the twenty-four participants interviewed experienced transformative learning. Eight of the twenty-two experienced transformation in more than one learning area. The program helped to foster transformative learning to varying extents based on where the program fell in one's individual and organizational contexts. In other words, for twelve participants the program triggered transformative learning, and for ten participants the program moved along or helped to integrate a previously started transformation. In all cases of transformation, the organizational context (i.e., job change) either triggered or helped to integrate the learning into their daily lives.

Sunny[19] exemplified those who had a transformation toward a broader, more global perspective:

> The program was the first time that I got to go abroad to be a *stranger in a strange land,* to get thrown in with people from totally different cultures, different backgrounds. I see myself more part of the world now ....I don't see my little corner of the world as important as it used to be. I identify more as a member of the human race and less as a member of the United States of America....Now when I say Volvo, I think of the whole world and what we can do on this end that ties into what they are doing 10,000 miles away that makes things better for the whole.

Lance illustrated participants who experienced a transformation in his overall leadership style from "power over" to "power with":

> I was convinced I was the owner of the truth ...I was too directive. After the program I said that nobody has the truth....It is possible for me to say or to think I was wrong.... Consensus is not in the French language. In France, I'm right or I'm wrong ...in the program I discover that it's more productive if I have others' points of view, and I change if they are right ....because you cannot—one man—think of everything.

The Global Financial Organization Action Learning Program, which used individual problems in the co-design, made use of similar data collection methods for evaluation that were used, as described above, in team project-focused programs.[20] As with the earlier co-designed programs discussed, the results of this research also demonstrated learning within the program, and the transfer to the workplace.

Global Financial Organization Action Learning Program

Seventeen participants were interviewed by telephone to obtain information about their experience in the AL program. The questions were:

- What do you believe was the most valuable thing learned?
- How were you able to use AL in your workplace?
- What enabled or deterred this learning and transfer?
- What are your ideas for program improvements?

Most of the participants indicated that they had gained new knowledge and insight about themselves and Global Financial Organization. One of the predominant learnings cited by all participants was the use of questioning insight. They used this learning both in the program and back on the job.

…that ignorant question sometimes can open somebody's eyes. I know that happened to me … one question can move you in a direction that you did not think about because you were in that box and you were not thinking …

Ask the "so what" question … and they (the clients) think about the "what?" and it isn't such a big deal. Now all of a sudden they have a realization and start questioning their initial decision.[21]

How Can Organizational Impact Be Measured?

The studies we have discussed thus far have focused primarily on individual change and development (although the Grace Cocoa program also looked at changes in the organization's culture). It is more difficult to determine the larger organizational impact when talking to or observing individuals. In order to assess organizational impact, a study would need to collect data from a sample of people throughout the organization affected potentially by impact, rather than talk only to those who participated more directly in the program. Culture surveys are known to reliably assess organizational-level data, so survey data from this kind of broader sample, if properly designed, could help an organization say something about system-level impact.

In absence of organization-level data, one strategy that has been used to get a sense of organizational impact is through analysis of AL project results. Some AL designs call for engaging groups in a discussion of how to evaluate project results at the beginning of their work together. Raelin discusses how this might be done and points out, in doing so, the value of collecting baseline data as well as post-program project data. Data collected can be numbers as well as changes in perceptions.[22] As mentioned in the Volvo Truck vignette, organizations "also wanted to achieve business results through the project teams solving critical business problems." Following is an example of PSE&G's work in evaluating project results.

PSE&G LIRW
Judy O'Neil, President, Partners for Learning and Leadership

As part of the co-design, it was decided that each project would be measured based on how well it met the project success criteria, which was co-developed by the team and sponsor. Each team and sponsor was asked to summarize ongoing project results

---

TABLE 52 LIRW Project Reports

Project Question	Results
How can we reduce the unit cost of overhead engineering and construction by 10–20 percent?	Savings of over $500,000 (over 30 percent) through changes in procedures within district. Statewide implementation.
What role can Distribution play in the communities in which we live and serve?	Establishment of guidelines for community proposals and necessary budget. Setup of four regional citizenship teams comprised of management and union. Each regional team identifies, reviews, and prioritizes the community proposals for implementation.

---

for the evaluation and report the information to the project director. Two illustrative reports appear in Table 52.

What About Efforts to Measure Return on Investment (ROI)?

O'Driscoll at IBM has looked at whether or not ROI and other studies of organizational impact serve either the Learning and Organization Development function or the organization itself. He points out that studies by ASTD suggest that only 8 percent of organizations evaluate impact at the organizational level, and that rather than considering this a failure, it might be looked at as an indication that evaluation of this kind is not really valued by the business-minded executives in organizations. Many evaluation designs aiming at organizational impact try to explain what did or did not happen after the fact according to O'Driscoll. Instead, he argues, business executives need predictive evaluation tools that "emphasize front-end strategic alignment and value articulation over back-end learning program value contribution." Predictive tools can aid in learning design and early decisions about value to the organization, but this calls for a very different approach to evaluation.[23]

Thinking on which O'Driscoll and others draw for this kind of evaluation involves causal chain analysis, that is, mapping in advance the chain of impact that interventions are expected to unleash.[24] Victoria Marsick and Martha Gephart have used causal-chain analysis to think about how to track progress toward strategic goals in the assessment work they have done at Otis Elevator to help the company identify ways to enhance networking at the company's flagship Otis University. The company seeks to improve business results gained through AL project work. Networking could be linked to improvements in behavior that could then be traced through a causal chain toward impact on business results.[25]

Seeking to simply prove that an AL intervention impacts the bottom line is, in a sense, a defensive action that is aimed more at retroactively justifying one's decision rather than proactively generating rich information that can improve results on an ongoing basis and be used to make better decisions about actions one should take throughout the life of an intervention. Preskill and Torres recommend ongoing evaluative inquiry that is built naturally into interventions in order to constantly learn from, and improve, actions in ways that are very consistent with AL aims and processes. "As each of the inquiry phases is implemented, organization members come together to engage in the learning processes of (a) Dialogue, (b) Reflection, (c) Asking Questions, and (d) Identifying and Clarifying Values, Beliefs, Assumptions, and Knowledge."[26]

As this chapter illustrates, there are many ways to help the organization see that their investment of time, talent, and resources is producing the intended results. As with any of the co-design elements discussed in chapter 2, it's important to choose the evaluation or research strategy that's right for the organization, one that meets its needs and fits its capacity. The chapter also shows that when a program is well co-designed, an organization will be pleased with the results that show up through the evaluation or research strategy. Our final chapter will look back at those important co-design elements to help determine how to apply them in your organization.

CHAPTER SIX

Pulling It All Together: Co-Designing Action Learning for *Your* Organization

"It is only when we forget all our learning that we begin to know."
—Henry David Thoreau
"In times of change, learners inherit the earth while the learned find themselves beautifully equipped to work in a world that no longer exists."
—Eric Hoffer

The variety of Action Learning (AL) programs and the considerations to be taken about how they are designed show how challenging it can be to decide whether or not AL is the right intervention for you. In the first chapter you used a questionnaire to decide whether or not AL was the right intervention for your organization's current needs. We also introduced the AL pyramid to describe different AL schools. In following chapters we discussed implications of choices around the co-design of AL programs. We highlighted what we and others have learned from experience and research about these choices.

In this chapter, we introduce a decision-support tool (Table 53),[1] that will help you review the choices you made in chapter 1.[2] We reproduce here the Action Learning Pyramid[3] to guide this discussion. We then identify and extract key considerations to help you think about how to co-design a program within your organization that will achieve the results you want. We'll use a review table to help you refer back to relevant sections of chapters in thinking about each consideration.

146

Which Is the Right School for You?

In chapter 1 you determined if AL was right for you, then chose an applicable school. You've gotten quite a bit of information since then, so Table 53 offers a review of these choices by using some of that newer information. To use the decision table, first answer "yes" or "no" to the questions in the first column of the table.

Answers to questions in the first column about organizational readiness must be answered "yes" to use AL, no matter which school you select. That is because all AL programs are designed to address compelling, ill-structured problems that require questioning insight as well as learning from experts. These problems lead to generative solutions that often involve systemic thinking and change across different parts of the organization. Senior leaders and managers must be on board to support new ways of thinking and working by employees on these challenges. If the program involves team projects, key leaders must be willing to champion and sponsor the projects, and to spend time with AL team members in thinking about the issues at hand.

FIGURE 7 Action Learning Pyramid

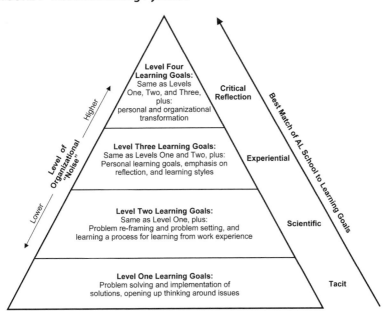

American Management Association

TABLE 53 Decision Table for Choosing an Action Learning Approach

Basic Questions (Answers Must All Be Yes)	Secondary Questions (Selecting an Approach)	If …	AL Approach (Most Appropriate)
Are managers and/or the organization confronted with compelling, unstructured questions?	a) Does the organization have a directive leadership culture that it doesn't wish challenged?		
Do members of the organization generally accept the need for improved organizational learning?	b) Are the desired learning outcomes centered around developing strategic thinking and/or answers to strategic questions?	If the answers to "a" and "b" are yes, then….	Tacit School
If team approach, are organizational leaders prepared to act as project sponsors?	c) In addition to "b" above, do desired formal learning outcomes include problem reframing, problem setting, and the learning of a problem resolution process?	If the answers to "a" is no, and to "c" is yes, then….	Scientific

Experiential

d) In addition to "b" & "c" above, do desired formal learning outcomes include personal development of participants?

If the answers to "a" is no, and to "d" is yes, then . . . .

e) In addition to "b," and "c," above, do desired learning outcomes include transformational individual and organizational learning?

If the answer to "a" is no, and to "e" is yes, then go to "f," "g," and "h," below

f) Is management prepared to accept a high level of uncertainty and ambiguity around learning outcomes?

If yes, go to "g"

g) Is there sufficient organizational justification for generating a high level of organizational *noise?*

If yes, go to "h"

h) Are senior leaders prepared to learn?

If yes, then . . . .

Critical Reflection

Keep in mind that making choices about AL programs is not a cut-and-dried process. You may have to talk with others and gather information in order to weigh one option against another. Some choices will be influenced by politics or resource constraints. Although questions in the decision table are close-ended, their use should stimulate thinking and conversation about goals, the needs of the organization or participants, and organization culture. For example, if you wish to use the program to develop individual leaders, stakeholders may emphasize personal development over organizational change. If you are designing the program for strategic leadership, stakeholders may emphasize the projects on which people work. Business demands might dictate a need for strategic transformation, but only within the parameters of an existing industry or organization culture.

Assuming your organization is ready for AL, in the second column of the decision-making tool you will find questions that differentiate among the four schools in the AL pyramid. The suggested school in the fourth column provides the best fit, depending on your answers.

Tacit School

If your answers to the first two questions ("a" and "b") in the second column are "yes," then the Tacit school of AL would work in your organization. The organizing idea for the Tacit school is bringing together smart people whom you ask to work on challenging tasks. The tacit approach encourages people to learn incidentally as a byproduct of their work on a challenge. The more meaningful the tasks, the more likely participants will be motivated to embrace them. The more visible the tasks, the more likely participants will be seen as valuable contributors and up-and-coming leaders.

A key consideration for the Tacit school is the degree to which the organization's leadership and culture support the status quo versus the degree to which there is openness to change. The Tacit AL design creates less *noise* in the organization, and hence, it is more suited to situations where the mandate is to develop people without radically changing how the organization functions. Participants ask questions but their curiosity is guided by the existing culture. Questions are directed at tasks and tactics rather than underlying values and norms.

Scientific School

If the organization's culture is not highly directive—and your answer to the third question ("c") in the second column is "yes"—then you might be interested in the Scientific school of AL. The organizing idea for the Scientific school is a full, systematic engagement in problem solving.

This school is powered by iterative cycles of inquiry. Information is collected as part of the process to shed light on problems under investigation. Scientific programs typically last over time so that the project group may even experiment with solutions they propose. The Scientific school is especially valuable when participants need skills in problem setting, problem reformulation, and problem resolution; and when the project on which they work is one that invites fact-finding and testing of proposed solutions.

Experiential School

If the organization's culture is not highly directive—and your answer to the fourth question ("d") in the second column is "yes"—then you might be interested in the Experiential school of AL. The organizing idea for this school is a strong focus on learning from experience for participants and the organization.

This school emphasizes questions and reflection before, during, and after action in order to help participants understand themselves, and the way they act, in different contexts and situations. It is predicated on the idea that one needs to learn from experience or else be condemned to having the same experience again and again. Without reflection, participants may not fully understand why they do what they do and how to change their actions. Self-insight and feedback from others about their experience will help them to respond differently in future situations. If personal development is as important as problem solving, then the experiential approach is preferred over the scientific approach. The Experiential school usually advocates for the use of learning coaches who create space for learning and provide feedback and thinking about alternative ways of behaving.

Critical Reflection School

If the organization's culture is not highly directive—and your answer to the fifth question ("e") in the second column is "yes"—then you might consider several options that lead toward the Critical Reflection school. The organizing idea for this school is whether capabilities developed in the program are expected to transform fundamental ways of thinking or working as an individual or organization. Many organizations need to transform aspects of the way in which work is done in the face of globalization, rapid changes driven by technology and market shifts, and business processes that are increasingly customer driven. The Critical Reflection school enables deep changes in individuals and the organization.

But as discussed earlier in this book, emphasizing critical reflection also introduces more *noise* in the organization. Critically reflective people are more likely to ask questions the organization may not want raised. Transformation also takes time. Although some leaders in the organization understand and support change, it may not yet be the time to seed the organization with AL graduates who are ready to move faster than the capacity of the organization to absorb change. Of course, this is a problem that *can* be addressed in the design of the program. So if the organization is serious about transformation, change management steps to support this direction can be included, and the program itself can be used as a driver of change.

So if your answer to questions "f" and "g" in the second column of our decision-support tool is "no," you may consider staying with the Experiential school choice. Questions "f" and "g" point to the readiness of senior leaders for accepting uncertainty and ambiguity in the program's design, the direction taken in project work, and in expected learning outcomes. Ambiguity characterizes critically reflective programs because control is shared with participants. Participants take a lead role in the direction taken in project work and choices about what is learned and in what ways. The program itself may become a self-organizing system and a transitional space where leaders can learn to act in ways that might not be consistent with the norms of the organization they are helping to change.[4] Organizational *noise* is created when participants use innovative strategies in their project work that might involve other parts of the organization that need to be on board for the solution of the project. Participants create *noise* because they begin to lead and manage differently.

The Critical Reflection school is a very good match if you are looking for a development initiative that supports organizational change. And for that reason, the last question ("h") in the second column of our decision-support table also needs to be affirmative. Senior leaders in the organization will need to be ready to learn along with participants in the program so that they can model and support the kinds of thinking and acting they expect of participants in this program. Senior leaders should expect to be surprised by the recommendations they receive from project work. And they should be ready to invite questions from participants about the way things are done in the organization that participants now understand might be counterproductive to the organization's new goals, strategy, or vision.

Blended Schools and Other Considerations

Some of the programs in this book could best be described as a blend of different schools. A blend of Tacit and Scientific schools encourages people to learn primarily on their own from work on an extended problem-solving project. A blend of Experiential and Critical Reflection schools can help managers transform some things about the way they work even though the organization as a whole does not change. The organization may choose to grow leaders with capacity for critical reflection and the ability to make decisions about when and how to exercise that capacity.

There can be a shadow side to choosing a model that reflects the organization's aspirations but is too far ahead of the organization's existing mandate or culture. Participants may feel that the organization has falsely raised expectations about how much they can contribute to change when they act in ways that meet with mixed response, or worse, appear to be punished. Cynicism can set in if project recommendations are not seriously considered, even if they cannot be implemented as proposed. And it could be harder to introduce change efforts further down the road if leaders feel they have "been there, done that" to no effect.

What Do I Have to Decide *First* in Designing a Program Within a Particular School?

Once you are clear about the school, or blend of schools, that is right for you, you can move on to *framing* decisions that influence other aspects of the program design. We summarize information about these framing decisions here from earlier chapters in this book. To find where to look for more information about these decisions, see Table 54. Framing decisions include:

• What role are senior leaders willing and able to play in the program? What do senior leaders think about the program and its strategic mandate?

TABLE 54 Review Table for Finding Information about Key Considerations in Using AL

Key Consideration for Co-Designing AL in *Your* Organization	Where in this book can I find more information
Is AL *right* for you? Which school best fits your goals and organization's needs/culture?	
Is Action Learning right for you?	Ch. 1, pp. 16–18
Which is the right school for you?	Ch. 1, pp. 18–21
Framing Questions to Consider	
What role are senior leaders willing and able to play in the program? What do senior leaders think about the program and its strategic mandate?	Ch. 2, pp. 26–33
What is the right focus, that is, the mix of individual development and organizational change for the part of your organization sponsoring the initiative?	Ch. 2, pp. 33–34
How does individual vs. organizational mix influence project choices?	Ch. 2, pp. 40–45 (team projects) Ch. 2, p. 51
Will you use learning coaches? What will be the role of the learning coach? Where and how will you find/train them?	Ch. 2, pp. 34–35 Ch. 4
Other Key Design Questions to Consider	
Who will the participants be?	Ch. 2, pp. 35–38
How will you get sponsors on board?	Ch. 2, pp. 38–40 Ch. 3, pp. 69–73
How long will the program be? How frequently will participants meet? What mix of face-to-face and virtual learning options should be used?	Ch. 2, pp. 45–51
What are the right strategies for success?	Ch. 3
What is the right mix of "P" and "Q" for this design?	Ch. 2, p. 52
Organizational Questions to Consider	
How will you prepare participants and the organization for the program?	Ch. 2, pp. 56–57 Ch. 3, pp. 73–76
How will you align and integrate the program with the HR and other organizational systems?	Ch. 2, pp. 57–60
What factors may most influence success or failure?	Ch. 3, pp. 94–98
How many programs will you have? How will you cascade multiple interventions throughout the organization?	Ch. 2, pp. 60–62
How will you check progress and evaluate success?	Ch. 5

- What is the right focus, that is, the mix of individual development and organizational change for the part of your organization sponsoring the initiative?
- How does the individual versus organizational mix influence project choices?
- Will you use learning coaches? What will be the role of the learning coach? Where and how will you find/train them?

Top Management Support and Strategic Mandate

What do senior leaders think the program's strategic mandate should be? And what role are senior leaders prepared to play in supporting this mandate? Answering these questions will help gain, ensure, and maintain top management support for the program. Experience suggests that it is better *not* to run a program unless leaders are open to learning from participants' new ideas and recommendations. Further, participants will be less motivated if leaders are not genuinely interested in the solutions and ideas they offer. Participants' managers also need to authorize time taken away from other work to engage in the program.

If strategic mandates involve transformative goals—changes to vision, goals, strategy, culture, or leadership itself—leaders need to check their receptivity to deep and fundamental change. Transactional goals—that revolve around challenges to day-to-day management and organization practices, climate, rewards, etc.—can also be unsettling, especially when changes involve consultation across boundaries with different parts of the business.[5]

You may not be designing a program that will reach the entire organization. Your sphere of influence, and the business leaders with whom you partner around your work, may dictate that the strategic mandate involves one small part of the business. The higher the level at which you work, the more likely you would involve business leaders across the organization and the more feasible it is to seek a mandate that enables project work that cuts across the organization.

Mix of Individual Development and Organizational Change

What is the right focus, that is, the mix of individual development and organizational change for the part of your organization sponsoring the initiative? The answer to questions about the right mix of focus on individual development or organizational change flows from the strategic mandate. Is your mandate about preparing bench strength? Locating and strengthening the capabilities of high potential managers? Improving knowledge and skills *now* for people who need to get behind new practices and integrate them more fully and skillfully in their work? Then you are probably interested first and foremost in individual development.

But if you are working with senior leaders across the organization, you may well be seeking broader organizational change or a mix of individual and organization development. Is your mandate to prepare leaders who also create breakthrough change or become more innovative in their product/service development? Do you want participants to improve business results in ways that might also mean changing work routines and practices? Do you want leaders to buy in to a new way of carrying out strategy by getting involved in setting directions? Are your participants expected to proactively seek customer views and bring them back to top management? Then you are likely concerned with organizational change that may also depend on new thinking and action on the part of individual participants.

You may be interested in a mix of both foci, but it is likely that you will be more interested in one rather than the other. If you focus primarily on individual development—with less interest in whether or not change will result from projects—you may want to cushion the interface between project work and the organization. This will create a safer environment for individuals to take risks from which they can learn through work on the project. You will still want senior leaders to respond to project recommendations, but those leaders should be coached to serve in mentor and development roles. You may choose to hold several report out and discussion sessions throughout the life of the projects to provide frequent feedback and exposure to the reasoning that organizational leaders would bring to making judgments about what the team presents.

If you focus on organizational change, you can also build in time for individual development through work on personal goals. When reviewing programs in many organizations, Conger and Benjamin found that "in the ideal case, projects would be chosen where individual development could be addressed while simultaneously tackling the business imperative."[6] If your focus is organizational change *and* individual development, arrange for exposure through projects to senior leaders and through strategic change opportunities. Build skills needed to be successful in these interactions, for example, consulting, influencing, and change management skills.

Project Choices

Choices about mix of individual and organizational development influence the nature of the project. In all cases, the project should be meaningful to participants and scoped to be actionable. Organizational change projects get best results when they are complex and solutions require work across boundaries. Participants will then engage many parts of the organization because reasonable people in leadership positions are likely to disagree about the right solution. Participants' experiences will push them beyond their typical sphere of influence.

No matter what the AL school, if team projects are selected, they should be influenced by the preferences of senior leadership and be in line with the program's strategic mandate. Conger and Benjamin found that sponsors want projects that "have a direct link to some business imperative." And participants value experiences where they have been "given primary responsibility for initiating a significant change or new venture."[7]

Many of the same criteria for team projects also apply to individual problems. Participants can suggest their own problems, but you will want to discuss their choices and help them pick a problem that provides for stretch and that fits the strategic mandate. The problem should be complex, but also scoped for action. To get the most out of individual problems for the organization, participants should discuss their problem with their manager. They should choose problems that enable them to be challenged yet supported by team members based on action taken in their AL groups that is relevant to their problem.

Choices about Coaches

Will you use learning coaches? What will be the role of a learning coach? Where and how will you find/train them? Co-designers grapple with these questions early on because if used, coaches must be recruited, selected, oriented or trained, and compensated. AL teams can learn without the help of coaches. But coaches can accelerate or deepen their learning because they bring a fresh eye to the team's dynamics. And, like all consultants, coaches are empowered to speak out about what they see going on that might otherwise not be named. Coaches add to the program's expense, but not using them may also be expensive, especially when the program is new to the organization.

No matter which school the design, AL is different from instructor-led training programs. Real life is at the heart of what happens, and real life cannot always be predicted. Participants are more active in making sense of the unpredictable, and in influencing what and how learning occurs. Experienced coaches can help you understand and prepare for inevitable bumps in the road that predictably emerge when learning from real-life projects. If cost is a consideration, ways can be found to build internal capacity. And, although it takes time, participants may eventually develop the skills within their team to be self-facilitating and self-managing.

The thinking you have done about the organization and its culture vis-à-vis choosing an AL school will also help you think about the kind of coach you need for your program. As discussed in chapter 4, the work the coach does with the team, and the capabilities he/she needs, should fit the school and the needs of the organization and program participants.

A frequent question in choosing coaches for any school is whether to hire them externally or find and train people internal to the organization for this role. This choice is partially one of cost and available expertise. Internal coaches have the advantage of knowing the organization's culture. But this same advantage may make it harder for them to speak freely or ask challenging questions. External coaches might see things people cannot see within the culture. But they may not have enough understanding of the context to make themselves clearly understood. In either case, coaches may need some orientation or skill building for their role. If internal coaches are used, they can function more like external coaches when they are not well known to the people they coach because they are freer to ask challenging questions and think outside the box.

What about Other Design Decisions?

What other design decisions do you need to consider once these framing questions have been settled? You need to ask yourself:

- Who will the participants be?
- How will you get sponsors on board?
- How long will the program be? How frequently will participants meet? Will the participants work on personal learning goals? What mix of face-to-face and virtual learning options will be used?
- What is the right mix of "P" and "Q" for this design?

Participants

The strategic mandate for the program influences who should participate and at what level. You may rely on mechanisms already in place for identifying, tracking, and developing participants for leadership roles in selecting the right pool of participants for your program. You may want to invite nominations by leaders, and ask senior leaders to send out letters of invitation to participate under their name.

You will also want to decide on how to help participants choose their project teams. You may be tempted to simply assign people to teams, but participants in the United States and Europe are more motivated when they have some choice in the team in which they work. The key to success is the diversity mix. People learn more and can be more creative when there are many differences in the team in age, gender, educational background, function, etc. Similarities may enable people to delve more deeply into the challenge, but they are also less likely to ask questions that cause the team to rethink assumptions and generate fresh views. If experts on the topic are in the mix, others will also defer to their point of view, which in turn, lessens learning and innovative solutions.

Getting Sponsors on Board

How do you get sponsors on board? Sponsors—project champions who "own" the problem—work with participants on a team project. Sponsors play a less visible role in individual programs because participants own the project. Managers to whom they report are in more of a support role than an owner role.

The ideal team project sponsor learns his or her role by involvement in an AL program. When this is not possible, for example, at start-up of a program, potential sponsors can get some exposure to AL through briefing on the role, contracting with the learning coach for development and specifically designed workshops. Sponsors find it helpful if roles and responsibilities are clarified up front and used to bring them on board.

Sponsors' roles may vary with different program designs, but all sponsors are called upon to champion the program, to interface between participants and other leaders and managers in the organization, and to ensure organizational commitment and resources. Sponsors often need help, even with prior experience in the program, in role modeling the behaviors and actions that participants are expected to acquire through the program. This is especially so when the program is designed to help bring about changes in organizational culture and practices.

Program Length and Meetings

How long will the program last? How frequently will participants meet? What mix of face-to-face and virtual learning options will be used? AL programs vary in length. The key consideration is how much time is needed to complete the project and to learn from the experience. Programs are longer when projects are more complex and/or involve cycles of different kinds of investigation and action. When goals include both project work and work on personal learning goals, time is usually balanced between the two activities. Time must also be allowed for "P" learning and any just-in-time learning sessions. Programs can meet in one or two concentrated sessions over a shorter period of time, or for chunks of time over a much longer period.

A sandwich design is typical, that is, short bursts of common meeting time sandwiched in between work on projects that parallels one's own regular work activities. Programs illustrated in this book typically meet face-to-face three to six times over a period of two to six months. These face-to-face meetings typically include all project teams linked together through a common mandate/purpose with anywhere from three to six weeks in between these sessions.

Project team members often schedule additional meetings in between sessions. Although amount of time and spacing between programs vary, teams need to meet frequently enough to ensure continuity. If the program is spread over time, and teams meet less often than once a month, they lose momentum and trust.

Increasingly, project teams meet virtually in between sessions for at least part of the work and learning they do together. As has also been found with respect to communities of practice and virtual teams, more progress can be made in project teams when time is invested up front for face-to-face meetings that build trust and rapport.[8] Most of the strategies discussed in chapter 3 can be used by teams meeting virtually once this trust and rapport has been established. Increasingly, project teams do much of their work virtually—via phone and video conferencing and/or web-based interaction—in between face-to-face sessions with other project teams in the program. The VNU Explorers program is a good example. AL programs are good vehicles for helping people learn how to work virtually in addition to accomplishing other program goals.

AL's purpose is *both* problem resolution and development, for individuals and/or for organizations. The investment of time and resources is justified because both purposes are to be addressed. So programs usually take longer than regular training interventions, but AL is not used when relatively routine, expert-based learning, or skill development is needed.

Strategies for Success and "P" Learning

Strategies for success are those elements of the co-design that help the program fit the school that best meets the needs of the organization. They are elements, such as definitions of roles and responsibilities, that help the players in the program better understand the expectations and objectives. They are processes that work toward developing skills in line with the focus of the program—processes for creating an environment for learning for personal development or the skill of reframing a project question to help an organization to change.

We have shared many strategies from our own experience and highlighted many from others' work. Good strategies can come from a variety of sources. Of particular relevance to the concept of "Q" learning are strategies from the practice of Action Science and the study of systems thinking.[9]

Program length depends both on the strategies chosen for "Q" learning or skill development and by how much "P" learning you want to add to the mix, a decision that is in turn driven by the strategic mandate, types of development intended, and desired learning outcomes. "P" learning is based on codified knowledge and expertise to differentiate it from discovery, question-driven, questioning insight ("Q"). Participants may need input to frame or execute on the projects. Leaders may want time to discuss the company's strategy and business issues. Development needs might require assessment-based, self-development sessions on, for example, Myers-Briggs leadership and communication styles, learning styles, or emotional intelligence. The company may want everyone to develop skills in the use of common company practices for running meetings or managing projects that are better done through a shared training session.

A cautionary note: It is tempting to fill time with "P" learning sessions, which are easier to control and explain. But the heart of AL is opportunity for questioning insight and self-directed learning from experience. Learning is maximized by interaction such as challenge and support within the team; dialogue around information gathered from the company and through benchmarking; and figuring out how to solve challenging problems together.

Therefore, the schedule needs to be open and flexible enough to let people set their own learning agendas and paths. Learning will take place differently amongst various project teams, even if some needs such as process skills in managing meetings, group leadership, conflict management, consulting skills, or presentation skills can be predicted. AL assumes that it is better to wait, and to help people seek and get the knowledge or skills they need "just-in-time" when they are motivated to learn.

Finally, all learning does not have to happen face to face, especially with the myriad online resources available today, as long as your participants are web-savvy. Participants can find what they need via Internet and Intranet searches and locate expert resources online or through blended learning options.

What about Other
Organizational Considerations?

Once the program has been designed, there are organizational questions to consider:

- How will you prepare participants and the organization for the program? How will you align and integrate the program with the HR and other organizational systems? What factors may most influence success or failure?
- How many programs will you have? How will you cascade multiple interventions throughout the organization?
- How will you check progress and evaluate success?

Preparation and Alignment

How will you prepare participants and the organization for the program? How will you align and integrate the program with the HR and other organizational systems? What factors may most influence success or failure?

Once the stage is set—strategic mandate and goals established, design laid out, participants selected and on board, sponsors lined up, and projects identified—you are ready for final preparations for the program. This may involve work with participants, managers, and other leaders affected by the program and links with other HR and organizational systems.

Participants need to get onboard for their work with projects, sponsors, and coaches. AL is experiential, real time, and highly visible. This kind of learning is unlike many prior structured learning and development interventions, and it involves interacting in new ways with peers, leaders, subordinates, and sponsors. In some AL designs, coaches are expected to support learning but not facilitate the team's work, which can run counter to their role in other task groups. Managers and peers may need to buy in to the extra work an AL program entails and the new behaviors expected of participants. Leaders and the organization may want to manage expectations to achieve unique program goals, particularly when organizational change is part of the desired outcome.

A combination of written communication, one-on-one meetings, and group sessions prior to the participant's involvement will help to prepare everyone for what to expect. Briefings with managers can be used to negotiate support, prioritize responsibilities, and delegate some jobs to subordinates as a development opportunity. Many organizations choose to launch the initiative with pre-program orientation sessions that provide an overview and a taste of the experience to help orient everyone to the experience and to new roles.

Finally, you will want to make sure the program is aligned and in sync with other HR systems and practices, for example, links to talent management and organization development. And you will want to think about your organization vis-à-vis factors for success or failure that others have confronted, particularly when the AL program is intended to go beyond individual development within existing boundaries and when the program is intended to support organizational change.

One final point to consider as you design your AL approach is the extent to which it should stand alone or be part of other development initiatives. For example, if development programs are being rolled out to support a particular strategy or organizational change, it may be possible to build in AL projects linked to those programs. Projects will then naturally relate to the focus of the change initiative. AL tools can be used to create a focus on learning as well as task accomplishment. We have also successfully used AL structured conversations, drawing on the protocols described in chapter 3, in other development initiatives to support reflective practice in pursuit of work goals.[10]

Cascading Rollout

How many programs will you have? How will you cascade multiple interventions throughout the organization? AL programs can be a one-time intervention. More often, organizations that have gotten into the AL habit choose to use this mode of development for a longer period of time. Questions arise, especially when launching the initiative, about critical mass and how quickly a group of key targeted participants can go through an AL experience and get onboard for the strategic mandate and desired outcomes. It is possible to orient a larger group of people to AL experiences in a short time and to use AL tools in various work situations. But a full-blown program, which entails project work extended over a period of time, and which is expected to result in deliberate work and behavior changes, takes time and often creates ripples in other parts of the organization that need to be managed.

If AL is to be a repeated intervention, it helps to have a cascading rollout plan that begins with experiences designed for senior leaders who need to champion the initiative. It is a good idea to run a pilot of the program before the cascade within the organization begins, particularly in programs involving organizational change. Depending on the length of each program, you will want to develop a plan that allows for cycles of program delivery that the organization can absorb and you can support.

Monitoring and Evaluation

How will you check progress and evaluate success? Start from the beginning by identifying what you think will be indicators of success and collecting baseline data against which to track change over time. There are many ways you can collect and analyze data. Even more important is to think about the kinds of changes you expect to find as outcomes of your intervention(s). You can then decide how to measure the current state so that you can later contrast the baseline with the changed state. You will also want to identify quantitative and qualitative metrics that will help you check to see if the intervention(s) is (are) taking place as planned, and with what result. Metrics can be used for course corrections throughout the program.

It is difficult to link learning interventions directly with changes in the bottom line. But what you can do is to collect data that will enable you to link your intervention with intermediate outcomes that are likely to grow out of your AL design. You can then link those changes to what they might likely affect, and so on up the ladder of changes to paint a picture of the path of impact that your AL intervention triggers. And you can use the collected data to both monitor and correct your course of action as well as to track changes over time as AL interventions are rolled out.

We'd like to end with some reflections on what we've learned from our work and what we've learned as we've been writing this book. First, what is the most difficult part of co-designing an AL program? Second, what is potentially the most important aspect in this design? Third, what is the easiest part of the work? Fourth, what have we found to be most fun and rewarding?

Often the most difficult part of a co-design is getting the right top management support and ensuring that it is demonstrable and ongoing. Not all programs require the backing of the CEO, but they do need the support of the key executives in the organization. *Support* needs to be sufficiently defined so the key executives understand what they are signing on for.

An equally important step is the recruitment and development of the right sponsors. Since they are the organization's most immediate contact with the AL participants, their actions and attitudes can potentially make or break a program and certainly impact the experience of their team. While a team can learn from a poor sponsor, the struggle of the experience and the resultant learning are probably not what you want from the program.

Easiest? If you engage all the right stakeholders in the co-design process right from the start of the work, you can probably overcome any issue, address any *noise,* and achieve success.

Finally, the most fun and rewards come from working with participants on personal learning goals. Our process has helped AL graduates bring about significant changes in both their work and personal lives—and that's a lot of what AL, and understanding it, is all about.

THEORY APPENDIX

"The purpose of learning is growth, and our minds, unlike our bodies, can continue growing as we continue to live.
—Morris Adler
"You cannot open a book without learning something."
—Confucius

This appendix is intended to provide additional understanding about some of the topics discussed in the preceding chapters.[1] It presents information and views from a number of theorists and authors and should be useful to readers wishing to delve further into the theory behind Action Learning (AL). We first discuss theory in more depth that informs the schools of AL (Table 55).

Schools of Action Learning

Tacit

In the Tacit school of AL the focus is primarily on action and results achieved through the project. The Tacit school is characterized by the assumption that learning will take place naturally as carefully selected participants work together, participate in team building, and are provided with information by experts both from within and external to the company.[2] Attention is usually not paid to how this learning happens, which makes the learning primarily tacit and incidental.[3]

166

TABLE 55 Comparison of the Schools of Action Learning[1]

School	Tacit	Scientific	Experiential	Critical Reflection
AL Theory	Incidental learning	Alpha, Beta, Gamma; P&Q=L	Learning from experience	Learning through critical reflection
Practitioners	Dotlich & Noel; Tichy	Revans	McGill & Beaty; Mumford	Marsick; O'Neil; Rohlin
Role for learning coach		(1)	X	X
Reflection		X	X	X
Groups/teams	X	X	X	X
Project/problem based in real work	X	X	X	X
Focus on group process	X	(2)	X	X
Questioning insight		X	X	X
"P" knowledge or teaching	X	(3)	X	X
Just-in-time learning		X	X	X
Individual problem		X	X	(4)
Group problem/project	X		X	X

(1) Revans says, "…there is a role for a supernumerary (set advisor) in the early days of the set, to help the five or so fellows find their feet in this somewhat artificial venture, by encouraging them to exchange their experiences at the periodic meetings in accordance with an intelligible programme."

(2) Revans explicitly says that action learning "is not group dynamics," but also refers to a need for participants to be involved in the "collective social process of the set."

(3) Revans says, "…this does not imply that action learning rejects all formal instruction; it merely recognises that, however necessary such instruction may be, it is by no means sufficient.…"

(4) Participants may have individual projects, but a group or team project is the norm.

[1]Adapted from O'Neil, "The Role of Learning Advisor in Action Learning," 20.

FIGURE 8 Formal and Informal Learning

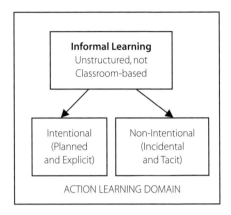

Informal and incidental learning both speak to learning outside formally structured, institutionally sponsored, classroom-based activities. . . . incidental learning is never planned or intentional, whereas informal learning can be planned or intentional . . . (incidental learning) is always tacit, whereas informal learning may be more or less tacit; and success in this kind of learning always depends on the ability of the person to frame the problem appropriately.[4]

All non-"P" learning in AL programs can be characterized as informal learning (Figure 8). The Tacit school can be differentiated from other schools by its lack of specific intentionality toward the process of learning. Although the program itself is a planned event, the lack of emphasis on planning for learning appears to place any learning into the incidental category.

In this school, the focus is more heavily on the project, while the Experiential and Critical Reflection schools stress the intentional nature of learning by positioning action and reflection as an equal reason for the AL team meeting.[5]

Benefits from the tacit type of AL program include lessons in teamwork, business strategy, and leadership, as well as payoff from valuable, fresh ideas on projects of importance for the business.[6] Participants may feel they have learned a lot in these areas as demonstrated by the voice of these participants from a Tacit school program. Participants ended a four week program feeling: "'It wasn't a game. Six groups of us

—total strangers were assigned real company issues to tackle. . . . And along the way, our groups became teams.'"[7]

Another aspect that reinforces the incidental nature of learning in the AL teams is the way in which the programs are staffed. The programs use business consultants, academics from business schools, and various feedback instrumentation to provide "P" learning.[8] While some authors[9] make a reference to action coaching and the role of a coach, they describe the role as meeting with individuals and teams at various points in the initiative and orchestrating team-building activities. Programs in the Tacit school often do not use a learning coach, nor do other staff help the AL team learn in ways that are explicit.

Although incidental learning may occur without explicit emphasis on learning, for incidental learning to systematically occur, the participants need to be able to "shift their attention to these byproduct messages and see them clearly."[10] "Trial-and-error learning from assignments is fraught with peril. Caught up in the action, immersed in the demands and challenges, the manager may have no time for reflection."[11] The Tacit school focuses on learning by doing. The 'doing' is a major requirement for learning, but it may not be sufficient. The complete process requires reflecting, theorizing, and retrieving from an experience.[12]

Scientific

The Scientific school is rooted in Revans's work and the theories that he developed early on.[13] He categorizes one theory as a "method for achieving managerial objectives" and calls it Systems Alpha, Beta, and Gamma. Given his early background as a physicist, these systems have a basis in the scientific method.[14] System Alpha refers to the strategy that a manager must devise when confronting a decision. Revans says that there are three key elements in that decision—the nature of the value system of the manager, the external system that affects the decision being made, and the internal system in which the manager works. System Alpha refers to the structured interplay of these three parts of a strategy decision.[15]

System Beta is the negotiation and implementation of that designed strategy. It overlaps with System Alpha in its first steps. System Beta, which Revans also refers to as SHEAR, is as follows:

• survey stage in which the data for System Alpha is identified

- hypothesis—a trial decision stage in which one of the alternative designs from System Alpha is chosen
- experiment—an action stage in which the trial decision is implemented
- audit—an examination stage during which the observed outcome is compared with the expected outcome
- review—control stage in which appropriate action is taken on the conclusions.[16]

Revans draws this system from the scientific method and equates the steps of System Beta with the learning process—"recognition, prima facie acceptance, rehearsal, verification, conviction."[17]

System Gamma refers to the manager's mental predisposition that he/she brings to the situation. The manager is continually checking his/her expectations of what should be happening against what is actually happening. "Insofar as he is able to identify the discrepancies between what he first took to be the condition and what experience suggests that the condition actually was, and insofar as he is able to change his perception accordingly, we may say that the manager is learning."[18]

One of the principal ways in which learning occurs is through asking questions. This concept leads to the second part of Revans's learning theory behind AL: L = P & Q (L = learning, P = programmed instruction, Q = questioning insight).[19] Questioning insight has been described as "discriminating questions,"[20] "fresh questions."[21] people questioning their direct experience,[22] "intuition, things crossing the mind, insight."[23] Revans feels that true learning is a combination of this "Q" plus "P." "P" is programmed knowledge, "the expert knowledge, knowledge in books, what we are told to do because that is how it has been done for decades."[24] Learning through AL happens only partially in finding the answer; the key is in finding the right question to ask.[25] Revans advocates that the starting questions for any problem are:

> What are we trying to do?
> What is stopping us from doing it?
> What can we do about it?[26]

Since AL requires that questions be posed in conditions of ignorance, risk, and confusion, Revans sees a role for a learning coach early in the program "to help the set develop an initial trustworthy cohesion through orderly debate; a catalyst of this kind, brought in to speed the self-integration of the set, must contrive that it gains independence of him at the earliest possible moment . . . ."[27] Given Revans's belief that an AL team, through working on a problem, will quickly reach the point of being able to ask these *fresh*, unusual questions themselves, the role of the learning coach in this school of AL is limited.[28]

Experiential

Many proponents of AL see Kolb's learning cycle as its theoretical base.[29] Kolb developed his approach in order to understand and maximize learning from experience. Kolb's experiential learning cycle[30] is comprised of four steps. Starting at the top/beginning of the cycle, a learner has an experience; in the next step clockwise, the learner reflects on that experience; in the third step, the learner draws new ideas and concepts from that reflection; and in the fourth step, the learner experiments with the new concept, which creates another experience, and so on.

Learning takes place because the opportunity to reflect on experience with the support of others, followed by action, means the members engage in learning from experience in order to change rather than simply repeating previous patterns. AL enables learning in each stage of the experiential learning cycle.[31]

The Experiential school differentiates itself from other forms of learning from experience, "accidental and informal,"[32] by its intentionality. Learning through action and reflection is the reason for the meeting. Legitimacy and formalization of events over an extended period of time with consistent team membership, as well as explicit discussion of learning processes, learning achievements, and so on, serve to reinforce the learning intention.[33] AL programs are designed to help create the ability to learn how to learn. This is done through scheduling time for learning reviews at each meeting; reviewing not only the problems and project/problems for learning, but also what the participants are learning; keeping learning logs, personal development plans, and learning agreements/contracts.[34]

Many proponents of the Experiential school also agree with Revans's L = P & Q equation.[35] Some of these proponents have further developed Revans's original equation. Since AL requires action to be taken, not just recommended, Inglis proposes L = P + Q + I—the "I" being implementation.[36] Mumford sees more than one opportunity for "Q".

The most effective learning is driven by the need to resolve a managerial problem Q (1). This leads to the acquisition of relevant knowledge (P)—which then stimulates the identification of further management opportunities Q (2). The revised equation is:

$$Q(1)+P+Q(2)=L.[37]$$

In the Experiential school, the learning coach is key to the AL team's learning throughout the cycle, and, as in the Scientific school, the coach is particularly important in the beginning of the life of the team. There is general agreement that the learning coach works toward a transfer of his/her skills to the team, and in some cases, actually works him/herself out of a job.[38] His/her roles include facilitating group process and facilitating learning.[39] The role differs from that of the traditional management trainer in that the coach doesn't teach, but instead provides conditions under which managers might learn themselves from their project work and from each other.[40] The learning coach tries to primarily use questions as the way of working with the team in order to model questioning insight.[41]

Reflection is also key to helping ensure that what is learned through the experience of working on a real project is explicit and planned, rather than erratic and half-hearted.[42]

The vast majority of opportunities for learning at work cannot be initiated or directed in this way. They arise in an unstructured, unplanned way. . . . They are . . . informal and accidental learning, often only partially understood and partially effective.[43]

Critical Reflection

Although many of the practitioners who fit in this school explicitly discuss Kolb,[44] they also believe that AL needs to go beyond the nature of reflection found in the Experiential school to a kind of reflection that pertains to problem posing as distinct from problem solving.[45] Mezirow calls this "reflection" on basic premises that underlie thinking "critical reflection." The explicit intention of fostering critical reflection is the primary differentiator of this school from that of the Experiential school.

In critical reflection, people recognize that their perceptions may be flawed because they are filtered through uncritically accepted views, beliefs, attitudes, and feelings inherited from one's family, school, and society. Such flawed perceptions often distort one's understanding of problems and situations. Taking time to reflect even in a surface fashion is powerful, and critical reflection is even more powerful because attention is directed to the root of the problem.[46]

Practitioners in the Critical Reflection school describe the process and results of critical thinking in different ways. Weinstein[47] talks about participants examining what they believe and value, and how they are changing and moving and gaining a better understanding of their own insights. When this kind of reflection takes place, she feels that the process may be deeply disturbing for those who don't want a change in the existing structures, status, and beliefs. Rohlin[48] and Marsick[49] speak to bringing real issues to the fore and subjecting them to scrutiny—allowing participants to call into question the rationale underlying their actions, challenging norms, and examining problems from multiple perspectives; while Dilworth and Willis[50] talk about asking fresh questions to lead to the *unfreezing* of underlying assumptions and the creation of new mental models. Critical reflection in AL can also go beyond the individual participant's underlying assumptions and can lead to the examination of organizational norms.[51] Reformulation, reframing, and transformation of the presenting project/problem happens because participants take action, then critically reflect on that action; and in so doing uncover misperceptions, norms, and expectations that were often hidden before the action and critical reflection.[52]

Learning coaches play a crucial role in the Critical Reflection school. Since a coach is not a team member, and often comes from outside the culture, he/she is often freer to ask questions from that outsider's perspective. Learning coaches help the team learn the following:

- how to frame, reframe or provide an alternative framing for the project/problem, since complex issues are seldom what they first seem
- how to identify, clarify, and test the participants' personal insights and theories about the project/problem
- how to reflect on the way in which the project/problem is formulated, tested, and solved.[53]

Authors in this school believe that not having a learning coach can lead to certain problems or pitfalls for a team. First, when there is no coach to work with the team the "whole focus of the set tends to shift to the solution of the problems . . . ."[54] Second, there is a danger of losing the learning dimension and the team becoming simply another project team.[55] "While the concept of learning-by-doing is easily understood in principle, executives either think that it is so simple that people can learn from experience without any outside help, or that it is so complex that the programmes would be hard to sell in their companies."[56]

All Schools

As evidenced by Table 55, Comparisons of the Schools of Action Learning, there are many similarities and differences in the four schools. Similarities include the fact that participants meet in small teams, also referred to as groups or sets depending on the school, of usually four to six members.[57] It is in the social process of these teams that "comrades in adversity"[58] or "fellows in opportunity"[59] are able to bring peer learning to its highest efficiency.

In each of these schools, the teams work on a project/problem that is based on real work.[60] The choice of the right problems is critical to the success of an AL program in all schools.[61] Another similarity across the four schools is a focus on group process. As noted in Table 55, Revans isn't clear regarding how much focus an AL team would give to their processes of working together.[62]

Practitioners in the Experiential and Critical Reflection schools speak much more explicitly about focusing on, and working with, group processes. Some of the processes mentioned include communication, conflict, consensus building, and leadership. The view expressed is that teams need to work together effectively in order to be able to learn together, and that the learning coach needs to play a role in enabling the team to develop effective processes.[63] The Tacit school also believes that group processes are developed in their AL programs but they are developed more often through specific team-building activities and through structured opportunities to give and receive feedback. The AL teams are able to more productively work together on the project as a result of these activities.[64]

A final similarity that the four schools share is agreement on the need to provide "P" in connection with their use of AL.[65] They differ in how and when that programmed knowledge is brought into the AL program. In the case of the Scientific school, the belief is that all "P" (with the exception of a short introduction to some basic AL concepts and terminology) should be provided as just-in-time learning, only after the participants have identified the need for the instruction.[66] In the

Experiential and Critical Reflection schools, there is agreement with the just-in-time philosophy, but there is also a belief that some instruction, such as information about the AL process or group dynamics, is usually needed, so should be built into the program.[67] In the Tacit school, "P" knowledge can be predetermined and much of the time it is provided at the start of the program prior to teams being formed to address an AL problem.[68]

Adult Learning Theories
Underlying Action Learning

AL is situated in the context of a variety of different approaches and conceptual frameworks of adult learning theories that influence the development and practice of AL.[69] These theoretical influences are shown in Figure 9, Adult Learning Theories Underlying Action Learning.

Practitioners in the Tacit school don't specifically refer to a theoretical base, but what is expressed in their writing seems to reflect the work of theorists in the area of social and situated learning. These theories also underlie scholarship on communities of practice.[70] Vygotsky's zone of proximal development, while discussed in terms of childhood, has implications for the tacit nature of learning in this school. According to Vygotsky, an important feature of learning is that it awakens a variety of internal development processes that are able to operate only when the individual is interacting with people in his environment in cooperation with his peers.[71]

Lave's situated learning, which has antecedents in Vygotsky's work, also appears to reflect some of the underlying assumptions in the Tacit school. For example, Lave says that knowledge needs to be presented in an authentic context; learning requires social interaction and collaboration; and situated learning is usually unintentional rather than deliberate.[72]

The concept of learning more intentionally from experience appears to have influenced several of the AL schools including the Scientific, the Experiential, and the Critical Reflection. Dewey, one of the first educators to discuss the connection between learning and experience, said that "the fundamental unity of the newer philosophy is found in the idea that there is an intimate and necessary relation between the processes of actual experience and education."[73] However, he did not believe that all experience is educational. Some experience could be

FIGURE 9 Adult Learning Theories Underlying Action Learning

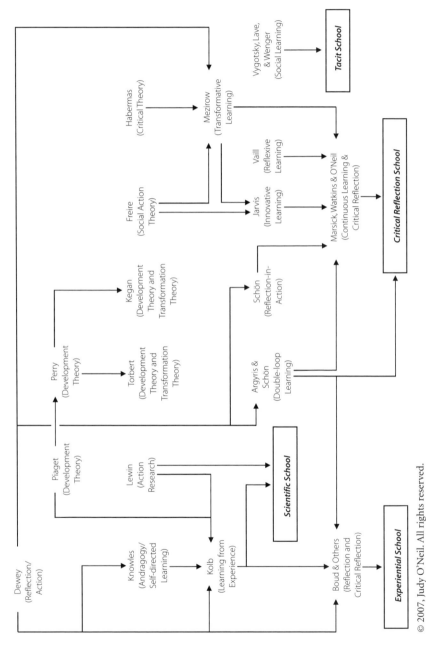

miseducative, arrested development, or distorted growth from future experience. As a result, Dewey believed that educators need to evaluate experiences to ensure attitudes conducive to continued growth and sympathetic understanding of individuals. Two factors need to be taken into account—the interaction and the situation. "Continuity and interaction in their union with each other provide the measure of the educative significance and value of an experience."[74]

Dewey was also one of the earlier educators to discuss the idea of reflection in connection with learning.

> When we experience something we act upon it, we do something with it, then we suffer or undergo the consequences . . . . When an activity is continued into the undergoing of consequences, when the change made by action is reflected back into a change made in us, the mere flux is loaded with significance. We learn something.[75]

He considered "reflective thought" or "reflective activity" to be a highly rational and controlled activity. Reflection can stop immediate impulsive action and help the individual to form a more comprehensive and coherent plan. Genuine reflection only follows times of more overt action and is used to organize what's gained from that action.

> To reflect is to look back over what has been done so as to extract the best meanings which are the capital stock for intelligent dealing with further experiences. It is the heart of intellectual organization and of the disciplined mind.[76]

Dewey offered a justification for learning by doing and reflection. He began to describe learning as having a kind of cyclic pattern—awareness of a problem, getting an idea, trying out a response, experiencing the results, and checking against previous conceptions to affirm or disconfirm.

Inspired by Dewey's ideas, Kolb linked this theory to practice. Kolb's theory of learning from experience is best expressed in terms of his learning cycle. He believes that learning is a cyclical process with four kinds of activities—a concrete experience; observations and reflection; formation of abstract concepts and generalizations; and testing the implications of the new concepts in new situations. He has taken Dewey's initial thoughts about learning as a process/cycle and given them more specificity. It is a fully integrated view of learning, so it is possible to begin anywhere and proceed through the cycle.[77]

Even though it is difficult, Kolb says that learners must proceed through the entire cycle in order to fully learn from experience. He believes that learning is a holistic process of adaptation that involves thinking, feeling, perceiving, and behaving. It is a process in which knowledge is created through the transformation of experience. Learning involves transactions between the individual and the environment—the individual's internal experience and the objective, external experience.[78]

Several AL practitioners discuss Kolb's learning cycle in connection with AL. Botham[79] agrees with Kolb's assertion that learners must go through the entire cycle. He calls for involvement cognitively, affectively, and behaviorally, and believes that the best way to ensure such involvement is to create a learning context in which the learner completes the Kolb cycle at least once. Mumford characterizes the internal and external processes for learning as the learning cycle (internal) and the task cycle (external) and says that both cycles need to happen in an AL program.[80]

In addition to Dewey, Kolb says he draws from the works of Lewin[81] and Piaget.[82] "Common to all three traditions . . . is the emphasis on development toward a life of purpose and self-direction as the organizing principle for education."[83] From Piaget, Kolb formulated the idea of the learning process as a dialectic between assimilation of experience and accommodating concepts to experience, as well as drawing from Piaget's work on epistemology. Kolb's view of learning is reflective of views described by Knowles, who developed the concept of andragogy and self-directed learning.[84]

Although Revans created his own underlying theory for AL, that is, Alpha, Beta, Gamma,[85] an examination of some of his writings on AL also reflects ideas in Kolb's work.

> An action learning programme should be designed to exploit these characteristics of the manager. It should oblige each participant to look critically at his past experience; whatever the deliberate content of his activity, whether a project (*concrete experience*) carried out elsewhere . . . his next move . . . should be so debated with his fellow participants that his first perceptions of his own experience are constantly under review (*observations and reflection*). . . . he will be constantly called upon to explain (*formation of abstract concepts*) why he suggests the course of action he does. . . . each participant will sooner or later run into a blind alley (*testing implications of new concepts*) . . . .[86]

Based on these types of similarities, and the discussion of Kolb's work by many theorists who also advocate Revans,[87] we see a theoretical foundation for the Scientific school in Kolb and his antecedents. Of particular note is the work of Kurt Lewin. Kolb's work draws on action research, based on the work of Lewin. Revans' scientific method follows steps similar to Lewin's action research approach.

In addition to the preceding theorists, Boud, Keough, and Walker[88] have written about focus on learning from experience that is intentional—in which learners are aware that they are learning, that the learning is experiential as opposed to classroom based, and that the learning is undertaken with a specific goal in mind. These authors have formulated five propositions about learning from experience.

> Proposition 1: Experience is the foundation of, and the stimulus for, learning.
> Proposition 2: Learners actively construct their experience.
> Proposition 3: Learning is a holistic process.
> Proposition 4: Learning is socially and culturally constructed.
> Proposition 5: Learning is influenced by the socio-emotional context in which it occurs.[89]

Similar to Dewey, Boud, Keough, and Walker recognize that not all experience is educative. They talk about barriers to learning from experience as "those factors which inhibit or block learners' preparedness for the experience, their active engagement in it, and their ability to reflect rationally on it with a view to learning from it."[90]

"Reflection consists of those processes in which learners engage to recapture, notice, and re-evaluate their experience, to work with their experience to turn it into learning."[91] Boud, Keough, and Walker feel they put more emphasis on reflection than Kolb does in his model. There are three elements to their reflective process—returning to the experience, attending to feelings, and re-evaluating the experience. They feel that the attention to feelings in this model serves to differentiate their view of reflection from Dewey, whom they see as being primarily cognitive. Reflection is not an end in itself. The objective is to help learners be ready for a new experience. Some benefits of reflection may be lost if they are not linked to action. "Action ends the reflective process for the time being."[92] Based on these specific discussions of reflection and its role in learning, we think that these theorists, as well as Kolb and his antecedents, have a theoretical influence on those who practice in the Experiential school of AL.

Boud, Keough, and Walker conceptualize reflection in ways that resemble the Critical Reflection school—questioning and challenging assumptions, values, and frames of reference.[93] They say that during reflection, the mindset of the learner can serve as a filter to the experience, which can serve to diminish the extent of learning. Learners need to become critically aware of how and why their assumptions about the world can constrain the way they think. Learners who choose to reflect will usually have a "deep approach" to learning. They also discuss being influenced by the work of Habermas, Mezirow, and Argyris, all theorists influencing critical thinking and transformative learning,[94] so while we think they influence the Experiential school, they also have an influence in the Critical Reflection school.

There are many other theorists who influence the Critical Reflection school through their work in critical thinking and transformative learning. We will discuss those whom we think may have had the most influence on practitioners in this school.

Two authors who have influenced some practitioners in the critical reflection school are William Torbert and Robert Kegan, both of whom built on the cognitive development theory of Jean Piaget and William Perry in their work with adults. Piaget conceptualized general periods of development up through adolescence based on active construction of knowledge that leads to increasingly more comprehensive ways of thinking. His stages included: 1) sensory-motor intelligence, 2) preoperational thought, 3) concrete operations, and 4) formal operations. Stages represent "increasingly comprehensive ways of thinking" that are followed in an *"invariant sequence—the same order"* (original italics).[95] Piaget's thinking influenced future cognitive developmental theorists, including William Perry, a professor and counselor at Harvard University who studied the development of college students. As did Piaget, Perry focused on "a process of new awareness of the self, of environmental influences on the self, and of the complex balance between this emerging awareness of the self and the external influences from the environment."[96] Perry and his colleagues identified nine positions of cognitive development that moved increasingly from dualism, multiplicity, relativism, and finally, commitment to relativism. Perry "chose to use the term position rather than stage . . . because they made no assumptions about the duration of the position."[97]

Torbert drew on the work of Piaget and Perry, but to this, he added a focus on personality development by drawing on the work of Jane Loevinger. Through his studies of the development of managers/

leaders, Torbert has created a theory of eight developmental stages that helps to form an underlying support for the theory of transformative learning. His theory is based on Loevinger's[98] earlier work on her stage theory of ego development. She proposed that people move through ten stages from birth through adulthood, each building on the one that precedes, and movement to the next stage occurs only when the individual has completed the development of the current stage. Torbert's stages account for how a manager views the world and him/herself—their focus of awareness, governing frame of the world, and characteristics of behavior.[99] The eight stages are shown in Table 56, Torbert's Stages of Development.

The first four stages of development are "a sequence of transformations through which persons can evolve."[100] Each stage has its own internally consistent logic and relates to certain objective realities as well. Each stage overturns the assumptions of the previous stage and "transforms them from their role of framing and governing reality to a new role as variables within a wider reality."[101] Although transformation takes place, individuals at the first four levels neither envision nor generate transformation of their own accord. It is not until the fifth, Achiever stage that managers/leaders begin to have a sense of the ability to transform, and at the sixth, Strategist stage "a person ceases to

---

TABLE 56 Torbert's Stages of Development[1]

Stage	Level of Personal Development
1. Impulsive	Impulses rule reflexes
2. Opportunist	Needs rule impulses
3. Diplomat	Norms rule needs
4. Technician	Craft logic rules norms
5. Achiever	System effectiveness rules craft logic
6. Strategist	Self-amending principle rules system
7. Magician/Witch/Clown	Process (interplay of principle/action) rules principle
8. Ironist	Intersystemic development rules process

[1]Adapted from Dalmar Fisher and William R. Torbert, *Personal and Organizational Transformations: The True Challenge of Continual Quality Improvement* (New York: McGraw-Hill, 1995).

take the existing overall structure of social systems for granted . . . and therefore becomes interested in what a normative (a best, a just) structure would be."[102] The Strategist is involved in explicit transformative learning.

> The Strategist realizes that all frames, including his or her own, are relative. With this realization, the Strategist, unlike the Achiever, is open to the possibility of "reframing" his or her viewpoint and purposes in a situation, and helping others to reframe, consciously seeking and choosing new frames that accommodate the disparities, paradoxes, and fluidity of multiple frames.[103]

At the higher developmental stages (Magician and Ironist) the power of self-challenging transformation comes naturally. A conclusion could be drawn that individuals at all three higher stages could be involved in transformative learning.

Kegan's developmental theory, while different from Torbert's, also contributes to support the theory of transformative learning and the Critical Reflection school. Kegan draws on cognitive development theory of Piaget and Perry, but Kegan also builds his thinking on Erik Erikson's psychodynamic stage theories and Lawrence Kohlberg's moral development stage theories.[104]

Kegan's theory addresses the forms of meaning making individuals use, the transformation of consciousness, the internal experience of these processes, and the role of the environment in this activity—a "view of human being as meaning-making and exploring the inner and outer contours of our transformations in consciousness throughout the lifespan."[105] His theory is a developmental theory of transformation—always gradual, always increasingly complex.[106] The levels are shown in Table 57, Kegan's Levels of Transformation.

While the first order of consciousness is all about the self, the first transformation an individual goes through is the ability to recognize something separate from the self; identifying that the phenomenon being considered has its own properties, which are elements of a class or set that has durable, ongoing rules; creating the concept of class membership; and regulating that membership. Kegan calls this the second order or "durable category"; it would be reflected in a behavior when we recognize that we need something from the other and are willing to negotiate to get it. It is also manifested in the pursuit of one's own needs

TABLE 57 Kegan's Levels of Transformation[1]

Underlying Structure	Order of Consciousness
Single point/immediate	1st
Durable category	2nd
Cross-categorical, trans-categorical	3rd
System/complex	4th
Trans-system	5th

[1] Adapted from Robert Kegan, *In Over Our Heads: The Mental Demands of Modern Life* (Cambridge: Harvard University Press, 1994), 94, 95, 126, 313.

at the expense of others, but only as long as the effort remains unseen, undetected. In the next developmental step, the third order of consciousness, individuals begin to make meaning through a reasoning process that honors relationships. Their identity is supported by how they think others see them. Individuals internalize values and norms, and behave in accordance with the expectations they believe others have about them. Kegan calls this new, higher order principle "cross-categorical" knowing. The construction of values, ideals, and broad beliefs requires the cross-categorical principle of mental organization, so it is at this level that individuals begin to use reflective thinking.[107]

Kegan feels that fourth order consciousness is needed to function in a post-modern world. At this level, individuals develop a different way of building the self that is no longer anchored in how we think others see us and what they expect us to be. We are able to hear other people's expectations but distance ourselves from them in order to make our own judgments. This process would appear to require a greater ability for self-reflection, and Kegan says that the fifth order of consciousness requires critical reflection. The fifth order allows individuals to see the systemic connections among all things. As with Torbert, it would appear that individuals who achieve the higher developmental levels in Kegan's theory, fourth and fifth orders of consciousness, could be involved in transformative learning.[108]

Many authors in the transformative learning literature have also been influenced by the work of Freire and Habermas. Underlying Freire's work as an adult educator is his theory of conscientization. In Freire's theory there are four levels of consciousness , the highest of which is conscientization—the process by which individuals learn "to perceive social, political, and economic contradictions, and to take action against the oppressive elements of reality."[109] At this level of consciousness, individuals can engage in "praxis"—action and critical reflection on that action—the combination of which can result in transformative learning.

Habermas[110] talks of three areas in which knowledge can be generated—the technical, the practical or communicative, and the emancipatory domains. Communicative action and learning—learning to understand what others mean and to make ourselves understood—can take place through rational discourse. As we elaborate below, Habermas says that so long as the optimal conditions for rational discourse exist, adults can become critically reflective, and therefore have the ability to engage in transformative learning.

Mezirow's transformative learning theory is based on work by Dewey, Freire, and Habermas, among others. He defines transformative learning as:

> The process of learning through critical self-reflection, which results in the re-formulation of a meaning perspective to allow a more inclusive, discriminating and integrative understanding of one's experience. Learning includes acting on these insights.[111]

In order to fully understand Mezirow's theory of transformative learning, it is necessary to examine the process. For Mezirow, there are two different types of learning, instrumental and communicative. Instrumental learning happens when we engage in task-oriented problem solving, i.e., how to do something or how to perform. In instrumental learning, we reflect on the content or procedural assumptions that guided our problem solving. We are able to use empirical evidence or informed consensus to ensure that our underlying assumptions are correct.[112]

Although Mezirow says that transformative learning is possible in both types of learning, he focuses in particular on communicative learning through rational discourse. Mezirow says that we view all of our experience through what he calls meaning perspectives and meaning schemes. A meaning perspective refers to the structure of cultural assumptions within which new experience is assimilated. These assumptions are generalized sets of habitual responses that act as perceptual and conceptual codes to form and limit how we think, believe, and feel.

Meaning schemes are the articulation of meaning perspectives. They make up our implicit, habitual rules for interpreting our experience. They are composed of the specific knowledge, beliefs, and value judgments that shape our particular interpretation. Both meaning perspectives and meaning schemes contribute to the frame of reference within which we engage in learning. We developed our ways of perceiving reality through meaning perspectives and schemes that were uncritically assimilated from our parents and society. As a result of this uncritical assimilation, we may need to question and challenge our schemes and perspectives in order for communicative learning, and possibly transformative learning to take place.[113]

In communicative learning—understanding the meaning of what others communicate concerning values, ideals, feelings, moral decisions, and concepts like freedom, justice, love, and democracy—a different kind of reflection is needed. Through critical reflection, we begin to question and challenge the assumptions, values, and frames of reference that formed our meaning perspectives and schemes.[114] Once we use critical reflection to raise our meaning schemes and perspectives to a conscious level, we must engage in what Mezirow and Habermas call rational discourse.[115] In this form of discourse—"a dialogue devoted to assessing reasons presented in support of competing interpretations, by critically examining evidence, arguments, and alternative points of view"[116]—we must rely on those whom we believe to be the most informed, objective, and rational in their ability to assess the arguments, examine the evidence, and arrive at the best consensus feasible, given what is known at the time. Since we are all trapped in our own meaning perspectives, it is primarily through this type of discourse that we are able to test validity. It is through critical self-reflection and rational discourse that the central concept of Mezirow's theory, perspective transformation, occurs.

Through transformative learning we become critically aware of how and why our presuppositions have come to constrain the way we perceive, understand, and feel about our world; we reformulate these assumptions to permit a more inclusive, discriminating, permeable, and integrative perspective and make decisions or otherwise act upon these new understandings. These are superior perspectives that adults choose if they can, because they are motivated to better understand the meaning of their experience. Mezirow speaks to how critical reflection and transformative learning should be fostered and supported. Education needs to be "learner-centered, participatory, and interactive, and it involves group deliberation and group problem solving."[117] His description of a facilitator of transformative learning very closely matches the description of a learning coach in the Critical Reflection school.

> The educator functions as a facilitator and provocateur rather than as an authority on subject matter. . . . models the critically reflective role expected of learners . . . . The facilitator works herself out of the job of authority figure . . . by progressively transferring her leadership to the group . . . .[118]

Like theorists already discussed, Jarvis believes that learning begins with experience. He also believes that experience is only a potential basis for learning and that unless there is a process that enables meaning to be attributed to experience, the experience can be meaningless.[119] He believes that reflection is an integral part of creating learning from experience.

> For a variety of reasons—possibly because the anticipated ends were not achieved through an action—either the monitoring or the retrospection might result in a situation being problematized. At this point, the process of reflection starts that sets learning in motion.[120]

Jarvis describes nine different routes that might be taken from an experience that might or might not result in learning.[121] When a path produces reflection that is critically aware—"a pluralism of interpretations of an experience"[122]—there is a possibility of breaking away from the established pattern of thinking and creating what Jarvis refers to as innovative learning. Jarvis compares this learning to Freire's authentic reflection in which people respond to challenge and have a perspective transformation, to Mezirow's transformative learning, and to Argyris and Schon's double-loop learning.[123] Double-loop learning probes underlying values, assumptions and beliefs that shape goals, intentions, and meaning making that underlie the actions we take to reach our goals. Single-loop learning involves simple changes in tactics when actions taken do not achieve desired results. Single-loop learning can be valuable as long as the diagnosis of the problem being solved is accurate. But when that is not the case, double-loop learning is needed to accurately understand the source of the problem. The terms, single-loop and double-loop, were adapted from cybernetics to show that the solution to a problem may require a double loop outside of the self-reinforcing circle that is part of the problem definition in the first place.[124]

Vaill describes seven qualities, or modes of learning, some of which track with the concepts of transformative learning. Reflexive learning is defined similarly to transformative learning in that it involves an awareness of ideas, patterns, and assumptions and enables individuals to reflect on their own learning. Vaill compares it to Argyris's double-loop learning.[125]

He also describes expressive learning as "doing things and learning in the process"[126] and online learning as "a learning process that occurs in the midst of work and of life rather than in an artificial, sheltered environment."[127] For Vaill, AL is one of the few learning systems that deals with expressive learning and has online learning at its core.

Schon writes about a kind of transformative learning that professionals engage in during their day-to-day work—reflection in action.

> When a practitioner reflects in and on his practice, the possible objects of his reflection are as varied as the kinds of phenomena before him and the systems of knowing-in practice which he brings to them. He may reflect on the tacit norms and appreciations which underlie a judgment, or on the strategies and theories implicit in a pattern of behavior. He may reflect on the feeling for a situation which has led him to adopt a particular course of action, on the way in which he has framed the problem he is trying to solve. . . .[128]

Professionals engage in reflection-in-action most particularly when their normally intuitive performance results instead in an outcome that is a surprise, either positive or negative. At those times reflection focuses interactively on the outcome that is the surprise, the action undertaken that has produced this surprise, and the intuitive performance that is implicit in the professional's action.[129]

As the professional practitioner engages in reflection-in-action, he/she "becomes a researcher in the practice context."[130] The practitioner carries out an experiment in which he/she reflects on the situation and the prior understanding implicit in his/her behavior. There is no need to separate thinking from doing; implementation is built into his/her inquiry. The outcome of the experiment is a new theory unique to the situation which practitioners integrate into their understanding of their practice.[131]

Argyris and Schon advocate a science of action, or "action science" that requires critical reflection:

> action science is an inquiry into social practice . . . that is interested in producing knowledge in the service of such practice. . . . requires that knowledge includes empirically disconfirmable propositions . . . also requires that these propositions be falsifiable in real-life contexts by the practitioners to whom they are addressed. . . . As a critical theory it aims to produce knowledge that evokes critical reflection among practitioners, so that they might more freely choose whether and how to transform their practice.[132]

As with Schon's discussion of practitioners' "surprises," when an individual encounters an outcome to an interaction that is not what he/she intended, there are different ways to approach the dilemma. "The mainstream epistemology of practice focuses on means-end rationality. Failure to achieve the intended ends leads to a reexamination of means and a search for more effective means."[133] Changing tactics to solve the problem involves single-loop learning.[134]

"The action science epistemology of practice focuses on framing or problem setting, as well as on means-ends reasoning or problem solving. Failure to achieve intended consequences may . . . lead to reflection on the original frame and the setting of a different problem.[135] The result of this type of inquiry can produce a change in individual assumptions and beliefs, and/or a restructuring of organizational norms and the strategies and assumptions associated with those norms. This approach is called double-loop learning.[136]

Watkins and Marsick see transformative learning coming about through critical reflection. They illustrate this kind of learning in a model of continuous learning that builds upon the problem-solving first cycle discussed by Dewey and later by Argyris and Schon in their work on action science.[137]

The Continuous Learning Model (Figure 10) consists of concentric inner and outer circles. In the middle of the circle are the challenges that one experiences day to day. The inner circle represents the simple steps of the problem-solving cycle—experience the problem, examine alternative solutions, produce the solution, and plan next steps. A level of learning is attainable by reflecting on the nature of the problem and using the problem-solving process, referred to by Argyris and Schon as single-loop learning.[138] The outer circle of the model represents the

FIGURE 10 Continuous Learning Model[1]

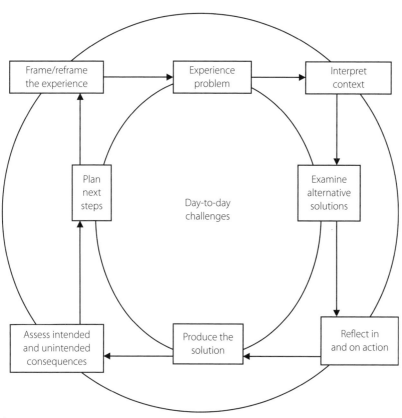

[1]Adapted from Karen E. Watkins and Victoria J. Marsick, *Sculpting the Learning Organization,* (San Francisco: Jossey-Bass (1993), 27.

deeper level of learning that is attainable by critically reflecting on the premises that underlie one's understandings and beliefs. This cycle is involved with surfacing and examining assumptions at each step—interpreting the context of the problem; reflecting both in and on action; assessing both intended and unintended consequences; and framing/reframing the experience.[139]

O'Neil and Marsick say that AL promotes critical reflection in several ways.[140] Their descriptions fall into the Critical Reflection school, where project teams are created with participants from diverse backgrounds in order to enable them to ask questions of one another that don't normally get asked. The learning coach "creates a climate that encourages dialogue, critique, and reflection by stopping the action periodically in order to help participants dig below the surface of their comments and behavior."[141] The learning coach introduces tools and methods to support and encourage critical reflection, and AL itself encourages action to test out individual and collective beliefs, hunches, and solutions.

ENDNOTES

Acknowledgments

1. Lyle Yorks, Judy O'Neil, and Victoria J. Marsick, Eds., *Action Learning: Successful Strategies for Individual, Team, and Organizational Development, Advances in Developing Human Resources,* 2 (San Francisco: Berrett-Koehler, 1999).

Introduction

1. Lyle Yorks, Judy O'Neil, and Victoria J. Marsick, "Action Learning: Theoretical Bases and Varieties of Practice" in *Action Learning: Successful Strategies for Individual, Team and Organizational Development,* eds. Lyle Yorks, Judy O'Neil and Victoria J. Marsick, 3 (San Francisco: Berrett-Koehler, 1999).

2. We owe a debt of gratitude to Gareth Morgan for the idea of including a Theory Appendix in this book, as he did in his book *Images of Organization* (Thousand Oaks, CA: Sage Publications, 1997).

3. National Center on Education and the Economy, *Tough Choices or Tough Times: The Report of the New Commission on the Skills of the American Workforce,* xviii (San Francisco: Jossey-Bass, John Wiley & Sons, Inc., 2007).

4. Rainer Maria Rilke, Letter 4, *Letters to a Young Poet,* 1903, translated Stephen Mitchel, downloaded 10 February 2007 from http://www.sfgoth.com/~immanis/rilke/letter4.html

Chapter One

1. Jay A. Conger and Beth B. Benjamin, *Building Leaders: How Successful Companies Develop the Next Generation* (San Francisco: Jossey-Bass, 1999) and Joseph A. Raelin, *Work-Based Learning: The New Frontier of Management Development* (Upper Saddle, NJ: Prentice Hall, Addison-Wesley OD Series, 2000).

American Management Association

2. Peter B. Vaill, *Learning As a Way of Being: Strategies For Survival in a World of Permanent White Water* (San Francisco: Jossey-Bass, 1996), 4; Karen E. Watkins and Victoria J. Marsick, *Sculpting the Learning Organization.* (San Francisco: Jossey-Bass, 1993).

3. Conger and Benjamin, *Building Leaders,* 211.

4. Rimanoczy, I. and Turner, E. *Action Reflection Learning: Solving Real Business Problems by Connecting Learning with Earning.* (Mountain View, CA: Davies Black® Publishing, Forthcoming 2008).

5. Robert L. Dilworth and Verna J. Willis, *Action Learning: Images and Pathways* (Malabar, FL: Krieger, 2003), 12; Mike Pedler, John Burgoyne, and Cheryl Brook, "What Has Action Learning Learned to Become?" *Action Learning: Research and Practice,* 2005, 2(1), 58–59.

6. Dilworth and Willis, *Action Learning,* 9.

7. "Who Was Reg Revans?," based on *Accrediting Managers at Work in the 21st Century* by Richard Teare and Gordon Prestoungrange, Prestoungrange University Press, 2004, retrieved May 29, 2006, from http://64.233.161.104/search?q=cache:kO70ogje 350J:www.imcasocrates.org/socrates/contentprev.asp%3Fpg%3D111602%26ft%3DP DF+Reg+Revans&hl=en&gl=us&ct=clnk&cd=3

8. Reginald W. Revans, *The Golden Jubilee of Action Learning* (Manchester, England: Manchester Action Learning Exchange, University of Manchester, 1989), 7.

9. Michael J. Marquardt, *Action Learning in Action: Transforming Problems and People for World-Class Organizational Learning* (Palo Alto, CA: Davies-Black, 1999), 19.

10. Ibid.

11. Dilworth and Willis, *Action Learning,* 9.

12. Victoria J. Marsick and Karen E. Watkins, *Informal and Incidental Learning in the Workplace* (NY: Routledge, 1992), 56; Lennart Rohlin, "The Story of MiL" *Earning While Learning in Global Leadership* (Lund, Sweden: MiL), 18.

13. Paul Froiland, "Action Learning: Taming Real Problems in Real Time," *Training,* January 1994, 31:1, 27–34.

14. Victoria J. Marsick and Lars Cederholm, "Developing Leadership in International Managers—An Urgent Challenge," *Columbia Journal of World Business,* 1988, 23:4, 3–11.

15. James L. Noel and Ram Charan, "Leadership Development at GE's Crotonville, *Human Resource Management,* 1988, 27:4, 433–447; Noel M. Tichy, *The Leadership Engine* (New York: HarperCollins, 2002).

16. Mike Pedler, *Action Learning for Managers* (London: Lemos & Crane, 1996), 13.

17. Reginald W. Revans, *The Origin and Growth of Action Learning* (London: Chartwell Bratt, 1982) 626–627.

18. Dilworth and Willis, 12.

19. Pedler, Burgoyne, and Brook, 58–59.

20. Lyle Yorks, Judy O'Neil, and Victoria J. Marsick, "Action Learning: Theoretical Bases and Varieties of Practice" in *Action Learning: Successful Strategies for Individual, Team and Organizational Development,* eds. Lyle Yorks, Judy O'Neil, and Victoria J. Marsick, 3 (San Francisco: Berrett-Koehler, 1999)

21. Ibid.

22. Ibid.

23. Krystyna Weinstein, *Action Learning: A Journey in Discovery and Development* (London: HarperCollins, 1995), 32.

24. Judy O'Neil, "The Role of the Learning Advisor in Action Learning", (Ed.D. diss., Teachers College, Columbia University, New York, NY, 1999), 19.

25. Judy O'Neil, "The Role of the Learning Coach in Action Learning" in *AHRD Conference Proceedings*, ed. O. A. Aliaga, 181 (Baton Rouge, LA: AHRD, 2001).

26. Yorks, O'Neil, and Marsick, "Action Learning: Theoretical Bases and Varieties of Practice," 12.

27. Marsick and Watkins, *Informal and Incidental Learning in the Workplace*, 33.

28. Reginald W. Revans, "The Managerial Alphabet". In *Approaches to the Study of Organizational Behavior*, ed. G. Heald. 141–161 (London: Tavistock, 1970).

29. Revans, "The Golden Jubilee of Action Learning," 102.

30. Weinstein, *Action Learning*, 44.

31. Mike Pedler, "Another Look at Set Advising" in *Action Learning in Practice*, 2d Ed., ed. Mike Pedler, 285 (Brookfield, VT: Gower, 1991).

32. Ian McGill, and Liz Beaty, *Action Learning: A Guide for Professional, Management and Educational Development* (London: Kogan Page, 1995).

33. McGill and Beaty, *Action Learning*, 31.

34. Jack Mezirow and Associates, ed., *Fostering Critical Reflection in Adulthood* (San Francisco: Jossey-Bass, 1990).

35. Victoria J. Marsick, "Action Learning and Reflection in the Workplace" in *Fostering Critical Reflection in Adulthood*, eds. Jack Mezirow and Associates, 23 (San Francisco: Jossey-Bass, 1990).

36. As we discuss later in the chapter, the GE model of AL can be characterized as Tacit because its focus is primarily on learning through work on the project.

37. Revans, "The Managerial Alphabet", 145.

38. David Casey, "Programme Outline" in *More Than Management Development: Action Learning at GEC*, eds. David Casey and David Pearce, 7 (Hampshire, England: Gower, 1984).

39. Nancy Foy, "Action Learning Comes to Industry," *Harvard Business Review*, (Sept–Oct) 1977, 55:5: 158; David Casey, "Programme Outline," 13; David Pearce, "Programme Development" in *More Than Management Development: Action Learning at GEC*, eds. David Casey and David Pearce, 25 (Hampshire, England: Gower, 1984).

40. Foy, "Action Learning Comes to Industry," 159; Pearce,"Programme Development," 25.

41. Pearce, "Programme Development," 19.

42. Foy, "Action Learning Comes to Industry," 166.

43. Don Howell, "This Is the Way to Unlock Resources" in *More Than Management Development: Action Learning at GEC*, eds. David Casey and David Pearce, 45 (Hampshire, England: Gower, 1984).

44. Mike Bett, "It's Opening Our Minds" in *More Than Management Development*, 116.

45. Ibid.

46. Tony Eccles, "Action Learning and the Company," 119.

47. Victoria J. Marsick and Karen E. Watkins, *Facilitating Learning Organizations: Making Learning Count* (Brookfield, VT: Gower, 1999), 123; Judy O'Neil, "Action Learning and Systems-Level Continuous Learning" in *AHRD Conference Proceedings*, ed. K. Peter Kuchinke, 159 (Baton Rouge, LA: AHRD, 1999).

48. Partners for Learning and Leadership changed its name from Partners for the Learning Organization in 2006.

49. Marsick and Watkins, "Facilitating Learning Organizations," 128; O'Neil, "Action Learning and Systems-Level Continuous Learning," 159.

50. Ibid.

51. Ibid.

52. Ibid.

53. Pedler, *Action Learning for Managers*, 31. Some of the questions in Table 3 are drawn from Pedler's questionnaire, "Organisational Readiness for Action Learning;" Lyle Yorks, Judy O'Neil, and Victoria J. Marsick, "Lessons for Implementing Action Learning" in *Action Learning: Successful Strategies for Individual, Team and Organizational Development*, eds. Lyle Yorks, Judy O'Neil and Victoria J. Marsick, 96 (San Francisco: Berrett-Koehler, 1999).

54. Yorks, O'Neil, and Marsick, "Action Learning: Theoretical Bases and Varieties of Practice," 14.

55. Pedler, *Action Learning for Managers*, 31.

56. Yorks, O'Neil, and Marsick, "Action Learning: Theoretical Bases and Varieties of Practice," 14.

57. Noel and Charan, "Leadership Development," 433–44.

58. Yury Boshyk, "Business Driven Action Learning: The Key Elements" in *Business Driven Action Learning: Global Best Practices*, ed. Yury Boshyk, xiv (London: Macmillan, 2000); Yury Boshyk, "Why Business Driven Action Learning?" in *Action Learning Worldwide: Experiences of Leadership and Organizational Development*, ed. Yury Boshyk, 39 (New York: Palgrave, 2002).

59. Judy O'Neil et al., "Life on the Seesaw: Tensions in Action Reflection Learning™" in *Action Learning in Practice*, ed. Mike Pedler, 339 (Brookfield, VT: Gower, 1997).

60. Alan Mumford, "Managers Developing Others Through Action Learning" *Industrial & Commercial Training*, 1995, 27(2), 19; Alan Mumford, "Effective Learners In Action Learning Sets" *Employee Counselling Today*, 1996, 8(6), 5.

61. Victoria J. Marsick and Judy O'Neil, "The Many Faces of Action Learning" *Management Learning*, 1999, 30(2), 163.

62. Raelin, *Work-Based Learning*, 101–107.

63. Conger and Benjamin, *Building Leaders*, 223–226.

Chapter Two

1. Partners for Learning and Leadership changed its name from Partners for the Learning Organization in 2006.

2. Edgar H. Schein, *Process Consultation Volume I: Its Role in Organization Development* (New York: Addison-Wesley, 1988), 5.

3. Judy O'Neil and Robert L. Dilworth, "Issues in the Design and Implementation of an Action Learning Initiative" in *Action Learning: Theoretical Bases and Varieties of Practice*, eds. L. Yorks, J. O'Neil, and V. J. Marsick, 34 (San Francisco: Berrett-Koehler, 1999).

4. Marsick and Watkins, *Facilitating Learning Organizations*, 127.

5. Partners for Learning and Leadership changed its name from Partners for the Learning Organization in 2006.

6. O'Neil and Dilworth, "Issues in Design and Implementation," 34.

7. Conger and Benjamin, *Building Leaders*, 226.

8. Michael Marquardt, *Optimizing the Power of Action Learning* (Palo Alto, CA: Davies-Black, 2004), 163.

9. O'Neil and Dilworth, "Issues in Design and Implementation," 24. Some of the criteria have been adapted from this chapter.

10. O'Neil and Dilworth, "Issues in Design and Implementation," 25.

11. Reginald W. Revans, *The A.B.C. of Action Learning: A Review of 25 Years of Experience* (Salford, England: University of Salford, 1978, reprinted in 1995), 13.

12. Revans, *The Origin and Growth of Action Learning.*

13. Mumford, "Effective Learners in Action Learning Sets," 5–12.

14. Christopher B. Dennis, Lars Cederholm, and Lyle Yorks, "Learning Your Way to a Global Organization," in *In Action: Creating the Learning Organization,* eds. Karen E. Watkins and Victoria J. Marsick, 165 (Alexandria, VA: ASTD, 1996).

15. Revans, *The Origin and Growth of Action Learning*; O'Neil and Dilworth, "Issues in Design and Implementation," 26.

16. Partners for Learning and Leadership changed its name from Partners for the Learning Organization in 2006.

17. O'Neil and Dilworth, "Issues in Design and Implementation," 27.

18. Ibid.

19. Ibid.

20. Marsick and Watkins, *Facilitating Learning Organizations,* 132.

21. Judy O'Neil, Eva Arnell, and Ernie Turner, "Earning While Learning: Volvo Truck Corporation," in *In Action: Creating the Learning Organization,* eds. Karen E. Watkins and Victoria J. Marsick, 155 (Alexandria, VA: ASTD, 1996).

22. Marsick and Watkins, *Facilitating Learning Organizations,* 129.

23. Conger and Benjamin, *Building Leaders*, 218.

24. Judy O'Neil and Victoria J. Marsick, "Becoming Critically Reflective through Action Reflection Learning," in New Directions for Adult and Continuing Education, 63, *The Emerging Power of Action Inquiry Technologies,* eds. Ann Brooks and Karen E. Watkins, 17 (San Francisco: Jossey-Bass, Fall 1994).

25. Lennart Rohlin, *Project Work in MiL* (Lund, Sweden: MiL, 1996).

26. Revans, *The A. B. C. of Action Learning*, 11.

27. For more information on "Exchange Options", see Reginald W. Revans, "Action Learning Projects." In *Management Development and Training Handbook,* edited by Bernard Taylor and Gordon Lippitt, 226–274. (New York: McGraw-Hill, 1983).

28. Conger and Benjamin, *Building Leaders,* 221.

29. McGill and Beaty, *Action Learning;* Weinstein, *Action Learning.*

30. Dennis, Cederholm, and Yorks, "Learning Your Way," 165; O'Neil, Arnell and Turner, "Earning While Learning," 153.

31. Noel and Charan, "Leadership Development at GE's Crotonville," 433.

32. Casey, "Programme Outline," 11.

33. Carter McNamara, "Evaluation of a Group-Managed, Multi-technique Managemet Development Program That Includes Action Learning" (Ed.D. diss, Graduate School of the Union Institute, Minn, MN, 1996).

34. O'Neil and Dilworth, "Issues in Design and Implementation," 28.

35. Ibid, 29.

36. Ibid.

37. Ibid, 31.

38. Casey, "Programme Outline," 11.

39. O'Neil and Dilworth, "Issues in Design and Implementation," 25.

40. An exception to the participant choosing a problem with which he/she has been struggling was in the GEC programme discussed earlier.

41. Marquardt, *Optimizing the Power*, 164.

42. Ian McGill and Anne Brockbank, *The Action Learning Handbook* (London: RoutledgeFalmer, 2004), 49.

43. Marsick and Watkins, *Facilitating Learning Organizations*, 124.

44. Dennis, Cederholm, and Yorks, "Learning Your Way," 167.

45. Marsick and Watkins, *Facilitating Learning Organizations*, 128.

46. Donald Kirkpatrick, *Evaluating Training Programs: The Four Levels* (San Francisco: Berrett-Koehler, 1994).

Chapter Three

1. Conger and Benjamin, *Building Leaders*, 218–235.

2. Watkins and Brooks provide the following description of action research in *The Emerging Power of Action Technologies: New Directions for Adult and Continuing Education* 63, eds. Anne Brooks and Karen E. Watkins (San Francisco: Jossey-Bass, 1994), 100. "Action research as a technology typically includes: formation of groups from among those who have the problem; reflection on problems in groups; collection of data around the problems; group analysis and group feedback; group-designed interventions to attempt to solve the problem."

3. Work on this project was partly supported by a grant from the U.S. National Science Foundation, Innovation and Change Division, and funding from the VA Learning University and Office of Resolution Management. Findings do not necessarily represent the views of these organizations.

4. The original design was a traditional expert consultation model, using a model developed from prior survey data, along with data gathered from the new survey to make recommendations regarding the issues that surfaced. Employing quasi-experimental design assessment methods, the project team would track effects over time, comparing where recommendations were implemented and were not implemented. As some members of the project team became increasingly aware of inherent limitations of this approach for producing change, a co-inquiry action research model was adopted by the project team. At this point a fourth academic with a background in adult learning was added to the project as a learning coach for the team. The team had adopted the language of Chris Argyris's work on Model II functioning, and realized their project was an example of Mode 2 research. (See Gibbons, et. al., *The New Production of Knowledge: The Dynamics of Science and Research in Contemporary Societies.* Sage Publications, 1994.) The project team and action teams were dealing with a practice focused question, were diverse both in terms of professional specialties and experience, socially distributed, and required the emergence of collaborative transdisciplinary relationships. In addition to the practitioner/academic diversity, the academics came with different

epistemic assumptions about research, and the project increasingly required the blending of different methodologies.

5. O'Neil and Marsick, "Becoming Critically Reflective Through Action Reflection Learning," 20.

6. MiL Institute, "MiL International Newsletter, 2d. ed., 1 (Lund, Sweden: MiL Institute, 1994).

7. O'Neil, "The Role of the Learning Advisor in Action Learning," 136.

8. Tom Bourner and Krystyna Weinstein, "Just Another Talking Shop? Some of the Pitfalls in Action Learning," *Employee Counselling Today,* 1996, 8(6), 66.

9. Ibid.

10. Judy O'Neil, "Facilitating Action Learning: The Role of the Learning Coach" in *Action Learning: Successful Strategies for Individual, Team and Organizational Development,* eds. Lyle Yorks, Judy O'Neil, and Victoria J. Marsick, 39 (San Francisco: Berrett-Koehler, 1999).

11. Conger and Benjamin, *Building Leaders,* 227.

12. Raelin, *Work-Based Learning,* 149.

13. Ibid., 44.

14. The Action Planning Cycle was derived from the Power Planning Cycle originally developed by Leadership in International Management (LIM).

15. Jack Mezirow, "Learning to Think Like an Adult" in *Learning as Transformation,* ed. Jack Mezirow, 16 (San Francisco: Jossey-Bass, 2000).

16. Ibid, 17.

17. Mike Pedler, "Another Look at Set Advising" in *Action Learning in Practice* (2^d ed.), ed. Mike Pedler, 285 (Brookfield, VT: Gower, 1991).

18. Robert. L. Dilworth, "Action Learning: Bridging Academic and Workplace Domains," *Employee Counselling Today,* 1996, 8(6), 48.

19. Marquardt, *Action Learning in Action,* 30.

20. Marilee C. Goldberg Adams, "Expert Question Asking: The Engine of Successful Coaching," *The Manchester Review,* retrieved from http://www.inquiryinc.com/knowledge/articles.html on July 29, 2006.

21. Conger and Benjamin, *Building Leaders,* 225.

22. David Boud, Ruth Cohen, and David Walker, "Understanding Learning from Experience" in *Using Experience for Learning,* eds. David Boud, Ruth Cohen, and David Walker, 9 (Buckingham, England: SRHE and Open University Press, 1996).

23. Jack Mezirow, *Transformative Dimensions of Adult Learning* (San Francisco: Jossey-Bass, 1991), 105.

24. O'Neil and Marsick. "Becoming Critically Reflective Through Action Reflection Learning" 17.

25. For those readers interested in additional material about simple and critical reflection see Raelin's discussion of tools and strategies for reflection in *Work Based Learning,* particularly Chapters 6–8.

26. Work on this project was partly supported by a grant from the U.S. National Science Foundation, Innovation and Change Division, and funding from the VA Learning University and Office of Resolution Management. Findings do not necessarily represent the views of these organizations.

27. O'Neil, Arnell, and Turner, "Earning While Learning," 159.

28. O'Neil and Marsick, "Becoming Critically Reflective Through Action Reflection Learning," 22.

29. Raelin, *Work-Based Learning*, 125.

30. O'Neil and Marsick, "Becoming Critically Reflective Through Action Reflection Learning," 26.

31. Marsick and Watkins, *Facilitating Learning Organizations*, 128.

Chapter Four

1. Judy O'Neil, "A Study of the Role of Learning Advisors in Action Learning" in *AHRD Conference Proceedings*, ed. E. F. Holton, 68 (Minneapolis, MN: AHRD, 1996); O'Neil, "The Role of the Learning Coach in Action Learning," 186.

2. Yorks, O'Neil, and Marsick, "Action Learning: Theoretical Bases and Varieties of Practice," 12.

3. David L. Dotlich and James L. Noel, *Action Learning: How the World's Top Companies Are Re-Creating Their Leaders and Themselves* (San Francisco: Jossey-Bass, 1998), 26.

4. Revans, *The A. B. C. of Action Learning*, 13.

5. Reginald W. Revans, "Notes on the Structure of Sets" (Unpublished manuscript. First Recommendation That Greater Manchester Council Should Start Action Learning in the Inner City, 1981).

6. Mike Pedler, "Another Look at Set Advising," in *Action Learning in Practice 2ᵈ ed.*, ed. Mike Pedler, 285 (Brookfield, VT: Gower, 1991).

7. Revans, *The A. B. C. of Action Learning*, 13.

8. Jean Lawrence, "Action Learning-A Questioning Approach" in *Handbook of Management Development 3rd ed.*, ed. Alan Mumford, 214 (Brookfield, VT: Gower, 1991).

9. Alan Mumford, Action Learning and Learning from Experience, Unpublished draft chapter from ILO Book, 1989), 26.

10. McGill and Beaty, "Action Learning."

11. Weinstein, *Action Learning: A Journey in Discovery and Development.*

12. O'Neil, "The Role of the Learning Advisor in Action Learning," 25.

13. Lyle Yorks, et al., "Boundary Management in Action Reflection Learning™ Research: Taking the Role of a Sophisticated Barbarian," *Human Resource Development Quarterly*, 1996, 7(4), 318.

14. O'Neil and Marsick, "Becoming Critically Reflective Through Action Reflection Learning," 20.

15. For a more complete discussion of the case, see Marsick and O'Neil, "The Many Faces of Action Learning," 167.

16. O'Neil, "The Role of the Learning Advisor in Action Learning," 135.

17. Ibid., 136.

18. Sharon Lamm, "The Connection Between Action Reflection Learning and Transformative Learning: An Awakening of Human Qualities in Leadership" (Ed.D. diss., Teacher's College, Columbia University, New York, NY, 2000).

19. Karen E. Watkins and Judy O'Neil, "Action Learning Toolkit" (Unpublished manuscript, Warwick, RI: Partners for the Learning Organization, Inc., 1997).

20. O'Neil, "The Role of the Learning Advisor in Action Learning," 68; Pedler, "Another Look at Set Advising."

21. Weinstein, *Action Learning: A Journey in Discovery and Development.*

22. Victoria J. Marsick, "Action Learning and Reflection in the Workplace," 30.

23. O'Neil, "The Role of the Learning Advisor in Action Learning," 164.

24. Chris Argyris, Robert Putnam, and Diane M. Smith, *Action Science* (San Francisco: Jossey-Bass, 1985).

25. Lyle Yorks, Sharon Lamm, and Judy O'Neil, "Transfer of Learning to the Organizational Setting," in *Action Learning: Successful Strategies for Individual, Team and Organizational Development,* eds. Lyle Yorks, Judy O'Neil, and Victoria J. Marsick, 63 (San Francisco: Berrett-Koehler, 1999).

26. David Casey, "The Role of the Set Advisor" in *Action Learning in Practice,* 2nd Ed., ed. Mike Pedler (Brookfield, VT: Gower, 1991), 263.

27. Marsick, "Action Learning and Reflection in the Workplace," 30.

28. Quotes in this section about saying nothing and being invisible are from O'Neil's research, "The Role of the Learning Advisor in Action Learning."

29. Weinstein, *Action Learning: A Journey in Discovery and Development.*

30. Judy O'Neil and Sharon L. Lamm, "Working as a Learning Coach Team in Action Learning" In *Team Teaching and Learning in Adult Education, New Directions for Adult and Continuing Education* 87, eds. Mary-Jane Eisen and Elizabeth J Tisdell, (Fall 2000):44.

31. For a more complete discussion of learning coach teams, see O'Neil and Lamm, "Working As a Learning Coach Team in Action Learning."

32. Marsick, "Action Learning and Reflection in the Workplace," 30.

33. Judy O'Neil, "Facilitating Action Learning: The Role of the Learning Coach," 51.

34. McGill and Beaty, *Action Learning;* Pedler, *Action Learning for Managers;* Weinstein, *Action Learning: A Journey in Discovery and Development.*

35. O'Neil, "The Role of the Learning Advisor in Action Learning," 222.

36. O'Neil, "Facilitating Action Learning: The Role of the Learning Coach," 52.

Chapter Five

1. Sharon Lamm, "The Connection Between Action Reflection Learning™ and Transformative Learning."

2. Raelin, *Work-Based Learning,* 200. See also John W. Boudreau and Peter M. Ramstad "Measuring Intellectual Capital: Learning from Financial History," *Human Resource Management,* 36: 3 (1997), 343–356.

3. Kirkpatrick, *Evaluating Training Programs: The Four Levels.*

4. George M Alliger et al., "A Meta-Analysis of the Relations among Training Criteria," *Personnel Psychology,* 50 (1997): 341.

5. Timothy T. Baldwin and J. Kevin Ford, "Transfer of Training: A Review and Directions for Future Research," *Personnel Psychology,* 41 (1988): 63.

6. Robert L. Dilworth, "Mapping Group Dynamics in an Action Learning Experience: The Global Team Questionnaire," in *AHRD 2001 Conference Proceedings,* ed. Oscar A. Aliaga, 20 (Tulsa, OK: AHRD, 2001).

7. Yorks, Lamm, and O'Neil, "Transfer of Learning to the Organizational Setting," 56–59.

8. No baseline data (data obtained before the program) were collected and no control groups (those as close as possible to the people being studied but not involved in the intervention) were used.

9. The concepts of single-loop and double-loop learning come from the work of Chris Argyris. These terms are defined in the Theory Appendix.

10. John C. Flanagan, "The Critical Incident Technique," in *Figuring Things Out: A Trainer's Guide to Needs and Task Analysis*, eds. Ron Zemke and Thomas Kramlinger, 277. (Reading, MA: Addison-Wesley, 1982).

11. Ibid.

12. No baseline data were collected and no control groups were used in this evaluation.

13. Yorks et al., , "Boundary Management in Action Reflection Learning™ Research: Taking the Role of a Sophisticated Barbarian," 313.

14. Ibid., 318. For a more comprehensive understanding of the observer-participant research role in this program and the nomenclature "sophisticated barbarian", see the complete journal article.

15. Dennis, Cederholm, and Yorks, "Learning Your Way to a Global Organization," 173, 175.

16. Mezirow, *Transformative Dimensions of Adult Learning*.

17. Lamm, "The Connection Between Action Reflection Learning™ and Transformative Learning."

18. See Lamm, "The Connection between Action Reflection Learning™ and Transformative Learning" for copies of the actual instruments.

19. Participant names are fictitious in order to protect the confidentiality of the actual program participants.

20. This study also depended on post-program self report without the use of baseline data or control groups.

21. Suzanne D. Butterfield, "Action Learning: Case Study of Learning and Transfer for Personal and Professional Development" (Ed. D. diss., Georgia State University, Atlanta, GA, 1999).

22. Raelin, *Work-Based Learning*, 209–213.

23. Tony O'Driscoll, "Redefining Learning's Business Value Contribution in the On Demand Era," paper delivered at the Academy of Management annual conference, Atlanta, GA, August 2006.

24. Dean R. Spitzer, for example, has identified an approach he calls Learning-Effective Measurement. See Greg G. Want and Dean R. Spitzer, "Human Resource Development Measurement and Evaluation: Looking Back and Moving Forward," in *Advances in Developing Human Resources*, 2005, 7(1), 5–15. For more information on theory-driven evaluation, see Huey-Tsych Chen, *Theory-Driven Evaluations*, Newbury Park, CA: Sage, 1990; and Leonard Bickman, ed., "Using Program Theory in Evaluation, *New Directions for Program Evaluation Series, 33* (San Francisco: Jossey-Bass, 1987).

25. See www.jmhuberinstitute.org for a brief description of the assessment done in partnership with Otis Elevator.

26. Hallie Preskill and Rosalie T. Torres, *Evaluative Inquiry for Learning in Organizations* (Thousand Oaks, CA: Sage Publications, 1999), 51.

Chapter Six

1. Yorks, Marsick, and O'Neil, "Lessons for Implementing Action Learning."
2. If you have not yet done so, please use the questionnaire in Table 3, chapter 1 to consider whether AL is right for your organization.
3. Yorks, O'Neil, and Marsick, "Action Learning: Theoretical Bases and Varieties of Practice," 14.
4. Lyle Yorks and Victoria J. Marsick, "Organizational Learning and Transformation" in *Learning as Transformation*, ed. Jack D. Mezirow (San Francisco: Jossey-Bass, 2000), 253–284.
5. For a deeper discussion of a research and practice-based framework that differentiates between transformational and transactional change factors in organizations, see W. Warner Burke and George H.Litwin, "A Causal Model of Organizational Performance and Change," *Journal of Management*, 1992, 18(31), 523–545.
6. Conger and Benjamin, *Building Leaders*, 219.
7. Ibid.
8. See, for example, Alexander Ardichvili, Vaughn Page, and Tim Wentling, "Motivation and Barriers to Participation in Virtual Knowledge-Sharing Communities of Practice, *Journal of Knowledge Management*, 2003, 7(1), 64–77. For additional strategies for virtual work see, Deborah L. Duarte and Nancy Tennant Snyder, *Mastering Virtual Teams: Strategies, Tools, and Techniques That Succeed* (San Francisco: Jossey-Bass, 2002).
9. O'Neil, "The Role of the Learning Advisor in Action Learning," 220.
10. Victoria J. Marsick and Terrence Maltbia, "Using Action Learning Conversations," in 'Where Is the Reflection in Action Learning?,'" presentation, Academy of Management, Atlanta, GA, August 14, 2006.

Theory Appendix

1. The authors acknowledge and thank Isabel Rimanoczy who co-authored this theory appendix with Judy O'Neil.
2. Yorks, Marsick and O'Neil, "Action Learning: Theoretical Bases and Varieties of Practice," 12.
3. Marsick and Watkins, *Informal and Incidental Learning in the Workplace*, 33.
4. Ibid., 7–8.
5. Marsick and O'Neil, "The Many Faces of Action Learning," 162; McGill and Brockbank, The Action Learning Handbook, 13.
6. Noel and Charan, "Leadership Development," 433.
7. Ibid., 434.
8. Thomas A. Downham, James L. Noel, and Albert E. Prendergast, "Executive Development" *Human Resource Management* 31, no. 1 & 2, (1992): 95–107.

9. Dotlich and Noel, "Action Learning," 26.

10. Marsick and Watkins, *Informal and Incidental Learning*, 14.

11. Morgan W. McCall, Michael M. Lombard, and Ann M. Morrison, *The Lessons of Experience: How Successful Executives Develop on the Job* (Lexington, MA: Lexington Books, 1988), 133.

12. Aaron Pun, "Action Learning for Trainer's Development," *Journal of European Industrial Training* 14, no. 9 (1990): 17; Revans, "The Managerial Alphabet," 141.

13. Ibid.

14. Revans, "The Managerial Alphabet," 145.

15. Revans, "The Managerial Alphabet," 145; Revans, "Notes on the Structure of Sets," 3.

16. Revans, "The Managerial Alphabet," 146.

17. Revans, *The A.B.C. of Action Learning*, 14.

18. Revans, "The Managerial Alphabet," 161.

19. Revans, *The Golden Jubilee of Action Learning*, 102.

20. Pedler, "Another Look at Set Advising," 285.

21. Dilworth, "Action Learning: Bridging Academic and Workplace Domains," 48.

22. John Morris, "Minding our P's and Q's," in *Action Learning in Practice, 2ᵈ Edition*, ed. Mike Pedler, 71 (Brookfield, VT: Gower, 1991).

23. Revans, *The Golden Jubilee of Action Learning*, 102

24. Weinstein, *Action Learning: A Journey in Discovery and Development*, 44.

25. Pedler, "Another Look at Set Advising," 285.

26. Revans, *The A.B.C. of Action Learning*, 17.

27. Ibid., 13.

28. Cliff Bunning, "Turning Experience into Learning," *Journal of European Industrial Training* 16, no. 6 (1992): 7.

29. Marquardt, "Optimizing the Power of Action Learning," 113; McGill & Beaty, *Action Learning*, 30; Alan Mumford, "Putting Learning Styles to Work," in *Action Learning at Work*, ed. Alan Mumford, 121 (London: Gower, 1997).

30. David Kolb, *Experiential Learning* (Englewood Cliffs, NJ: Prentice-Hall., 1984).

31. Bunning, "Turning Experience into Learning," 7; McGill and Beaty, *Action Learning*, 30.

32. Alan Mumford, 1991 Action Learning Moves On. Unpublished manuscript.

33. McGill and Beaty, *Action Learning*, 31.

34. Mumford, "Effective Learners in Action Learning Sets," 6.

35. Scott Inglis, *Making the Most of Action Learning* (Brookfield, VT: Gower, 1994), 8; McGill and Beaty, *Action Learning*, 173; Mumford, "Managers Developing Others through Action Learning," 22.

36. Inglis, *Making the Most of Action Learning*, 10.

37. Mumford, "Managers Developing Others through Action Learning," 20.

38. Inglis, *Making the Most of Action Learning*, 143; McGill and Beaty, *Action Learning*, 75; Mumford, "Action Learning and Learning from Experience."

39. Mumford, "Action Learning and Learning from Experience."

40. O'Neil, "The Role of the Learning Advisor in Action Learning," 181; Lawrence, "Action Learning," 214; Mumford, "Action Learning Moves On;" Pearce, "Programme Development," 14.

41. McGill and Beaty, *Action Learning,* 140; McGill and Brockbank, *Action Learning Handbook,* 70; Marquardt, *Optimizing the Power of Action Learning,* 142.

42. Inglis, *Making the Most of Action Learning,* 14.

43. Mumford, "Action Learning."

44. Weinstein, *Action Learning: A Journey in Discovery and Development,* 50.

45. Mezirow, "Fostering Critical Reflection in Adulthood," xvi; Jack Mezirow, "Learning to Think Like an Adult: Core Concepts of Transformation Theory" in *Learning As Transformation,* ed. Jack Mezirow and Associates, 24 (San Francisco: Jossey-Bass, 2000).

46. O'Neil and Marsick, "Becoming Critically Reflective," 20; Marsick and O'Neil, "Many Faces of Action Learning," 163.

47. Weinstein, *Action Learning: A Journey in Discovery and Development,* 169.

48. Lennart Rohlin. 1993. "Fifteen Years and 350 Learning Projects Later: What Are We Learning about Learning?" Unpublished manuscript.

49. Marsick, "Action Learning," 30.

50. Dilworth and Willis, *Action Learning,* 31–32.

51. Marsick and O'Neil, "Many Faces of Action Learning," 163; Weinstein, *Action Learning: A Journey in Discovery and Development,* 146.

52. Marsick and Watkins, *Informal and Incidental Learning in the Workplace;* Pedler, *Action Learning for Managers,* 47; Weinstein, *Action Learning: A Journey in Discovery and Development,* 146.

53. Joseph A. Raelin, "The Persean Ethic: Consistency of Belief and Actions in Managerial Practice," *Human Relations,* 46, no. 5 (1993): 580; O'Neil and Marsick, "Becoming Critically Reflective," 21.

54. Bourner and Weinstein, "Just Another Talking Shop?," 6.

55. Ibid.

56. Marsick, "Action Learning," 59.

57. Marsick, "Action Learning," 25; McGill and Beaty, *Action Learning,* 122; Noel and Charan, "Leadership Development," 434; Revans, *The A.B.C of Action Learning,* 14.

58. Revans, *The Golden Jubilee of Action Learning,* 6.

59. Mumford, "Effective Learners in Action Learning Sets," 7.

60. Lawrence, "Action Learning," 216; McGill and Brockbank, *Action Learning Handbook,* 28; Noel and Charan, "Leadership Development," 440; Pedler, *Action Learning for Managers,* 56.

61. Lawrence, "Action Learning," 216.

62. Revans, *The A.B.C. of Action Learning,* 13.

63. Weinstein, *Action Learning: A Journey in Discovery and Development,* 155; Pedler, "Action Learning for Managers," 46; McGill and Beaty, *Action Learning,* 131.

64. Downham, Noel, and Prendergast, "Executive Development," 100.

65. Judy O'Neil, "Changing Whole Systems: Leadership Is Real Work at Public Service Electric & Gas" in *Facilitating Learning Organizations: Making Learning Count,* by Victoria J. Marsick and Karen E. Watkins, 120–136 (Brookfield, VT: Gower, 1999); Noel and Charan, "Leadership Development," 440; Revans, *The A.B.C of Action Learning,* 17; Weinstein, *Action Learning: A Journey in Discovery and Development,* 230.

66. Revans, *The A.B.C. of Action Learning,* 12.

67. Lawrence, "Action Learning," 220; Raelin, "The Persean Ethic," 580; Watkins and Marsick, *Sculpting the Learning Organization,* 126.

68. Noel & Charan, "Leadership Development," 440; Albert A. Vicere, "Executive Education: The Leading Edge" *Organizational Dynamics* (Autumn, 1996): 68.

69. O'Neil, "The Role of the Learning Advisor in Action Learning," 78; Isabel Rimanoczy, "Action Reflection Learning: A Learning Methodology Based on Common Sense," *Industrial and Commercial Training,* 2007, 39(1), 43; Deborah Dewolfe-Waddill and Michael Marquardt, "Adult Learning Orientations and Action Learning," *Human Resource Development Review,* 2003, 2(4), 406.

70. For more information, see Etienne Wenger, *Communities of Practice: Learning, Meaning, and Identity* (Cambridge, MA: Cambridge University Press, 1998).

71. Lev S. Vygotsky, *Mind in Society* (Cambridge, MA: Harvard University Press, 1978).

72. Jean Lave and Etienne Wenger, *Situated Learning: Legitimate Peripheral Participation* (Cambridge, UK: Cambridge University Press, 1990).

73. John Dewey, *Experience and Education* (New York: Collier, 1938), 7.

74. Ibid., 43.

75. John Dewey, *Democracy and Education* (New York: Free Press, 1917), 139.

76. Dewey, "Experience and Education," 110.

77. Kolb, 17.

78. Ibid.

79. David Botham, "Human Learning and Human Nature." Unpublished manuscript, April 1987.

80. Mumford, "Managers Developing Others through Action Learning," 22.

81. Albert J. Marrow, *The Practical Theorist: The Life and Work of Kurt Lewin.* (New York: Basic Books, 1969).

82. Jean Piaget, *Genetic Epistemology.* (New York: Columbia University Press, 1970).

83. Kolb, 18.

84. Malcolm Knowles, *The Modern Practice of Adult Education: Andragogy Versus Pedagogy.* (New York: Association Press, 1970).

85. Revans, "The Mangerial Alphabet", 145.

86. Revans, *The ABC of Action Learning,* 6, italics added.

87. Botham, "Human Learning and Human Nature"; Mumford, "Action Learning and Learning from Experience"; Weinstein, *Action Learning: A Journey in Discovery and Development.*

88. David Boud, R. Keogh, and David Walker, eds. *Reflection: Turning Experience into Learning.* (London: Kogan Page., 1985), 2.

89. Boud, Cohen, and Walker, "Understanding Learning," 8–14.

90. David Boud and David Walker. "Barriers to Reflection on Experience," in *Using Experience for Experience,* eds. Boud and Walker.

91. Boud, Cohen, and Walker, *Understanding Learning,* 9.

92. Boud, Keogh, and Walker, *Reflection,* 35.

93. Mezirow, "Fostering Critical Reflection in Adulthood," xvi.

94. Boud, Keough, and Walker, *Reflection,* 40.

95. William Crain, "Piaget's Cognitve-Developmental Theory," *Theories of Development: Concepts and Applications,* 3rded., (Englewood Cliffs, NJ: Prentice-Hall, Inc., 1980), 102–103.

96. Patrick G. Love and Victoria L. Guthrie, "Perry's Intellectual Scheme," in *Understanding and Applying Cognitive Development Theory, New Directions for Student Services, 88* (Winter, 1999), 6.

97. Love and Guthrie, Perry, 6–7.

98. Jane Loevinger, *Ego Development* (San Francisco: Jossey-Bass, 1976).

99. William R. Torbert, *The Power of Balance: Transforming Self, Society and Scientific Inquiry*. (Newbury Park, CA: Sage, 1991).

100. Ibid., 46.

101. Ibid., 42.

102. Ibid., 51.

103. Dalmar Fisher and William R. Torbert, *Personal and Organizational Transformations: The True Challenge of Continual Quality Improvement* (New York: McGraw Hill, 1995), 78.

104. Patrick G. Love and Victoria L. Guthrie, "Kegan's Orders of Consciousness," in *Understanding and Applying Cognitive Development Theory, New Directions for Student Services, 88* (Winter, 1999), 65.

105. Robert Kegan, *In Over Our Heads: The Mental Demands of Modern Life*. (Cambridge, MA: Harvard University Press, 1994), 1–2.

106. Ibid.

107. Kegan, *In Over Our Heads,* 94, 95, 126 312.

108. Ibid.

109. Paulo Freire, *Pedagogy of the Oppressed* (New York: Continuum, 1970), 19.

110. Jurgen Habermas, *Knowledge and Human Interests* (Boston: Beacon, 1971).

111. Mezirow, "Fostering Critical Reflection in Adulthood," xvi.

112. Ibid., 30.

113. Mezirow, "Fostering Critical Reflection in Adulthood, "Transformative Dimensions of Adult Learning."

114. Jack Mezirow. 1993. "Toward a Transformation Theory: Speculations on Understanding and Facilitating Adult Learning." Unpublished manuscript, Teachers College, Columbia University, New York.

115. Ibid.

116. Jack Mezirow, "Transformative Learning: Theory to Practice," in *Transformative Learning in Action: Insights from Practice. New Directions for Adult and Continuing Education, 74,* ed. Patricia Cranton, 6 (San Francisco: Jossey-Bass, 1997).

117. Ibid., 10.

118. Ibid., 11.

119. Peter Jarvis, *Adult Learning in the Social Context* (New York: Croom Helm, 1987), 111.

120. Peter Jarvis, *Paradoxes of Learning* (San Francisco: Jossey-Bass, 1992), 57.

121. Jarvis, *Adult Learning in the Social Context,* 112.

122. Ibid., 111.

123. Ibid.

124. Argyris, Putnam, and Smith, 232.

125. Vaill, *Learning As a Way of Being*.

126. Ibid., 65.

127. Ibid, 76.

128. Donald Schon, *The Reflective Practitioner: How Professionals Think in Action* (New York: Basic Books, 1983), 62

129. Ibid.

130. Ibid., 68.

131. Ibid.

132. Argyris, Putnam, and Smith, 232.

133. Ibid., 53.

134. Chris Argyris and Donald Schon, *Organizational Learning: A Theory of Action Perspective* (Reading, MA: Addison-Wesley., 1978), 50.

135. Argyris, Putnam, and Smith, 53.

136. Argyris and Schon, 55.

137. Watkins and Marsick, *Sculpting the Learning Organization*, 27.

138. O'Neil and Marsick, "Becoming Critically Reflective," 20.

139. Watkins and Marsick, *Sculpting the Learning Organization*, 27.

140. O'Neil and Marsick, "Becoming Critically Reflective," 23.

141. Ibid.

BIBLIOGRAPHY

Alliger, George M., Scott I. Tannenbaum, Winston Bennet Jr., Holly Traver, and Allison Shotland. "A Meta-Analysis of the Relations among Training Criteria." *Personnel Psychology,* 50 (1997): 341–358.

Ardichvili, Alexander, Vaughn Page, and Tim Wentling. "Motivation and Barriers to Participation in Virtual Knowledge-Sharing Communities of Practice," *Journal of Knowledge Management,* 7:1 (2003), 64–77.

Argyris, Chris, and Donald Schon. *Organizational Learning: A Theory of Action Perspective.* Reading, MA: Addison-Wesley, 1978.

Argyris, Chris, Robert Putnam, and Diane M. Smith. *Action Science.* San Francisco: Jossey-Bass, 1985.

Baldwin, Timothy T., and J. Kevin Ford. "Transfer of Training: A Review and Directions for Future Research." *Personnel Psychology,* 41 (1988): 63–105.

Bett, Mike. "It's Opening Our Minds." In *More Than Management Development: Action Learning at GEC,* eds. David Casey and David Pearce, 116–118. Hampshire, England: Gower, 1984.

Bickman, Leonard. ed. "Using Program Theory in Evaluation." *New Directions for Program Evaluation,* 33. San Francisco: Jossey-Bass, 1987.

Bierma, Laura L. Action Learning Quick Guide. Paper distributed at IFAL Conference, Arlington, VA, 1999.

Boshyk, Yury. "Business Driven Action Learning: The Key Elements." In *Business Driven Action Learning: Global Best Practices,* ed. Yury Boshyk, xi–xvii. London: Macmillan, 2000.

———. "Why Business Driven Action Learning?" In *Action Learning Worldwide: Experiences of Leadership and Organizational Development,* ed. Yury Boshyk, 30–52. New York: Palgrave, 2002.

207

Bossert, Ron. "Johnson & Johnson: Executive Development and Strategic Business Solutions through Action Learning." In *Business Driven Action Learning: Global Best Practices*, ed. Yury Boshyk, 91–103. London: Macmillan, 2000.

Botham, David. Human Learning and Human Nature. Unpublished manuscript, April, 1987.

———. Discussion Paper: Relationships Between. Unpublished manuscript, Manchester Polytechnic, Department of Management, MSc Think Tank, England, January, 1991.

Boud, David, and David Walker. "Barriers to Reflection on Experience." In *Using Experience for Learning*, eds. David Boud, Ruth Cohen, and David Walker, 73–86. Buckingham, England: SRHE and Open University Press, 1996.

Boud, David, R. Keogh, and David Walker, eds. *Reflection: Turning Experience into Learning*. London: Kogan Page, 1985.

Boud, David, Ruth Cohen, and David Walker. "Understanding Learning from Experience." In *Using Experience for Learning*, eds. David Boud, Ruth Cohen, and David Walker, 1–17. Buckingham, England: SRHE and Open University Press, 1996.

Boudreau, John W., and Peter M. Ramstad. "Measuring Intellectual Capital: Learning from Financial History." *Human Resource Management* 36, 3 (1997), 343–356.

Bourner, Tom, and Krystyna Weinstein. "Just Another Talking Shop? Some of the Pitfalls in Action Learning." *Employee Counselling Today*, 8, 6 (1996): 57–68.

Brooks, Anne and Karen E. Watkins. *The Emerging Power of Action Technologies, New Directions for Adult and Continuing Education, 63*, eds. Anne Brooks and Karen E. Watkins. San Francisco: Jossey-Bass, John Wiley & Sons, Inc., 1994.

Bunning, Cliff. "Turning Experience into Learning." *Journal of European Industrial Training*, 16, 6 (1992): 7–12.

Burke, W. Warner and George H. Litwin. "A Casual Model of Organizational Performance and Change." *Journal of Management*, 18:31 (1992), 523–545.

Butterfield, Suzanne D. Action Learning: Case Study of Learning and Transfer for Personal and Professional Development. Unpublished doctoral diss., Georgia State University, Atlanta, GA, 1999.

Casey, David. "Programme Outline." In *More than Management Development: Action Learning at GEC*, eds. by David Casey and David Pearce, 7–13. Hampshire, England: Gower, 1984.

———. "The Role of the Set Advisor." In *Action Learning in Practice 2d ed.*, ed. Mike Pedler, 261–273. Brookfield, VT: Gower, 1991.

Chen, Huey-Tsych. *Theory-Driven Evaluations.* Newbury Park, CA: Sage Publications, 1990.

Conger, Jay A., and Beth B. Benjamin. *Building Leaders: How Successful Companies Develop the Next Generation.* San Francisco: Jossey-Bass, 1999.

Dennis, Christopher B., Lars Cederholm, and Lyle Yorks. "Learning Your Way to a Global Organization." In *In Action: Creating the Learning Organization,* eds. Karen E. Watkins and Victoria J. Marsick, 165–177. Alexandria, VA: ASTD, 1996.

Dewey, John. *Democracy and Education.* New York: Free Press, 1917.

———. *Experience and Education.* New York: Collier, 1938.

Dewolfe-Waddill, Deborah, and Michael Marquardt. "Adult Learning Orientations and Action Learning." *Human Resource Development Review, 2,* 4 (2003): 406–429

Dilworth, Robert L. "Action Learning: Bridging Academic and Workplace Domains." *Employee Counselling Today,* 8, 6 (1996): 48–56.

———. "Mapping Group Dynamics in an Action Learning Experience: The Global Team Questionnaire." In *AHRD 2001 Conference Proceedings,* ed. Oscar A. Aliaga, 20–25. Tulsa, OK: AHRD, 2001.

Dilworth, Robert L., and Verna J. Willis. *Action Learning: Images and Pathways.* Malabar, FL: Krieger, 2003.

Dotlich, David L., and James L. Noel. *Action Learning: How the World's Top Companies Are Re-Creating Their Leaders and Themselves.* San Francisco: Jossey-Bass, 1998.

Downham, Thomas A., James L. Noel, and Albert E. Prendergast. "Executive Development." *Human Resource Management,* 31, 1 & 2 (Spring/Summer, 1992): 95–107.

Duarte, Deborah L., and Nancy Tennant Synder. *Mastering Virtual Teams: Strategies, Tools, and Techniques that Succeed.* San Francisco: Jossey-Bass, 2002.

Eccles, Tony. "Action Learning and the Company." In *More than Management Development: Action Learning at GEC,* eds. David Casey and David Pearce, 119–123. Hampshire, England: Gower, 1984.

Fisher, Dalmar, and William R. Torbert. *Personal and Organizational Transformations: The True Challenge of Continual Quality Improvement.* New York: McGraw-Hill, 1995.

Flanagan, John C. "The Critical Incident Technique." In *Figuring Things Out: A Trainer's Guide to Needs and Task Analysis,* eds. Ron Zemke and Thomas Kramlinger, 277–317. Reading, MA: Addison-Wesley, 1982.

Foy, Nancy. "Action Learning Comes to Industry." *Harvard Business Review,* 55, 5 (1977, September–October): 158–168.

Freire, Paulo. *Pedagogy of the Oppressed.* New York: Continuum, 1970.

Froiland, Paul. "Action Learning: Taming Real Problems in Real Times." *Training*, 31:1 (1994): 27–34.

Gelb, Michael J. *How to Think Like Leonardo da Vinci.* New York: Dell, 2000.

Gibbons, Michael, Camille Limoges, Helga Nowotny, Simon Schwartzman, Peter Scott, and Martin Trow. *The New Production of Knowledge: The Dynamics of Science and Research in Contemporary Societies.* Thousand Oaks, CA: Sage Publications, 1994.

Habermas, Jurgen. *Knowledge and Human Interests.* Boston: Beacon, 1971.

———. *The Theory of Communicative Action, Vol. 1: Reason and the Rationalization of Society,* trans. T. McCarthy. Boston: Beacon Press, 1984.

Howell, Don. "This is the Way to Unlock Resources." In *More than Management Development: Action Learning at GEC,* eds. David Casey and David Pearce, 45–47. Hampshire, England: Gower, 1984.

Inglis, Scott. *Making the Most of Action Learning.* Brookfield, VT: Gower, 1994.

Jarvis, Peter. *Adult Learning in the Social Context.* New York: Croom Helm, 1987.

———. *Paradoxes of Learning.* San Francisco: Jossey-Bass, 1992.

Kegan, Robert. *In Over Our Heads: The Mental Demands of Modern Life.* Cambridge: Harvard University Press, 1994.

Kirkpatrick, Donald L. *Evaluating Training Programs: The Four Levels.* San Francisco: Berrett-Koehler, 1994.

Knowles, Malcolm. *The Modern Practice of Adult Education: Andragogy Versus Pedagogy.* New York: Association Press, 1970.

Kolb, David. *Experiential Learning.* Englewood Cliffs, NJ: Prentice-Hall, 1984.

Lamm, Sharon. The Connection Between Action Reflection Learning™ and Transformative Learning: An Awakening of Human Qualities in Leadership. Unpublished doctoral diss., Teachers College, Columbia University, 2000.

Lave, Jean and Etienne Wenger. *Situated Learning: Legitimate Peripheral Participation.* Cambridge, UK: Cambridge University Press, 1990.

Lawrence, Jean. "Action Learning-A Questioning Approach." In *Handbook of Management Development 3rd ed.,* ed. Alan Mumford, 214–247. Brookfield, VT: Gower, 1991.

Lewin, Kurt. "Action Research and Minority Problems." *Journal of Social Issues* 2:4 (1946): 34–46.

Loevinger, Jane. *Ego Development.* San Francisco: Jossey-Bass, 1976.

Marquardt, Michael J. *Action Learning in Action: Transforming Problems and People for World-Class Organizational Learning.* Palo Alto, CA: Davies-Black®, 1999.

————. *Optimizing the Power of Action Learning*. Palo Alto, CA: Davies-Black, 2004.

Marrow, Albert. J. *The Practical Theorist: The Life and Work of Kurt Lewin*. New York: Basic Books, 1969.

Marsick, Victoria J. and Lars Cederholm. "Developing Leadership in International Managers—An Urgent Challenge." *Columbia Journal of World Business*, 23:4 (1988): 3–11.

Marsick, Victoria J. "Action Learning and Reflection in the Workplace." In *Fostering Critical Reflection in Adulthood*, eds. Jack Mezirow and Associates, 23–46. San Francisco: Jossey-Bass, 1990.

Marsick, Victoria J., Lars Cederholm, Ernie Turner, and Tony Pearson. "Action-Reflection Learning." *Training and Development* (August 1992): 63–66.

Marsick, Victoria J., and Judy O'Neil. "The Many Faces of Action Learning." *Management Learning* 30, 2 (1999): 159–176.

Marsick, Victoria J., and Terrence Maltbia. "Using Action Learning Conversations," Panel on "Where is the Reflection in Action Learning?" Academy of Management, Atlanta, GA, August 14, 2006.

Marsick, Victoria J., and Karen E. Watkins. *Informal and Incidental Learning in the Workplace*. NY: Routledge, 1992.

————. *Facilitating Learning Organizations: Making Learning Count*. Brookfield, VT: Gower, 1999.

McCall, Morgan W., Michael M. Lombard, and Ann M. Morrison. *The Lessons of Experience: How Successful Executives Develop on the Job*. Lexington, MA: Lexington Books, 1988.

McGill, Ian, and Liz Beaty. *Action Learning: A Guide for Professional, Management and Educational Development*. London: Kogan Page, 1995.

McGill, Ian, and Anne Brockbank. *The Action Learning Handbook*. London: Routledge Falmer, 2004.

McNamara, Carter. Evaluation of a Group-Managed, Multi-Technique Management Development Program that Includes Action Learning. Unpublished doctoral diss., Graduate School of the Union Institute, Minneapolis, MN, 1996.

Mercer, Stephen. "General Electric's Executive Action Learning Programmes." In *Business Driven Action Learning: Global Best Practices*, ed. Yury Boshyk. London: Macmillan, 2000.

Mezirow, Jack and Associates. *Fostering Critical Reflection in Adulthood*. San Francisco: Jossey-Bass, 1990.

————. *Transformative Dimensions of Adult Learning*. San Francisco: Jossey-Bass, 1991.

————. Toward a Transformation Theory: Speculations on Understanding and Facilitating Adult Learning. Unpublished manuscript, Teachers College, Columbia University, New York, 1993.

————. "Transformative Learning: Theory to Practice." In *Transformative Learning in Action: Insights from Practice, New Directions for Adult And Continuing Education, 74,* ed. Patricia Cranton, 5–12. San Francisco: Jossey-Bass, 1997.

———— "Learning to Think Like an Adult." In *Learning as Transformation,* ed. Jack Mezirow, 3–33. San Francisco: Jossey-Bass, 2000.

MiL Institute. MiL International Newsletter, 2d ed., June 1, 1994.

Morris, John. "Minding our P's and Q's." In *Action Learning in Practice 2d ed.,* ed. Mike Pedler, 71–80. Brookfield, VT: Gower, 1991.

Mumford, Alan. Action Learning and Learning from Experience. Unpublished draft chapter from ILO book, 1989.

Alan Mumford, "Putting Learning Styles to Work." In *Action Learning at Work,* ed. Alan Mumford, 121. London: Gower, 1997.

————. Action Learning Moves On. Unpublished manuscript, 1991.

————. "Managers Developing Others through Action Learning." *Industrial & Commercial Training* 27, 2 (1995): 19–27.

————. "Effective Learners in Action Learning Sets." *Employee Counselling Today* 8, 6 (1996): 5–12.

————. *Action Learning at Work.* London: Gower, 1997.

National Center on Education and the Economy. *Tough Choices or Tough Times: The Report of the New Commission on the Skills of the American Workforce.* San Francisco: Jossey-Bass, John Wiley & Sons, Inc., 2007.

Noel, James L., and Ram Charan. "Leadership Development at GE's Crotonville." *Human Resource Management* (1988): 433–447.

O'Driscoll, Tony. "Redefining Learning's Business Value Contribution in the On Demand Era," paper delivered at the Academy of Management's annual conference, Atlanta, GA, August, 2006.

O'Neil, Judy. "A Study of the Role of Learning Advisors in Action Learning." In *AHRD Conference Proceedings,* ed. Ed F. Holton, 65–71. Minneapolis, MN: AHRD, 1996.

O'Neil, Judy. "Action Learning and Systems-Level Continuous Learning." In *AHRD 1999 Conference Proceedings,* ed. K. P. Kuchinke, 159–165. Baton Rouge, LA: AHRD, 1999.

————. "Facilitating Action Learning: The Role of the Learning Coach." In *Action Learning: Successful Strategies for Individual, Team, and Organizational Development, Advances in Developing Human Resources* 2, eds. Lyle Yorks,

Judy O'Neil, and Victoria J. Marsick, 39–55. San Francisco: Berrett-Koehler, 1999.

———. The Role of the Learning Advisor in Action Learning. Unpublished doctoral diss., Teachers College, Columbia University, 1999.

———. "Changing Whole Systems: Leadership Is Real Work at Public Service Electric & Gas." In *Facilitating Learning Organizations: Making Learning Count*, by Victoria J. Marsick and Karen E. Watkins, 119–136. Brookfield, VT: Gower, 1999.

———. "The Role of the Learning Coach in Action Learning." In *AHRD 2001 Conference Proceedings*, ed. Oscar A. Aliaga, 181–188. Tulsa, OK: AHRD, 2001.

O'Neil, Judy, Eva Arnell, and Ernie Turner. "Earning While Learning: Volvo Truck Corporation." In *In Action: Creating the Learning Organization*, ed. Karen E. Watkins and Victoria J. Marsick, 153–164. Alexandria, VA: ASTD, 1996.

O'Neil, Judy, and Robert L. Dilworth. "Issues in the Design and Implementation of an Action Learning Initiative." In *Action Learning: Successful Strategies for Individual, Team and Organizational Development, Advances in Developing Human Resources* 2, eds. Lyle Yorks, Judy O'Neil, and Victoria J. Marsick, 19–38. San Francisco: Berrett-Koehler, 1999.

O'Neil, Judy, and Sharon L. Lamm. "Working As a Learning Coach Team in Action Learning." In *Team Teaching and Learning in Adult Education, New Directions for Adult and Continuing Education* 87, eds. Mary-Jane Eisen and Elizabeth J. Tisdell, 43–52. San Francisco: Jossey-Bass, Fall 2000.

O'Neil, Judy, and Victoria J. Marsick. "Becoming Critically Reflective through Action Reflection Learning." In *The Emerging Power of Action Inquiry Technologies, New Directions for Adult and Continuing Education* 63, eds. Anne Brooks and Karen E. Watkins, 17–30. San Francisco: Jossey-Bass, 1994.

O'Neil, Judy, Victoria Marsick, Lyle Yorks, Glenn Nilson, and Robert Kolodny. "Life on the Seesaw: Tensions in Action Reflection Learning." In *Action Learning in Practice 3rd ed.,* ed. Mike Pedler, 339–346. Brookfield, VT: Gower, 1997.

Pearce, David. "Programme Development." In *More than Management Development: Action Learning at GEC*, eds. David Casey and David Pearce, 14–27. Hampshire, England: Gower, 1984.

Pedler, Mike. "Another Look at Set Advising." In *Action Learning in Practice 2d ed.,* ed. Mike Pedler, 285–296. Brookfield, VT: Gower, 1991.

———. *Action Learning for Managers.* London: Lemos and Crane, 1996.

Pedler, Mike, John Burgoyne, and Cheryl Brook. "What Has Action Learning Learned to Become?" *Action Learning: Research and Practice*, 2:1 (2005): 49–68.

Piaget, Jean. *Genetic Epistemology.* New York: Columbia University Press, 1970.

Preskill, Hallie, and Rosalie T. Torres. *Evaluative Inquiry for Learning in Organizations.* Thousand Oaks, CA: Sage Publications, 1999.

Pun, Aaron. "Action Learning for Trainer's Development: A Design for Post-Graduate Studies." *Journal of European Industrial Training,* 14, 9 (1990): 17–23.

Raelin, Joseph A. "The Persean Ethic: Consistency of Belief and Actions in Managerial Practice." *Human Relations* 46, 5 (1993): 575–621.

———. *Work-Based Learning: The New Frontier of Management Development.* Upper Saddle, NJ: Prentice Hall, Addison Wesley OD Series, 2000.

Revans, Reginald W. "The Managerial Alphabet." In *Approaches to the Study of Organizational Behavior,* ed. G. Heald, 141–161. London: Tavistock, 1970.

———. *The A. B. C. of Action Learning: A Review of 25 Years of Experience.* Salford, England: University of Salford, 1978, reprinted in 1995.

———. Notes of the Structure of Sets. Unpublished manuscript. First Recommendation that Greater Manchester Council Should Start Action Learning in the Inner City, 1981.

———. *The Origin and Growth of Action Learning.* London: Charwell Bratt, 1982.

———. "Action Learning Projects." In *Management Development and Training Handbook,* eds. Bernard Taylor and Gordon Lippitt, 226–274. New York: McGraw-Hill, 1983.

———. *The Golden Jubilee of Action Learning.* Manchester, England" Manchester Action Learning Exchange, University of Manchester, 1989.

———. *Disclosing Doubts.* London: First International Action Learning Mutual Collaboration Congress, 1995.

Rimanoczy, Isabel. "Action Reflection Learning: A Learning Methodology Based on Common Sense." *Industrial and Commercial Training,* 39, no. 1 (2007): 43–51.

Rimanoczy, Isabel, and Ernie Turner. *Action Reflection Learning: Solving Real Business Problems by Connecting Learning with Earning.* Mountain View, CA: Davies Black® Publishing, Forthcoming, 2008.

Rohlin, Lennart. Fifteen Years and 350 Learning Projects Later: What Are We Learning about Learning? Unpublished manuscript, 1993.

———. *Project Work in MiL.* Lund, Sweden: MiL, 1996.

———. "The Story of MiL." In *Earning While Learning in Global Leadership: The Volvo MiL Partnership,* 17–22. Lund, Sweden: MiL, 2002.

Schein, Edgar H. *Process Consultation Vol. 1: Its Role in Organization Development.* New York: Addison-Wesley, 1988.

Schon, Donald. *The Reflective Practitioner: How Professionals Think in Action.* New York: Basic Books, 1983.

Sewerin, Thomas. April, 1997. The MiL Learning Coach, MiL Concepts. Lund, Sweden: MiL Institute.

Teare, Richard and Gordon Prestoungrange. *Accrediting Managers at Work in the 21st Century.* Prestopans, East Lothian, Scotland: Prestoungrange University Press, 2004.

Tichy, Noel M. *The Leadership Engine.* New York: HarperCollins, 2002.

Torbert, William. R. *The Power of Balance: Transforming Self, Society and Scientific Inquiry.* Newbury Park, CA: Sage, 1991.

Vaill, Peter B. *Learning As a Way of Being: Strategies for Survival in a World of Permanent White Water.* San Francisco: Jossey-Bass, 1996.

Vicere, Albert A. "Executive Education: The Leading Edge." *Organizational Dynamics* (Autumn 1996): 67–81.

Vygotsky, Lev S. *Mind in Society.* Cambridge: Harvard University Press, 1978.

Want, Greg G., and Dean R. Spitzer. "Human Resource Development Measurement and Evaluation: Looking Back and Moving Forward." *Advances in Developing Human Resources,* 5–15, 7(1), 2005.

Watkins, Karen E., and Judy O'Neil. 1997. Action Learning Toolkit. Unpublished manuscript. Warwick, RI: Partners for the Learning Organization, Inc.

Watkins, Karen E. and Victoria J. Marsick. *Sculpting the Learning Organization.* San Francisco: Jossey-Bass, 1993.

Weinstein, Krystyna. *Action Learning: A Journey in Discovery and Development.* London: HarperCollins, 1995.

———. *Action Learning: A Practical Guide.* London: Gower, 1998.

Wenger, Etienne. *Communities of Practice: Learning, Meaning, and Identity.* Cambridge, MA: Cambridge Universty Press, 1998.

Yorks, Lyle, Sharon Lamm, and Judy O'Neil. "Transfer of Learning to the Organizational Setting." In *Action Learning: Successful Strategies for Individual, Team and Organizational Development,* eds. Lyle Yorks, Judy O'Neil, and Victoria J. Marsick, 56–74. San Francisco: Berrett-Koehler, 1999.

Yorks, Lyle and Victoria J. Marsick. "Organizational Learning and Transformation." In *Learning as Transformation,* ed. Jack D. Mezirow, 253–284. San Francisco: Jossey-Bass, 2000.

Yorks, Lyle, Victoria J. Marsick, and Judy O'Neil. "Action Learning: Theoretical Bases and Varieties of Practice." In *Action Learning: Successful Strategies for Individual, Team and Organizational Development,* eds. Lyle Yorks, Judy O'Neil, and Victoria J. Marsick, 1–18. San Francisco: Berrett-Koehler, 1999.

————. "Lessons for Implementing Action Learning." In *Action Learning: Successful Strategies for Individual, Team and Organizational Development*, eds. Lyle Yorks, Judy O'Neil, and Victoria J. Marsick, 96–113. San Francisco: Berrett-Koehler, 1999.

Yorks, Lyle, Judy O'Neil, Victoria J. Marsick, Glenn E. Nilson, and Robert Kolodny. "Boundary Management in Action Reflection Learning™ Research: Taking the Role of a Sophisticated Barbarian." *Human Resource Development Quarterly* 7, 4 (Winter 1996): 313–329.

INDEX

217